Ruin
and Resilience

Southern Literary Studies

SCOTT ROMINE, SERIES EDITOR

Ruin and Resilience

Southern Literature and the Environment

DANIEL SPOTH

LOUISIANA STATE
UNIVERSITY PRESS
BATON ROUGE

Published by Louisiana State University Press
lsupress.org

DESIGNER: Andrew Shurtz
TYPEFACE: Eldorado

COVER PHOTOGRAPH: Alcovy Railroad Trestle,
Social Circle, Georgia. Photograph by Lee Edwin Coursey.
https://flic.kr/p/2jsGP5q.

Library of Congress Cataloging-in-Publication Data
Names: Spoth, Daniel, author.
Title: Ruin and resilience : Southern literature and the environment /
    Daniel Spoth.
Description: Baton Rouge : Louisiana State University Press, [2023] |
    Series: Southern literary studies | Includes bibliographical references
    and index.
Identifiers: LCCN 2022042825 (print) | LCCN 2022042826 (ebook) |
    ISBN 978-0-8071-7936-9 (cloth) | ISBN 978-0-8071-8003-7 (epub) |
    ISBN 978-0-8071-8004-4 (pdf)
Subjects: LCSH: American literature—Southern States—History and
    criticism. | Environmentalism in literature. | Ecocriticism in literature. |
    Southern States—In literature. | LCGFT: Literary criticism.
Classification: LCC PS261 .S67 2023 (print) | LCC PS261 (ebook) |
    DDC 810.9/3553—dc23/eng/20230217
LC record available at https://lccn.loc.gov/2022042825
LC ebook record available at https://lccn.loc.gov/2022042826

for my parents, Tom and Jean Spoth

"The best of all breathing and forever the best of all listening."

CONTENTS

ACKNOWLEDGMENTS

It is, of course, customary to remark that my debts are many, and this project has been sufficiently long in coming to consign some of those debts beyond memory. As such, I would like to offer acknowledgments to those that memory preserves, with the understanding that there are many others whose anonymous and unpredictable influence on this text I understand only as the leaf understands the hurricane.

More than anything else, this volume owes its existence to the dozens of students who have avidly participated in my "Southern Literature and the Environment" class at Eckerd College: their range of reactions to the involved texts, from flamboyant appreciation to bored disdain, have illuminated my own readings consistently over the last ten years of teaching.

My colleagues at Eckerd, especially Julienne Empric and Jared Stark in the Literature discipline, also deserve my thanks. Their ceaseless support for my research and teaching interests influenced the direction that the book oriented itself toward in immeasurable ways.

The final years of this project were graciously supported by a Chapin Fellowship administered by Eckerd, and I owe the college, and Lloyd Chapin himself, a considerable debt of gratitude. The staff at the Rose Library at Emory University and the J. D. Williams Library at the University of Mississippi were exceptionally helpful in allowing access to original sources regarding O'Connor and Faulkner, respectively.

As ever, I am in constant reliance on (and frequently in awe of) the sharp intellect and wise council of my partner, Amanda Hagood. The influences that she had on this text are impossible to accurately enumerate, from suggestions of primary and secondary texts to address to new and insightful comments on sources that I had thought I fully understood.

Ruin
and Resilience

Against Ruin

The tradition of the oppressed teaches us that the "state of
emergency" in which we live is not the exception but the rule.
We must attain to a conception of history that is in keeping
with this insight.

— WALTER BENJAMIN,
"Theses on the Philosophy of History" (257)

LATE IN THE EVENING, a hand-painted gondola makes its cautious way
through the flooded streets of what was once Miami, a badly effaced plaque
on the crumbling planetarium the only definite clue as to the city's identity.
The vessel contains two people: a gondolier (Janelle Picaro, better known as
"Blister") and her passenger. This man does not reveal his true name (Blister
refers to him as "the Missing Person," an alias she borrows from a poster),
though he is forthcoming about his history: he lived here, once, when the city
was composed of land rather than water. He was responsible for constructing
the failed seawalls that were supposed to contain the encroaching ocean. The
lives of his wife and two sons were the price of that failure. He is sick, visibly
and grievously, and has elected to spend his last moments atop the ruins of
the seawall on the anniversary of his family's death. Blister describes him as
"a man who has written the last scene of his life," and it is distinctly a tragedy
(224). As the gondola inches toward the seawall in the teeth of a rising storm,
the Missing Person seems compelled to recite his own culpability, eagerly
expecting Blister's confirmation of his guilt: "We all knew the end was coming. Don't let anybody tell you otherwise. . . . We ate up the whole horizon.
We left you a ghost town. Not even a town. A toxic slough—" which Blister
finally interrupts: "This is our home . . . and we are not ghosts."

I begin with this scene from Karen Russell's "The Gondoliers" (2018) because the respective standpoints of its two main characters correspond precisely to the two poles of southern environmental philosophy and rhetoric that I will be engaging with over the course of this volume. The perspective of the Missing Person is the narrative of ruin—through an excess of hubris, incompetence, and myopia, humans (himself in particular, but also those of his generation) are "criminals" who have "ruined the world," and survivors of the cataclysm are inhuman freaks, "the birds of Chernobyl," sentenced to short lives of disease and dysphoria (216, 218). When Blister looks out over the same flooded landscape, however, she sees transformation rather than destruction, an environment that requires new skills and adaptations to navigate and a population that is proving itself adequate to the task.[1] This latter position, which I simply call "resilience," prioritizes human survival at all costs, reacting to environmental change with durability and adaptability. The correct course of action under the narrative of resilience is always the one that offers the highest chance of survival and maintenance of human life. Resilience is morally neutral; it does not contemplate whether behaviors are good or evil, only whether they preserve life. The contrary perspective, the narrative of ruin, sees large-scale environmental change as destruction, an irrevocable loss from which humankind can never recover. Moreover, this destruction is phrased as tragedy: ruin does not share resilience's neutrality, instead dwelling upon a set of errors, failures, or sins committed in the past.

I will return to "The Gondoliers" later in this Introduction, but it is worth noting, at this point, that Blister's philosophy of resilience runs against the grain of environmental sentiment in the South, and in South Florida especially; for some time, the dominant rhetoric has been that of ruin, loss, and the suffering of both human and nonhuman nature. In this sense, the Missing Person's perspective is reinforced by the weight of common wisdom. On numerous occasions, he instructs Blister on how she *should* feel: betrayed, angry, deprived, corrupted. The ruination visited upon Miami *should* be tragic, a monument to human hubris and inaction. In the US South, however, the rhetoric departs somewhat from this androcentric perspective, frequently regarding the land *itself* as not simply the victim of human misuse, but in fact already condemned, forsaken, ruined—in Faulkner's phrase: "a land primed for fatality and already cursed with it" (*Absalom, Absalom!* 16). For Faulkner, this "fatality" stemmed from both atrocities inflicted upon the human inhabitants of the region by the legacy of slavery and (later in his career) by the physical scars left upon the landscape by industry and agriculture. In Faulkner, there is seldom (if ever) the notion that these losses can be compensated for or alleviated; they are permanent stains, the "original sin" to which his work perpetually alludes. Why does the work of the South's highest-profile author continually insist on the ruination of his home region?

A better question might be: why is it useful, and perhaps even attractive, for southern authors, not to mention critics and historians dealing with the region, to think of the landscape as despoiled, tainted, and, in a word, "ruined"? Such rhetoric is frequently predicated on an exaggerated representation of the "unspoiled" character of the landscape prior to a cataclysmic turning point (a war, a natural disaster, a new invention). Christopher Rieger, in *Clear-Cutting Eden* (2009), correctly notes that southern literature seems obsessed with "the sense of a lost golden age" located in "an irrecoverable past . . . rather than an actual place of the present or future," suggesting that this particular ecological notion is intentional and serves a social function, but what might that function be (4)? Proceeding along the lines of southern self-fashioning— that is, what narrative the South chooses to follow in order to promote its own sense of coherence—pioneered by Michael Kreyling in *Inventing Southern Literature* (1998) and subsequently exploded by Scott Romine in *The Real South* (2008), what does the repeated claim of the southern landscape's "ruined" state say about how authors wish to represent the historical and current state of southern environments? Just as Leo Marx identifies Robert Beverly's designation of Virginia as "one of the 'Gardens of the World'" in *History and Present State of Virginia* (1705) as evincing contrary desires for "an Edenic land of primitive splendor inhabited by noble savages" and "an abundance produced by work [or] improvement," we must be aware that ruinous environmental rhetoric reveals more about the interpreter of landscapes than the landscapes themselves (85).[2] Embracing the narrative of ruin, the present volume argues, enables easily legible patterns of (tragic) misuse to emerge out of the complexities of historical contingency while simultaneously relegating southern environmentalism to a dominantly symbolic role.

This book contends that the helical interchange between ruin and resilience constitutes one of the fundamental touchstones of southern environmentalism, but these large conceptual categories are by no means confined to the South exclusively, and "the South" itself is a highly fluid signifier, signifying something different (or, in some cases, nothing at all) to a range of readers and audiences. To what extent, then, does it make sense to discuss "ruin and resilience in the South"? I would answer: to the extent that these qualities shape a narrative that those who seek to delineate the borders of the region (including myself) find explanatory. That is to say, speaking of each of these individual terms ("ruin," "resilience," and "the South") has utility insofar as they help to account for the actions of an ill-defined and diverse population that has acted in correspondingly inconsistent manners toward the environment. Discussing "ruin" and "resilience" in "the South," then, does not constitute an attempt to fortify or disassemble any hard-and-fast definition of those terms, but rather to offer them as, to paraphrase Faulkner, a means of extracting order against the turgid background of a horrible and bloody mischancing of environmental affairs.

Frequently this order, it must be said, takes the form of declension—not an unusual master narrative for accounts of settler colonial interactions with the environment. Joseph Meeker contended, in *The Comedy of Survival* (1974), that we tend to favor erroneously tragic conceptions (heavily influenced by morality, agency, and heroism) of our relationship with the environment. The rigidity of the tragic mode, its emphasis on human flaws and sins, and its disastrous conclusion align with latter-day narratives of slow, inevitable anthropogenic environmental decline culminating in destruction, extinction, or (at the very least) a radically reshaped planet. However, conceiving of environmental use—especially in the South—as irredeemably tragic also forecloses on the possibility of recuperating damaged landscapes; if the land is always already doomed, there is little to be done beyond a blind execution of the fated decline.

Yet the dominance of southern tragic environmentalism is less intractable than it might appear in literature and criticism. Scott Romine writes that southern narrative is a constantly shifting "archive of improvisations grounded in space and time, a register of imagined relations to artificial territorialities, themed spaces, virtual terrains, built environments, localities, and 'the global'" (*The Real South* 17). And Suzanne Jones and Sharon Monteith, in *South to a New Place* (2002), similarly define southernness as a fluid, ongoing process toward forming imagined communities, "a matter of *language* and *communal ritual*, the human habit of positioning the self with the help of the word and others, giving a local habitation and a name to things to secure their and our identity" (xxi, emphasis theirs).

In short: when we discuss the southern environment no less than when we discuss the South itself, how we phrase that discussion and what sorts of

4

narratives we attach to the region are concerned less with any fundamental truth at its core than with what we *want* or *desire* the place to represent. As Dana Phillips writes in *The Truth of Ecology* (2003), American authors and thinkers have perennially "attempted to define the basic character of historical processes in terms of the unfolding and eventual fulfillment of grand narrative designs," and the resulting stories that they developed (Turner's Frontier Thesis, for instance) "are . . . ways of giving shape to what otherwise might seem like anarchic or chaotic processes" (55–56). When we discuss narratives of ruin and resilience in the South, we are in essence discussing *stories* of environmental collapse or endurance—stories that are subject to interpretation, reworking, and change.

Thus, this book's intent is to propose alternatives to the popular ruin-narrative in the South, to reinterpret southern environmental texts—some familiar, others quite recent—in light of the massive changes that have attended the Anthropocene Era, to articulate manners in which resilience might be teased out of ruin. The time frame of this book ranges from John Muir's travelogues in the years immediately following the Civil War to contemporary narratives of climate change. Though I begin with Muir's 1867 *A Thousand-Mile Walk to the Gulf* in order to illustrate proto-environmentalist articulations of lack toward the southern landscape, and discuss several landmarks of Modernist and late Modernist southern environmental literature along the way, my primary purview is the late twentieth and early twenty-first centuries. While it is true that the discourse of vulnerability—that is, the notion that certain aspects of the region that have been implicitly static are in fact imperiled—has been deployed in service of southern culture (or, rather, a wide range of ideological bents that are subsumed within the lumpy category of capital-S "Southern culture") by Agrarian, pseudo-Agrarian, and neo-Agrarian authors through the middle of the twentieth century, these writings generally eschew a true environmental ethos, preferring abstract ideas of "the land" or "the soil." It is only when the human pressures that spurred first-wave environmentalism in the West (large-scale urban development, corporate-controlled extractive industries, construction of modern roads) finally swept across the South that the region's authors and artists began to respond in earnest—and, by that point, many of the West's nightmares (poor agricultural practices, "removal" of Native Americans, deforestation, etc.) had already come true in the South. From the beginning, then, southern environmental writers have always been conscious of their late arrival on the stage—a major contributing factor to the prevailing attitude of ruin. In the late twentieth and early twenty-first centuries, however, as the threats to the region (particularly the coast, but also the South as a whole) come into ever-sharper focus, southern writers begin to tentatively imagine alternatives to ruin.

―――――

Before putting forth detailed examples of resilience and ruin in southern literature, it may be valuable to survey the state of southern ecocriticism—its brief history and its many challenges and potentialities. Considering the South's cautious approach toward embracing environmental precepts, it is perhaps unsurprising that existing critical studies of the region's environment tend toward a focus on proven, though oftentimes somewhat outmoded, generic concepts: nature writing, for instance, pastoralism, regionalism, or (unique to the South) Agrarianism. A short, though by no means comprehensive, list of texts that have dealt in some capacity with southern literature and the environment might include Lewis Simpson's *The Dispossessed Garden: Pastoral and History in Southern Literature* (1975), Louise Westing's *Sacred Groves and Ravaged Gardens: The Fiction of Eudora Welty, Carson McCullers, and Flannery O'Connor* (1985), two volumes of proceedings from the annual Faulkner and Yoknapatawpha conference, *Faulkner and the Natural World* and *Faulkner and the Ecology of the South* (1999, 2005), Suzanne Jones and Sharon Monteith's *South to a New Place: Region, Literature, Culture* (2002), and Christopher Rieger's *Clear-Cutting Eden: Ecology and the Pastoral in Southern Literature* (2009). The latter few sources do emerge after the dawn of ecocriticism narrowly conceived (the publication of Lawrence Buell's *The Environmental Imagination* in 1995), though they are, by and large, concerned with rectifying the field's reactionary tendencies and principles—the aforementioned entanglement of environmental and racial rhetoric, for example, the problematic work of the Agrarians, or the fetishization and appropriation of the southern "sense of place" for all manner of political and intellectual aims.

If the field had been, if not cleared, at least prepared for the advent of southern ecocriticism proper by scholars of the first decade of the twenty-first century, a new surge in southern environmental history texts and nature writing reinforced the impression. A (partial) survey of such works would include such titles as Thomas D. Clark's *The Greening of the South: The Recovery of Land and Forest* (1984), Bob Bullard's *Dumping in Dixie* (1990), Albert E. Cowdrey's *This Land, This South: An Environmental History* (1996), Mikko

Saikku's, *This Delta, This Land: An Environmental History of the Yazoo-Mississippi Floodplain* (2005), Donald E. Davis's *Homeplace Geography: Essays for Appalachia* (2006), Jack Temple Kirby's *Mockingbird Song: Ecological Landscapes of the South* (2008), Paul Sutter and Christopher J. Manganiello's *Environmental History and the American South: A Reader* (2009), Dorinda G. Dallmeyer's *Elemental South: An Anthology of Southern Nature Writing* (2009), and Erin Stewart Mauldin's *Unredeemed Land: An Environmental History of Civil War and Emancipation in the Cotton South* (2018). What is particularly remarkable about these works is, quite simply, their tardiness; though regional natural histories centered around other US regions such as the West and the Northeast became common in the late 1980s and early 1990s, similar studies of the South tended to lag a decade, if not two, behind the trend.

Nonetheless, the preponderance of these works, the majority of which emanate from the early twenty-first century, suggest that the time for a full-formed southern ecocriticism has come, an intimation that has been reinforced by the publication, in 2019, of Zackary Vernon's *Ecocriticism and the Future of Southern Studies.* Vernon acknowledges, in his introduction, that even in the recent past, "only a small percentage" of articles in top southern studies journals "addresses [sic] either past or present ecological concerns, and most are not firmly grounded in ecocriticism or environmental studies" (3). Though Vernon marks the aim of his volume as similar to the existing corpus of proto-ecocritical works, to wit, "complicat[ing] traditional conceptions of 'nature' and 'sense of place,'" the exceptional number of disciplinary perspectives represented therein suggest innumerable future paths for southern ecocriticism (6). Vernon's volume positions itself at the beginning of, rather than amidst, a corpus of works of southern ecocriticism, indicating that the field still has a long road ahead of it.

What can the South and its literature contribute to ecocriticism writ large? Christopher Rieger contends, in *Clear-Cutting Eden*, that the region can offer valuable lessons in shaking off old stereotypes toward the environment. Twentieth-century southern authors, Rieger argues, "reject the static, passive conception of nature implied in the traditional pastoral garden," instead positing "a network model of the natural world that includes humans, placing people and their environments in a reciprocal relationship" (7). Bart Welling has also claimed, in "A Meeting with Old Ben" (2002), that "as ecocriticism works to extend its geographical, historical, canonical, and theoretical horizons 'beyond nature writing' of the traditional varieties, it will profit greatly by confronting the challenges presented by southern authors" (461). The specific character of those challenges, Welling claims, is a vision of nature "that has always really been a set of contested *places*—never simply 'virgin,' forever locked in (over)heated dialogue with the forces of language and culture" (462). It is the explicit *lack* of any kind of perfected past that animates the main issues of southern ecocriticism, the lack itself being informed in part by the region's difficult history and in part as a backlash against the romanticization of that past by postbellum authors. In a 2012 essay, Welling goes on to claim that southern environmentalism is interesting precisely because it never had a preservationist ethos and has always lacked an idealized natural past to return to: "Southern ecocriticism will participate actively in the important scholarly task of making sense of the non-sublime and ecologically degraded . . . places where most of the Earth's inhabitants, human or not, actually live" (132). Though I believe both Rieger and Welling are correct insofar as they note how southern ecocriticism challenges traditional preservationist ideas of "the pastoral" and "the sublime," balancing the field on a notion of lack or ruin makes the region perhaps more homogenous than is desirable—what about southern authors and artists who *do* have a preservationist ethos? Or those who still believe even in outmoded concepts such as "the sublime"?

On two major points regarding southern environmental history and activism the aforementioned scholarship tends to agree: first, the South has always had a weaker environmental tradition than most, if not all, of the country's other regions. Second, and perhaps as a consequence of the aforementioned weakness, less attention has been paid to the region by environmental writers, thinkers, activists, and historians. Albert G. Way puts the matter succinctly in a 2009 article: "The West's role in the national conservation movement is beyond reproach, and the Northeast has recently received more attention, but we usually view the South as a conservation backwater" (Sutter & Manganiello 284). Correspondingly, Mikko Saikku writes in *This Delta, This Land* that, until recently, "the American South was largely neglected in environmental historiography when compared to other major regions of the United States, especially the West" (3). Though individual landscapes in the South tend to be further from the Romantic ideal of sublimity in nature than the great national park sites of the West are, the West is not a *place* in any greater capacity than other regions and, in a manner of speaking, does not have a greater *quantity* of environment than any other. If foundational US environmentalism was predicated on the fragility of landscapes, their vulnerability to human misuse, how is it that its thinkers tended to pass over the South, a region that had already endured centuries of that same misuse?

The challenges that environmental perspectives on southern literature and culture face are thus twofold: difficulties in dealing with both *nonhuman* and *human* nature. In regard to the former, the South offers landscapes that are frequently difficult to reconcile with traditional ideals of Romanticism and preservationism. Jon Smith writes, in a 2003 article, that the southern region "resists figurations of identity-bestowing American 'wilderness' simply because it is *hot:* swampy, snaky, roiling with deadly, engulfing agency" and, as a result, southern environmental thought finds it immensely difficult to "negotiate between the discourses of Muir and Humboldt, spirit and body, mountains and coast, temperate and tropical, sublime global-northern wilderness and marvelously real global southern jungle" (116–17). The swamp, for Smith as well as for Anthony Wilson in *Shadow and Shelter* (2006), becomes metonymic for the region as a whole: mysterious, complex, dangerous, and, above all, recalcitrant, resistant to attempts to contain or fully comprehend it.

These impediments, however, also represent crucial points of inflection through which we might reconceive our relationship not only to the South, but to environmentalist methodologies more broadly. With local, grassroots environmental hazards repeatedly overshadowed by looming planetary catastrophes, ostensibly "useless" regions that were once marginalized on aesthetic, economic, or social grounds such as the swamp, the tundra, the polar regions, and the open ocean have become increasingly visible, powerful, and threatened. It is correspondingly becoming more and more unfashionable, in environmental thought, to hold prejudices against subaltern landscapes. Jay Watson, in a 2016 article, acknowledged that "ecocriticism and environmental studies . . . have historically underrepresented the scruffy South in favor of more sublime landscapes and literatures," but that, precisely owing to the scruffy/sublime distance, "Southern studies and environmental studies can thus take each other to new places on southern ground" (158). It may be that studying the South through an environmental lens can aid in one of US environmentalism's most prominent and persistent ideological quandaries: how to divorce itself from the idea of certain partitioned and designated sublime "natural areas" with vast wastes of urban or rural decay separating them.

Yet, difficult as it may be to align southern landscapes with the stereotypical vistas that have preoccupied traditional environmentalism, the region's social structure—the human difficulties I have alluded to above—presents an even more formidable boundary to southern ecocriticism. To some extent, these difficulties are adumbrated by political characteristics of the region with which anyone acquainted with the leanings of the New South should be familiar: conservatism, states' rights, and rapid industrialization, for instance. Paul Sutter attributes the dearth of environmental studies of the South to precisely these human failings: "While the environmental crises of the interwar years produced an early though abortive move toward southern environmental history, it was the postwar environmental movement that produced the field, and that movement was weak in the South. In a disproportionately poor and rural region renowned for being friendly to migrating industries and slow to regulate environmental impacts, southern environmentalists have had a hard time getting traction" (4). Understanding how these factors originate and constellate in the South, however, requires extensive attention to human factors that have, historically, been tarred with the brush of longstanding reactionary politics, racism, and corruption. Though Sutter is correct to associate the South's relative absence from the nascent environmentalist movement with post-WWII New South policies, the roots of the region's anti-environmentalism run deeper than this—as deeply as disenfranchisement of Black people from property ownership, for instance, or as deeply as agricultural mismanagement of land. In other words, as deeply as a number of things that we think of as "always having been a problem in the South."

From this perspective, southern ecocriticism is hobbled before it leaves the gate. One of the critical school's hairiest bugbears is the idea that, if the traditional targets of environmentalism are dramatic, unusual, and exceptional regions, the constituency of environmentalism is exceptional people—specifically wealthy, liberal, educated, and, implicitly, white activists. The South is none of these things, or, at least, is not dominantly associated with them. This deterministic perspective, which suggests that environmentalists and their causes *have always been* a certain kind of person and a certain kind of cause, and that the South *has always been* interested in different kinds of people and different kinds of causes, sockets seamlessly into much of the logic that governs southern discourse on "place"—specifically, "place" as something construed according to an intractable natural order. Literary regionalism in the South for a very long time relied on dubious linkages between places or climates and the (often racially coded) people who inhabit them. Such connections oftentimes reach back into history for historical treatises that affirm biases of the present. Take, for example, Montesquieu's *The Spirit of the Laws* (1748), books 17 and 18 in particular, in which the author studies the relationship between climate and government and agriculture and government, respectively.[3] The central contention of these two chapters can be adumbrated by the author's claim that "the effeminacy of the people in hot climates has almost always rendered them slaves; and that the bravery of those in cold climates has enabled them to maintain their liberties." Montesquieu's analysis is, as one might expect, highly deterministic, taking as given the fact that "political servitude does not less depend on the nature of the climate than that which is civil and domestic" and that the fertility of the soil naturally encourages "subjection and dependence."

The ideas of Montesquieu and other Enlightenment-era thinkers would prove to have a surprisingly lengthy half-life in the South; Christopher Morris, in "A More Southern Environmental History" (2009), has traced the progress of such early attempts to equate environment and behavior in the South during the nineteenth and early twentieth centuries, noting that William Elliott of South Carolina "declared in 1848 that slavery would 'endure as long as the climate which called it into being; which sustains it, and at the same time justifies it'" (585). To some extent, such a rhetorical move is unsurprising; reactionary political elites have repeatedly attempted to construe their own power, especially power over othered populations, as arising out of some kind of essentialized relationship with the environment. What *is* surprising is that this rhetoric lingers in the South long after the conclusion of the Civil War—though the Vanderbilt Agrarians are most often tarred as perpetuating the fetishized link between (implicitly white) southerners and their environment, Morris also notes Robert R. Russel's belief, as articulated in a 1938 essay, that "Southern economic progress or lack thereof owed more to climate, topography, and natural resources than it did to slavery," ideas that "were modified and repeated decades later by Robert William Fogel and Stanley L. Engerman" (586).[4] In these accounts, to return to Montesquieu's language, political effects are essentially grafted onto natural causes in the interest of making the former as deterministic and objective as the latter, and to the detriment of both.

In 2002, Scott Romine noted that "traditional" conceptions of regionalism imply "a kind of geographical determinism; a regional text is assumed to display certain characteristics deriving from place" (*South to a New Place* 27). Though this permits southern literature to be considered as a corpus, with its own distinctive set of tropes (such as Jerry Leath Mills's semihumorous contention that each work of southern literature must include at least one dead mule), it also imprisons the field of southern environmentalism within a ceaseless cycle of racism, poverty, and bad logic. After all, how could studies of the southern environment be taken seriously when the field has effectively been poisoned by its own history? Sutter contends, in *Environmental History and the American South* (2009), that the "burden" of southern environmentalism is "to insist upon the efficacy of environmental analyses while also confronting their past misuse" (3). Southern ecocritics would thus seem, out of necessity, to be trapped in a cycle of anxiety toward the region's previous failed attempts to deploy environmentalist methodologies, not to mention the almost incalculable harm inflicted on southern landscapes.

———

This rather dolorous view of southern ecocriticism could be interpreted as guiding the contemporary reader toward the dominant narrative of ruin rather than toward resilience; if the problems facing the field are problems that have proven intractable over the course of the region's history, if southern ecocritical study is hampered by both human and inhuman prejudices, and if the very metadiscourse of the field itself has been rendered toxic by decades (perhaps even centuries) of bad science, regressive politics, and iconoclasm, why attempt southern ecocriticism at all?

The first answer that I would offer is that, at long last, the time is right. Mainstream environmentalism, having upheld the stereotype I advanced above (that of the environmentalist as implicitly wealthy, educated, liberal, and white), has in recent years come around to the notion that other voices might contribute to the conversation. In 2014, a landmark study by Dorceta Taylor noted the startling lack of diversity in environmental organizations; in a 2018 interview, Taylor stated: "If environmental organizations continue to ignore 35 percent to 40 percent of the population, they're going to be in a world of hurt in terms of finding talent as we move toward a majority minority country" (Toomey). Similarly, in July 2020, the Sierra Club made the controversial decision to distance itself from John Muir, the club's founder, whose derogatory remarks about Black and Native Americans in his nature writing troubled his preservationist legacy. "We must," wrote executive director Michael Brune, "take this moment to reexamine our past and our substantial role in perpetuating white supremacy," noting Muir's longstanding friendship with Henry Fairfield Osborn, one of the founders of the American Eugenics

Society (Brune). Karen Bell's *Diversity and Inclusion in Environmentalism* appeared in early June 2021, signifying a new interest in environmentalism's race, gender, age, and other biases. If environmentalism is becoming more egalitarian, learning to accept not only alternative landscapes, but alternative voices, it stands to reason that even regions that have traditionally been regarded as acting antithetically to environmental aims should receive attention.

More to the point: it has become clear in recent years that collapsing the boundary between "humanity" and "nature," as advocated by William Cronon and many others, assumes a certain homogeneity of the former category, and, in reality, such cognitive breakthroughs are deeply imbricated in race, class, and gender identities that must be unpacked and analyzed. As ecocriticism sharpens its focus on environmental racism and environmental justice, the South's long history of struggles, reforms, and, yes, failures in those realms can prove instructive. Moreover, the region's history of such failures reveals unique ways in which the past weighs down upon the environmental racism of the present. A resident of Geismer, Louisiana (in the center of the infamous "Cancer Corridor" between New Orleans and Baton Rouge), speaking with Bob Bullard, claims: "We are all victimized by a system that puts dollars before everything else. That's the way it was in the old days when the dog and whips were masters, and that's the way it is today when we got stuff in the water and air we can't even see that can kill us deader than we ever thought we could die" (104). Bullard's *Dumping in Dixie* (1990), a landmark of the environmental justice movement, contends that there is a vast gulf between the environmental concerns of people of color living in segregated urban areas or near hazardous industrial sites and the ideology of "traditional" environmentalists concerned with wilderness and wildlife.[5] This gap, in the South, is as deep and profound as the color line.

The intractability of environmental racism in the South means that Bullard's work could easily follow the dominant narrative of ruin; he notes that, for liberal northern audiences, the South is still predominantly "a backward land, based on its social, economic, political, and environmental policies," that consequently was used as a "sacrifice zone" for the rest of the nation's waste (97). The "colonial mentality" of the South, brought on by "the legacy of slavery, Jim Crow, and white resistance to equal justice for all," not only inflicted economic and social damage, but "left the region's air, water, and land the most industry befouled in the United States" (97). However, Bullard's work implies that the pervasiveness of environmental racism in the South does not necessarily mean that environmentalism itself should be abandoned; rather, it indicates that the region needs a different environmental methodology. Resilience needs to be dragged out of the shadow of ruin, however strange the former and however entrenched the latter might be. For the communities that Bullard studies, as for other victims of environmental injustice across the South, this process involves not the scrappy and self-motivated protests and direct action of second-wave environmentalism, but the acquisition of tools that have historically been denied to those communities: competent legal counsel, independent environmental testing, and media coverage. Only in the last few decades have these tools even begun to be leveraged by disenfranchised groups in the South; only recently has resilience, for them, come to constitute more than bare survival, more than being diseased, oppressed, imperiled—but alive.

———

The storm over what was once Biscayne Bay worsens. Blister wants to turn back, but the Missing Person will have none of it; he is "furious that his stage directions are getting eaten by the wind" (227). Their struggle is ended by a rogue wave that sweeps the Missing Person overboard; Blister hears him laboring through the water toward the seawall, but his death is not narrated. If he conceives of himself as the director of the final act of his life's play, as Russell's frequent allusions to dramaturgy suggest, it is a performance delivered to an empty theater. Instead, the final pages of the story focus on Blister, her reunion with her sister Viola, and their struggle to escape the "dead spot" near the seawall. Hope comes in the form of alien nocturnal voices that overload the sisters' echolocation with the insistence that *"this is not the end of the world"* (233). Blister knows that she must attune herself to these sounds, but fears what will happen when she does: "I am afraid of the voices lifting out of the dark. I am afraid to join them. But perhaps we will have to, if we want to survive" (233). These are the last words in the story—the fate of the sisters, foundering in a distant backwater of New Florida as the night deepens and the storm rolls in, is left uncertain.

The ending of "The Gondoliers" is, of course, about survival in a landscape that has experienced and is still experiencing rapid anthropogenic change, change on a scale that the title characters find terrifying. Resilience is not a choice for Blister and Viola; it is a necessity. The alternative to resilience is ruin, the theatrical self-destruction pursued by the Missing Person.

The mood of the story's conclusion might be called perilous optimism: a deep sense of trepidation coupled with the understanding that the gondoliers, like all of the other organisms native to New Florida, will perform the necessary adaptations to go on living. Whatever comes next for Blister and Viola, whatever new trials await them, they (and, implicitly, the besieged and endangered communities of South Florida) will rise to the challenge. And, even if they fail, the struggle to adapt and react to the environment's demands, however painful, is presented as clearly preferable to the Missing Person's nihilistic perspective. Resilience struggles against ruin and achieves a fragile, reluctant victory in this short story; it is not an attractive alternative, but the only viable one.

In reference to this indelible twinning of ruin and resilience, both within "The Gondoliers" and in this volume *in toto:* it will no doubt be remarked that a dualistic division of southern environmentalism into parallel categories of ruin and resilience is too simplistic, unnuanced, and absolute. Indeed, it is easy, in a story like "The Gondoliers," to establish binarisms: Blister's cautious optimism versus the Missing Person's crushing pessimism, for instance, or the younger generation's futurity versus the older generation's fatalism, or communality and familial support versus a single consuming ego. Resilience versus ruin. But I would like to suggest that neither resilience nor ruin are what we might believe them to be on the surface of things and, moreover, that there is not necessarily a hierarchical relationship between the two any more than there is a hierarchy of the future and the past. Nor are the two mutually exclusive; though "The Gondoliers" casts the future of South Florida as a choice between the Missing Person's defeatism and Blister's endurance, with a clear preference for the latter, both are equally powerful narrative and rhetorical stratagems. And, in their capacity as rhetoric, they do not necessarily operate in wholly logical, deterministic manners; ruin can result even from well-laid plans, and resilience can arise when all hope seems lost. Environmentalists use the term "global weirding" to describe the unpredictable sets of changes that arise seemingly at random—a town in Colorado might experience record cold temperatures while a heat wave bakes the Southwest—when worldwide systems such as the climate are disrupted, and the machinations of ruin and resilience follow similarly chaotic patterns.

Blister is reluctant to listen to the "new voices" at the end of "The Gondoliers." It would be easier to remain within the familiar confines of wind, water, and eroded concrete. The nocturnal voices are strange, incomprehensible, menacing, but they also offer the only hope for survival. Environmentalism in the age of global weirding means, through either necessity or simple abnegation, an acceptance of nonlinear, even chaotic narratives. Thus, the theme of this book is not how ruin pervades southern environmental literature, or how resilience supplants ruin. Rather, it is about how, as the twentieth century has given way to the twenty-first, inseparable these narratives have become. Resilience and ruin, rather than remaining externalized stories "told by history" or "proven with science," become internalized accounts of how unpredictably, and occasionally how haphazardly, humans have approached the environment. And the South is a uniquely promising region in which to explore such narratives.

Though several of the ensuing chapters provide close readings of nonfiction writing and films, my focus is dominantly on literature. The reasoning for this is simple: literature has, historically, been the locus of the environment in the southern imaginary. Christopher Morris notes that twentieth-century southern natural historians and biologists "saw in their research a scientific foundation for southern distinctiveness," suggesting the nascence of an organized study of southern landscapes (588). However, these sources "have largely been ignored by Southern historians, who are quick to draw on the region's literary but not its scientific traditions. A Southern environmental historian is more likely to read William Faulkner's stories of the Big Woods than the Odum brothers' *Fundamentals of Ecology* (1953)" (588). The first task of southern ecocriticism, then, is narrative—taking account of the shape and texture of southern nature as it has been depicted in literature and other confabulative forms and considering the implications of such representations. This book, therefore, pays broad attention to texts with both self-avowed literary aims and those that adopt a more popular perspective. In the South, environmental ethoi and aesthetics may appear in the region in ways that are unexpected, sudden, or unpredictable. They may appear, for example, in the discourse surrounding "traditional" foodways in the South, or in science-fiction novels, by the roadside and buried in the mud rather than whispering through majestic redwoods. Such a methodology is vital for any ecocritical approach to the South.

My first chapter, "The Region in Ruins," makes the case that the dominant mode of conceiving of the southern environment in postbellum history, literature, and criticism has been the familiar narrative of ruin. The South's land and people, the ruin-narrative tells us, have been repeatedly misused, oppressed, and tormented to the extent that the damage to the region is tragic and irreparable. And, since a tragedy is nothing without the fundamental flaws of its characters, the ruination of the region can be easily traced back to simple human failures—greed, for instance, or hubris, or cruelty—that form broadly legible patterns of loss. The dominance of this narrative is reinforced by Faulkner's enunciation, in what has become the most widely read triad of all southern environmental texts, of a tragic fate for the region's wildernesses. In my reading of "The Old People," "The Bear," and "Delta Autumn," I detail how Faulkner's writing does indeed chronicle the region's ruin, though only through an antiquated, binaristic preservationist lens. As an alternative to the declensionary direction of southern environmentalism, I also study Natasha Trethewey's *Native Guard* (2006), which exists in the shadow of both Faulkner's writing and the institution of southern literature overall, con-curring with this literary tradition's tragic narratives in many ways. However, Trethewey insists that such a narrative is insufficient, offering a resilience that is informed, rather than precluded, by ruin.

My second chapter, "Resilient Routes," opens with the thesis posed by the recent film *General Orders No. 9* (2009), to wit, that the widespread con-struction of interstate highways in the South represented an irreparable de-struction of aesthetically pure southern landscapes and ways of life, a different articulation of the ruin-narrative. While the rural infrastructure of the South symbolized a certain harmony of humans and landscape, the film argues, the interstate is an imposition that trivializes that same landscape. With this contention in mind, I examine the approach of two major southern authors, Eudora Welty and Flannery O'Connor, specifically their novels and short stories dealing most directly with roads and travel. In Welty's work, my read-ing of *The Robber Bridegroom* (1942), *The Optimist's Daughter* (1972), and several short stories finds, we observe scant trace of the highway as a wedge driven between humans and nature—rather, the travel enabled by roadways in the South frequently acts as a means of establishing and fortifying such connections. In O'Connor's work, however, we see a far more dualistic vision of the function of roads in the South, with infrastructure frequently symbol-izing the disruption of an order that a higher power has put in place. These two writers' texts, taken in tandem, show how the large-scale mobilization of the South that accompanied the rise of democratized interstate travel led to environmental narratives of ruin and resilience, loss and transformation, with the latter frequently arising unexpectedly from the former.

My third chapter, "Of Yams and Canned Pasta," interrogates the concept that specific foods and their consumption compromise a means of affiliating oneself with southern nature in an unproblematic manner. Not only does the globalization of southern foodways frequently downplay the racial and historical contexts that gave rise to the cuisine, it also tends toward an appeal to a visceral sense of place and belonging that attempts to compensate for the region's lack of effective environmental policy. This argument concurs with southern natural-historical narratives of ruin that claim the failure of "traditional" environmentalism in the region, though it offers the ostensibly racially and politically neutral sphere of foodways as a means of rehabilitation and compensation. To see this argument in action, I turn to two recent novels, Toni Morrison's *Home* (2012) and Fannie Flagg's *Fried Green Tomatoes at the Whistle-Stop Cafe* (1997). Morrison deploys traditional southern foodways talismanically against both racism and the erosion of identity that accompanies late capitalism more broadly, using (as she does in many of her other novels) its origin, preparation, and ingredients to label particular landscapes as natural ("home") or artificial ("elsewhere"). My reading of Flagg's novel, conversely, shows that what appears to be a visceral equation of food, place, and identity is in fact an acute awareness of the discursivity of southern foodways and their dialogic production out of a multitude of various—oftentimes conflicting—notions of what constitutes home and authenticity. If southern foodways are bent to an ecocritical intent, I suggest, neither traditionalist narratives of loss and recovery or more global synthetic conceptions of southern cuisine can be discarded—ruin and resilience are symbiotically connected.

My fourth chapter, "Leaving the Ruins," posits the aftermath of major natural disasters such as floods and hurricanes as better predictors of any hypothetical southern environmentalism than more traditional romanticizations of human/natural relationships. I begin with a brief account of how the impact of natural disasters, particularly in the South, are greatly exacerbated by human factors: mismanagement of natural resources and critical landscapes, structural violence inflicted upon social others, and limited mobility. It is simple to read such elements as reinforcing the southern ruin-narrative, though one school of ecocritical thought among southern scholars contends that the recovery period following natural disasters represents an opportunity to transcend these challenges and affirm a strong connection between southerners and their environments. However, my reading of Faulkner's "Old Man" (1939), Zora Neale Hurston's *Their Eyes Were Watching God* (1937), and Benh Zeitlin's film *Beasts of the Southern Wild* (2012) suggests not only that such recovery periods tend to *reveal* more structural violence than they obscure, but also that they challenge the entire idea of southern regionalism itself. In a sense, rather than suggesting a rehabilitation or reinforcement of southern environmentalism, these texts reveal the ways in which the center was never as stable as it was, perhaps, presumed to be. Their resilience is predicated on a rapidly shifting notion of place that only becomes more indefinite over time.

My fifth chapter, "Glimpses of the Whole," moves from regional cataclysms to the far more wide-reaching and slow-moving phenomenon of anthropogenic climate change. This transition produces intense cognitive difficulties, however; most analyses mark the scope and scale of the problem as one of the primary obstacles standing in the way of effectively conceiving of and addressing climate change. For this reason, climate fiction frequently turns to personal, individual stories rather than to narratives that encompass the globe. I close-read three examples of southern climate-change fiction that do precisely this: Barbara Kingsolver's *Flight Behavior* (2012), Sherri Smith's *Orleans* (2013), and Omar El Akkad's *American War* (2017). These sources, as we have seen in other southern environmental texts, represent the southern environment as not only fundamentally broken beyond repair, but also *fragmented* into a variety of unparseable pieces. However, these volumes also rely upon a significant imbalance of knowledge between the reader and their main characters, suggesting that, if the world is irredeemably fragmentary for these protagonists, the reader themselves may be able to put the pieces together. If contemporary southern climate fiction is predicated on the notion of ruin (as climate fiction oftentimes is), it also leverages distinctive place-based environmental elements that make that ruin legible; the southern climate novel is essentially a dialogue between the text's ruination and the reader's resilience.

My final chapter, "No Straight Lines in Nature," performs short readings of four postapocalyptic novels set in the South: Pat Frank's *Alas, Babylon* (1959), William Forstchen's *One Second After* (2009), Holly Goddard-Jones's *The Salt Line* (2017), and Michael Farris Smith's *Rivers* (2013). I discuss each of these novels in turn as variations on the "fantasy of return" in the South: the notion that, with various apocalyptic events as a catalyst, the region might conceivably start over—reinvent itself from its organic, eco-friendly origins. Such a revival would seem to elide the competing narratives of ruin and resilience for the region by essentially constituting a reset button for southern history, a chance to alleviate the environmental failures of the past. However, the fantasy of return is predicated on the presence of walls, physical or symbolic boundaries within which such a resurrection can take place. And the walls in these four novels either fail catastrophically or come to enclose dystopias, their failures marked by some essential moral and ethical flaw on the part of their creators. Thus, the fantasy of return simply marks a newer incarnation of the southern ruin-narrative, which seeks to attribute environmental failures to easily identified human errors. Yet Jeff VanderMeer's *Southern Reach* trilogy (2014), which portrays a similar enclosed postapocalyptic zone in which history is unspooled to form a closer bond between human and nonhuman nature, posits that attempting to build a wall between the resilient new state of nature and the ruination of the surrounding world may be a doomed enterprise to begin with.

Ultimately, this volume is an attempt to make sense not only of trends in southern literature and ecocriticism, but also of the approach I have seen in myself and my students to reading those same texts. It is motivated by a reluctance to accept the narrative of ruin that threatens, with each successive day of the twenty-first century that passes, to pervade our shared existence. Here, in this tiny liberal arts college on the rainswept verge of Tampa Bay, with hurricanes ricocheting around the Gulf of Mexico like billiard balls, resilience is all we have. But one of the lessons of the Anthropocene is that even positions that have always thought themselves secure may find the ground crumbling unexpectedly beneath them, the water lapping at their doorstep. Across the South, and elsewhere.

ONE

The Region in Ruins

William Faulkner and Natasha Trethewey

Like history, the novel is thus an exercise in making the past
coherent. Like history, it explores the respective contributions of
character and circumstance to forming the present. By doing so,
the novel suggests how we may explore the power of the present to
produce the future. This is why we have this thing, this institution,
this medium called the novel.

   — J. M. COETZEE,
     Elizabeth Costello

In visiting Florida in dreams, of either day or night, I always came
suddenly on a close forest of trees, every one in flower, and bent down
and entangled to network by luxuriant, bright-blooming vines, and
over all a flood of bright sunlight. But such was not the gate by which
I entered the promised land. Salt marshes, belonging more to the sea
than to the land; with groves here and there, green and unflowered,
sunk to the shoulders in sedges and rushes; with trees farther back,
ill defined by their boundary, and instead of rising in hilly waves and
swellings, stretching inland in low water-like levels . . .

   — JOHN MUIR,
     A Thousand-Mile Walk to the Gulf

JOHN MUIR ENTERED FLORIDA on October 15, 1867, with visions of vibrant
flowers and welcoming forests filling his head. He left in January 1868, having spent the majority of his time in the state barely surviving a three-month

battle with malaria. In place of "flowering trees" and "blooming vines," he discovered smothering swamps, ravenous wildlife, impenetrable palmetto thickets, and hostile backwoods folk. Though, like the polar explorers of the previous century who described mundane bits of the landscape in luminous terms in order to justify the cost of the expedition, Muir repeatedly tries to put a positive spin on his discoveries—he pens a lengthy adoration of a palm tree—his suffering and disappointment pervade the Florida chapters of *A Thousand-Mile Walk to the Gulf.* Though Muir at times admires the southern landscape (primarily the Appalachian Mountains), he never issues the sort of statements on its behalf that would make him famous as a preservationist in the West. Since *Thousand-Mile Walk* emanates from the earliest stages of Muir's career as a naturalist, and we do not see, in its pages, the same full-throated preservationist ethos that appears in his later career, the reader might be forgiven for believing that Muir admires southern landscapes but does not judge them worthy of the attentions of environmentalists. In a broader sense, the long history of human use and the scars and schisms brought about by slavery and war that inhered in southern landscapes tended to redirect attention from naturalists such as Muir away from nonhuman nature and toward social and political strife.[1] The South appears in Muir's writing not as an untouched garden, but as a tainted and exploited space, even its relatively "wild" spaces suffering from human attention.

What Muir found in the South, in a word, was a region that would not conform—not to his expectations of a place innocent of human attention nor to his understanding of what a *lack* of human attention should look like.[2] Scott Obernesser writes that, for Muir, "it is ultimately not regional distinction that drives [him] west but rather encroaching industrial modernity. Muir, who had left the North in search of wilderness spaces, finds the South a much closer reflection of the North than he anticipated" (Vernon 74). Though Muir frequently attempts to *represent* his encounters with southern landscapes as dramatic revelations, in reality he finds the countryside he traverses either brought low through slavery and economic exploitation (Tennessee, Georgia) or a horrifying swamp vastly at odds with his preconceptions of wilderness (Florida). Weary of Wisconsinian factoryscapes, Muir expects "the promised land," but finds a region where industry is already entrenched, where Tennessean landowners have taken to "bust[ing]" open mountainsides in search of minerals now that the depleted soil no longer supports agriculture, where residents regard him with suspicion and where strangers repeatedly attempt to rob him on the road (84). No critical mass of the soaring Romantic prose that Muir is known for can conceal his despondence toward the land he traverses; no quantity of flowers can conceal the malarial swamp.

Ruined by the war, ruined by industry, ruined by the people who inhabit it, the South appears in *A Thousand-Mile Walk* as a region fundamentally gone astray—though a different eye than Muir's might interpret its people and its environment as struggling to survive after the shattering events of the previous six years: a landscape of resilience. Thus, the purpose of this chapter is to introduce "ruin" as the dominant school of thought in regard to the southern environment in both history and literature, yet with the notion that this narrative varies widely and is subject to significant reinterpretation. I propose to begin with a brief account of how historians have approached the issue of the southern environment and the narratives that they have attempted to craft from the evidence at hand—narratives, as we will see, that curve overwhelmingly toward the notion of ruin. This theme is deepened and expounded upon by perhaps the most commonly referenced works of southern environmental literature: William Faulkner's trilogy of "Big Woods" short stories in *Go Down, Moses* (1942). However, it is possible to find resilience within ruin, as Natasha Trethewey does in *Native Guard* (2006), a text that is saturated with Faulknerian images of tragedy and ruin, but endeavors to supplant the tragic narrative by regarding ruin as a transitional phase rather than as a terminus. Trethewey does not dispute the South's past mistakes—indeed, they are abundantly and painfully visible to her—but she also suggests that, if we are to live with those mistakes, we need a vastly revised understanding of southern nature.

And it is true that, in the South as elsewhere, if an untouched, unspoiled, virgin landscape is the aspirational metric by which we assess the health or value of environments, we are apt to be disappointed, repeatedly and emphatically.[3] Greg Garrard, in *Ecocriticism* (2004), among others, has placed the origin of this idealized vision of "nature in a state uncontaminated by civilisation" within the industrial era in Europe, when urban subjects sought "the promise of a renewed, authentic relation of humanity and the earth, a post-Christian covenant," which they "found in a space of purity, founded in an attitude of reverence and humility" (59). Though the sense of nature as inherently pure and capable of peaceful coexistence with humanity was useful in a variety of ways to the Romantics, Modernism and first-wave environmentalism quickly came to regard natural spaces as inevitably ruined by human greed, hatred, and myopia. Into unspoiled, virgin wildernesses, so the narrative goes, intrude the nefarious human subjects, bound by their very nature to waste what has been given. This narrative is so common that Robin Veldman, writing in 2012, is able to typify it into three discernable "acts," from the first, in which humans "are depicted as living in idyllic harmony with nature," through the intermediate phase of "subdu[ing] and dominat[ing] the earth, penetrating her secret depths with mines and ploughs, blighting her surface with dams and cities," and finally, in the present, "reap[ing] the misfortune [humanity] has sown" in the loss of both human and nonhuman nature (12). And, as William Cronon argues in the seminal "The Trouble with Wilderness" (1995), that very action represents the dissolution of wilderness, which "quietly expresses and reproduces the very values its devotees seek to reject . . . if we allow ourselves to believe that nature, to be true, must also be wild, then our very presence in nature represents its fall" (80–81). Cronon's invocation of the biblical fall here is deliberate, since the Garden of Eden is one of the most persistent tropes used to address an ostensibly "perfect" environmental system invaded, mismanaged, and ruined by humans.[4]

Postlapsarian rhetoric proliferates in southern environmentalist accounts to a somewhat lesser extent than in writing about New World colonialism as a whole, in which it has become a nearly meaningless signifier.[5] However, it is worth noting that one varietal of this rhetoric is particularly pervasive in the region: the utopian idea of economic, rather than aesthetic or biological, perfection inherent in southern landscapes. William F. Byrd, in his unambiguously titled 1733 *Journey to the Land of Eden*, describes reconnoitering a plot of his own land near the Virginia–North Carolina border (close to present-day Danville, VA) in unmistakably Edenic terms: "The air is wholesome, and the soil equal in fertility to any in the world. The river is about eighty yards wide, always confined within its lofty banks, and rolling down its waters, as sweet as milk, and as clear as crystal. There runs a charming level, of more than a mile square, that will bring forth like the lands of Egypt, without being overflowed once a year."[6] Byrd's effusions depart markedly from latter-day paeans to unspoiled wilderness; though he rhapsodizes on the beauty of the region, his aims are explicitly economic and contingent on agricultural exploitation, more in keeping with Renaissance-era exploration literature than the categorical natural histories of the Enlightenment. Jack Kirby, in *Mockingbird Song* (2008), takes note of how the first Europeans to set foot in the South "called it virgin land, a paradise, an Eden enchanting almost beyond expression. Not so, of course; for the Eden of Genesis was untouched, and we know that for thousands of years, the South had been both extensively and intensively managed by the first Southerners" (74).

In its origins, then, the utopian conception of southern landscapes was strongly associated with economic potential, with natural beauty usually as the proof of that potential rather than an autonomous good in itself. Anthony Wilson, in *Shadow and Shelter* (2006), notes that Virginia "conceived of its role with a mixture of pastoral idealism and acute commercial consciousness" (xvii). It is hardly worthwhile to point out the impracticality of the coexistence of these concepts; indeed, Lewis Simpson has already done so, in *The Dispossessed Garden* (1975), contending that southern treatments of nature in early New World settlements were a utopian (and thus doomed) attempt to marry boundless productivity and picturesque, bucolic landscapes. Early settlers, Simpson suggests, quickly found themselves replacing "paradise lost" with "paradise improved" (*Dispossessed* 2, 17). Southern environmental consciousness, for Simpson, begins with Virginia's acknowledgment of the loss of any notion of utopian pastoralism as "a necessity of [the state's] involvement in the empirical development of the modern marketplace economy . . . its role in history was to propagate, not the gospel, but tobacco" (119). Yet the abandonment of the pastoral ideal simply suggests a subtle movement of the goal posts established by the binaristic "unspoiled/despoiled" principle of land—if the South was not fated to be a pastoral realm free of Old World corruption, it was at least an ideal place to produce enormous quantities of hugely profitable crops, which is a certain very narrow kind of utopia, for a certain very small quantity of people.[7]

What is important about the lapsarian rhetoric as deployed by southern authors is not necessarily its perfection, but its pastness—"paradise" implies "loss," and for any narrative of ruin to hold power, the ruination must be irrevocable. Lucinda MacKethan claims, in *The Dream of Arcady* (1980), that utopian environmental rhetoric in the South produced "a world committed in both imagery and ideology to the preservation of the simple, good life, to a working respect for nature, and to the practice of neighborliness," a world that, by its very nature, is always already vanished.[8] The profitable harmony with nature that white landowners in the region attempted to lay claim to was, moreover, contingent on a vast network of human suffering and exploitation; ironically, the slaves (who held no such utopian ideals toward the region) who were actually working the land understood its processes much more completely than those who marveled at the "paradise" of the South. According to Mart Stewart, "in plantation districts, both the cultivated and uncultivated environments were often better known by slaves than by their masters," and, on the whole, "slave experiences with the environment were profoundly social ones—they moved into nature to enact social meanings, at the same time that they did not make the sharp distinction between the human and nonhuman worlds that were common for whites. For African Americans in the South, nature was negotiated, it was kin, and it was community" (Sutter & Manganiello 201, 211). The narrative of the Edenic—and thus necessarily fallen—southern environment both establishes an utterly inevitable fate for the region and effaces the voices of those who might otherwise be able to speak with some knowledge of the place. Not even the South's most reactionary defenders in academia in the early twentieth century could unironically deploy such rhetoric again.

Indeed, the widespread realization that the economic "paradise" that the South seemed to represent to early colonists was dependent on catastrophic crimes perpetuated on the land and those who worked it induced a rhetorical shift, in the years following Reconstruction, toward metaphors of waste, loss, and ruin.[9] Teresa Farris notes that "early settlers wrote poetically of the South's fertile soil and abundant vegetation, evoking a New World Arcadia that promised the Jeffersonian ideal of yeoman prosperity," but also that this ideal was ultimately doomed: "Within a few short decades, their overzealous deforestation and imprudent farming practices depleted the southwestern frontier's soils and created devastating widespread erosion" (74). Farris's language ("overzealous," "imprudent," "devastating") emphasizes human error rather than divine retribution; the ruination of the region is the fault of its people. Max Edelson makes much of the same point as Farris, with a similar use of rhetorical flourishes: "The arrival of Europeans in Florida, Virginia, Carolina, and elsewhere along the coast put an end to the sustainable pattern of development initiated by Native Americans. Europeans left an indelible mark on southeastern landscapes, whether measured by the smoke pouring from burning woodlands or the dilating swath of cleared farmland that always followed" (Sutter & Manganiello 107). The bleak images with which Edelson concludes his contention drive home the sense of loss articulated in this passage, and the intractability of that loss—the environmental potential of the past is here, literally, burnt away.[10] Edelson's insistence on the "indelibility" of settlers' presence on the land invokes tragic histories, irredeemable losses, irrecoverable ruin. In fact, remorse and ruefulness seem to be the default rhetorical modes for environmental histories addressing the South; Donald Davis dolefully remarks that "when settling the Southern landscape no one asked enough questions of themselves, the environment, or each other" (*Southern United States* 219). The spectator of southern environmental history, then, might as well be a member of the audience for a classical tragedy, sorrowfully wondering how the events they have witnessed could have played out differently, what better choices might have been made, what futures the players might have possessed if not for the errors they committed.

Other, more focused natural histories of the region frequently adopt the language of ruin—the sense of irrecoverable loss—to drive home the enormity of environmental changes across the South. Davis's *Where There Are Mountains: An Environmental History of the Southern Appalachians* (2005), one of the first volumes to perform a rigorous, regionally focused analysis of southern landscapes, for example, discusses the catastrophic loss of the American chestnut to blight, setting the scene with early explorers of the region encountering "what to us would be an unimaginable landscape of old-growth timber, impenetrable canebrakes, and deep woodland meadows" (11). Davis's sharp break between the wilderness and the wasteland is not simply temporal, but epistemological—the untouched southern landscape is "unimaginable" to modern readers.[11] Though the loss of the chestnut was only marginally due to human action, Davis nonetheless sees its vanishing as a moment of irrevocable loss: "The death of the chestnut symbolized the end of a waning, albeit arguably vital, subsistence culture in the mountains. . . . The rural mountaineers turned increasingly to milltowns and urban centers for economic salvation. . . . With the death of the chestnut, an entire world did die, eliminating cultural practices that had been viable in the southern Appalachians for more than four centuries" (198). The language here emphasizes the intractability of the loss, the abrupt dissolution of, in Davis's phrase, "an entire world," a world that could never conceivably return.

The narrative of ruin curves toward notions of human error, hubris, myopia, and sin with the same inevitability as literary tragedy, as Joseph Meeker points out in *The Comedy of Survival*. Moreover, transposing human shortcomings onto natural history can force nonhuman nature to conform to the same ethical and emotional patterns of behavior that we expect from literary plot arcs. Erin Mauldin's *Unredeemed Land*, an environmental history of the cotton industry, uses the concept of "redeeming" farmland, that is, switching it back from monoculture to more varied and sustainable crops, as a central metaphor. "During the postwar years," she writes, "it was no longer practical or feasible to pursue [redemption]. The dramatic and irreversible changes to the landscape during the war made the negotiation between farmer and nature more difficult than ever, and because of the ecological legacies of the Civil War and emancipation, the Southern environment remained unredeemed" (7). In this passage, Mauldin proceeds from a quite specific notion of redemption as an agricultural practice to a much more widespread condemnation of southern environmental policy, with the notion of "unredemption" standing in for a battery of poor decisions. Thus, the South cannot be *agriculturally* redeemed because it was never *ethically* redeemed. Whether overtly or subtly, histories that produce narratives of ruination attempt to persuade the reader that the environment is an archive that records and remembers human failures—those failures inscribed indelibly upon the land.

If there is a defining characteristic of the histories I have collected here, it must reside within the repeated emphasis on the South's major environmental battles having already been fought and, tragically, lost. Whether couched in the language of the biblical fall or the invocation of apocalyptic turns of phrase, these accounts overwhelmingly center on the region's ruin. Though there are alternatives to the historical narrative of ruin, they frequently involve an act of imagination. Rick Bass writes, in 2004, that environmentalism in the American West tended to view the natural world as "a line in the sand, with every day a fierce and holy battle," while southerners must instead imagine "a reconstructed future in which ecological passions are fierce and wild rather than muted and downtrodden . . . what a burden that is, and what a responsibility; and what an amazing opportunity. Southerners get to start over because they *have* to" (Dallmeyer 146). In Bass's analysis, environmental battles in the West are still being fought, while in the South they have already been lost—a story that should, by this point, be familiar. However, Bass regards the ruination of the South as presenting an opportunity rather than imposing a curse. Bass's work presages more contemporary attempts to rethink traditionally marginalized southern landscapes—regions that were once thought useless or blighted—as sites of human resilience rather than a set of tragic failures.[12] Anthony Wilson, in *Shadow and Shelter* (2005), discusses one such landscape—the swamp—in the service of showing the mutability of such varied geographical features. "Landscape is essentially an imaginative creation," Wilson writes. "Depending on the values a culture imports, the swamp's character changes drastically . . . the effort to transform its natural state into the pastoral garden, however, transforms the swamp into a deadly and intractable foe. Approached with a romantic sense of nature as inherently benevolent, the swamp becomes a shady paradise."[13] The same swamp that Muir found so hellish in *A Thousand-Mile Walk to the Gulf* becomes a "paradise" for Wilson—ruin and resilience, far from being intractable, are patterns derived *by humans* from history, frequently saying more about the former category than the latter.

At this point, it may be valuable to condense these ruinous histories into a set of assertions about the dominance of the ruin-narrative in southern environmental thought. The southern environment is construed as ruinous for a vast assortment of complex reasons, but those reasons tend to fall broadly into three conceptual categories.

The region has always had the weakest environmental policy in the nation. For many generations (arguably, still today), rural regions in the South have been locked into cycles of exploitation and collapse in a wide variety of agricultural and extractive industries. Exploitation leads to collapse, with the catastrophic failure of the South's cotton crop offering the most widely-cited parable of the region's environmental shortcomings, and collapse necessitates discovering another resource to exploit. The South's insistence on "strong states' rights" and hostility toward federal regulations permitted widespread corporate malfeasance, to the detriment of the health of both the environment and its inhabitants, human and otherwise. The New South's friendliness to industry, low land prices, and a surfeit of unskilled labor encouraged further environmental depletion, while regressive political action ensured that nothing changed. Faced with such a history, it is not uncommon to hear the region spoken of as "ruined," "lost," or "backward," an opinion that may be shared by even those who care deeply about both local and global environmental issues.[14]

The region's humanitarian record of cruelty precludes environmental concerns. Chief among such cruelties, of course, is the institution of slavery, which establishes a precedent that, for many contemporary readers, the region can never effectively overcome. For such readers, who continue to witness the marginalization and hatred directed toward Americans of color in the South, the region may be called "cursed," "doomed," "worthless," or "corrupted," and it follows that any place laboring under such an onus will act in similarly cruel manners toward the natural world. Intersectional environmentalism depends on the notion that oppression based on race, class, and gender (among other prejudices) is structurally identical to oppression of the environment. My students in particular are sensitive to the presence of such defiant, perverse treatments of nature: why do the hunters not return Old Ben's paw to him? Why do the families in Agee's *Let Us Now Praise Famous Men* treat their domestic animals so poorly? Agee himself makes mention of the "unconscious, offhand, and deliberated cruelty, in relation toward extra-human life and toward negroes, terrible enough to freeze your blood or to break your heart or to propel you toward murder," and admonishes himself to "realize that it is at least unlikely that enough of the causes can ever be altered, or pressures withdrawn, to make much difference" (190). Agee implies that such actions, though deplorable, are also intractable, part of a long pattern of abuse endured and inflicted by southerners. Such a thesis, in essence, condemns the region to repeat its mistakes, leading down an ever-steepening path to ruin.

The internalization of cyclical tragedy in southern narratives permits damaging beliefs toward the environment. The persistence of narratives of suffering in the South is perhaps the most enduring marker of its borders; the region is hit hardest by economic slumps, natural disasters, and disease, among other afflictions (at the time of this writing, the COVID-19 pandemic is engulfing the South, despite the wide availability of vaccines). Internalizing such patterns makes environmental ruin a self-fulfilling prophecy. The implication of seeing echoes of the 1927 Mississippi River flood in a hurricane occurring nearly a century later is clear: the place is somehow *destined* for ruination; it is "cursed," as the Compson children claim in *The Sound and the Fury.* Whether such devastation is attributed to a higher (or lower) power or not, however, positing an unbreakable cycle of suffering visited upon the region normalizes such suffering, permitting it to continue. Eventually, the preponderance of such disasters leads to the specious conclusion that it is the destiny of the region itself to remain ruined.

It is as impossible to discuss the current state of environmentalism in the South without taking account of these ruinous factors as it would be to discuss, say, Jean Toomer's work without an understanding of the institution of slavery. Yet if the narrative of ruin is one particular pattern that is drawn from history by its interpreters, it also acts as a constriction of that history, foreclosing on possibilities for the future. If all of the important environmental decisions in the region have already been made, what motivation apart from bare self-preservation could inspire action in the present? And, more importantly, who does the narrative of ruin overlook? Where does this narrative place southerners who did *not* make the tragic decisions vis-à-vis the environment that the historians decry, whether through lack of agency or an actual environmental consciousness? Where does it place the lives of Black southerners, who have, in the past, literally lacked the right to determine how the environment should be used, and even in the present have that right severely restricted? The answers to these questions are found in literature, in the ways in which we approach—and try to make sense of—the environmental legacy that the region and its chroniclers leave us.

———

Making the case for a region as possessing a distinct environmental ethos virtually requires major figures—authors, artists, philosophers—who can extract narrative from history. And, with what can seem at times like grim predictability, the first name on the list is the same that appeared when the region (or, according to Laurence Schwartz's *Creating Faulkner's Reputation* (1990), the country writ large) required a major Modernist to legitimize itself: William Faulkner. Albert E. Cowdrey wrote, in 1996, that "Faulkner inevitably draws the eye of anyone seeking a nature poet" among southern authors (Cowdrey 199). Whether this process is "inevitable" because all roads eventually lead to Faulkner, because there are few other contenders for the vaunted title, or because "The Bear" remains required reading on syllabi across the country is unclear, but I suspect Cowdrey is *not* singling out Faulkner for his Thoreauvian appreciation for wilderness. On the contrary, with the exception of the "Big Woods" stories in *Go Down, Moses* and elsewhere, as well as certain well-known sections of the Snopes trilogy, nature in Faulkner's writing is hardly sublime. His primary landscapes are blasted, unproductive fields (the hellscape of *As I Lay Dying* and the menacing darkness of "That Evening Sun"), flood-swollen and devouring rivers, and weed-infested yards—mud, dirt, dung.[15] These are hardly appropriate environs for a "nature poet."

As a result, at the top of every reading list covering Faulkner's interest in nature are his most unambiguous defenses of "pure" wilderness: the "Big Woods" stories of *Go Down, Moses*. Christopher Rieger writes that "the issues of land ownership and destruction of wilderness in *Go Down, Moses* makes this work one of the most significant American novels to tackle environmental themes" (136). Rieger is likely correct, though I might suggest that his definition of "environmental themes" is somewhat normative—narratives centered about individual experiences of sublime nature—in the way that many readers of "The Bear" in particular are normative. As far back as 1966, during the first wave of Faulkner criticism, John MacLachlan effusively proclaimed: "Faulkner's Yoknapatawpha County is a far place. There is nothing between its folk and the elemental forces of the universe . . . no overwhelming manmade technology, because the doings of man are dwarfed, as are his machines, by the immensities around them" (*A Southern Renascence* 107). MacLachlan's perspective, like much Faulkner criticism of the period, endeavors to divorce the author's concerns from the petty social concerns of the "real" world (that is to say, race, class, gender, economics, industry, etc.) in favor of the headier air of "the elemental forces of the universe," as if Yoknapatawpha were a sort of Dixiefied Narnia.

Such ideas, which would strike most ecocritics today as somewhat naïve, have a surprisingly long half-life in Faulkner studies. Francois Pitavy, speaking at the 2003 Faulkner and Yoknapatawpha conference, calls the Big Woods "a sublime space, that is, of an order different from that of the garden, beyond the threshold . . . an unchristian metaphor of divinity, a myth divested of religious meaning but not of the sense of the sacred—a secularized version of the Old Testament God" (*Faulkner and the Ecology of the South* 90). Pitavy's "sublime space" is not unlike MacLachlan's "far place" in that both interpret southern landscapes as largely significant not ecologically, but in reference to human religious and philosophical concerns. In a departure from contemporary ecocriticism's skepticism of the divide between "humans" and "nature," Pitavy insists that "the wilderness must remain unknowable, tremendous and indifferent, like God, unapproachable, like a dream, and man must remain alone, cut off from his dream . . . the Arcadian dream of a blessed interrelatedness between man and nature must remain just the impossible dream of man's desire to inhabit an eternity which his temporal condition, his heritage, precludes" (94). Pitavy's frequent references to "myth," "eternity," and "man" in the abstract suggest much more of a conceptual address of Faulkner's ecological concerns than the more specified attention to individual environments and wariness toward "wilderness" as sacred space adopted by contemporary ecocriticism. From this perspective, Faulkner is essentially congruent with John Muir, or Thoreau, or any number of other "nature poets" aligned with traditional "sublime nature" environmentalism.

And, if the reader approaches the Big Woods stories in *Go Down, Moses* expecting to find a heady and tragic account of the inevitable destruction of nonhuman nature by wrongheaded humans (which sockets cleanly into the southern ruin-narrative), the trilogy provides them with exactly that. It is worth remembering, however, that Ike absorbs his set of ethics from Sam Fathers in "The Old People," and Sam's own relationship with his environment is marked (in Ike's view) by a sense of irrecoverable loss. He teaches young Ike of his kin, "who had vanished from [the earth] now with all their kind, what of blood they left behind them running now in another race and for a while even in bondage and now drawing toward the end of its alien and irrevocable course, barren, since Sam Fathers had no children" (157). What Ike gains from Sam is "an unforgettable sense of the big woods—not a quality dangerous or particularly inimical, but profound, sentient, gigantic and brooding, amid which he had been permitted to go to and fro at will, unscathed, why he knew not, but dwarfed and, until he had drawn honorably blood worthy of being drawn, alien" (167). Twice in "The Old People" Faulkner uses the word "alien," once to describe the "barrenness" of Sam's genealogical line and once to articulate Ike's lack of comprehension of the wilderness prior to killing his first deer—in both cases, Ike is presented with a distinct lack brought on by the presence of the unknown, an "alien" human *and* ecological spectrum with only Sam's own narratives to guide him. From Sam, Ike derives the notion of history, especially natural history, as declension, a steady eradication of green spaces and their original inhabitants. Sam's "barren" history, a botanical as well as familial designator, makes this plain, as does the near-simultaneous death of Sam, Lion, Old Ben (who fall, in the hunt's climactic scene "all of a piece, as a tree falls"), and the last remnant of the Big Woods themselves (228). This sense of steady and irrecoverable loss is a major theme in Faulkner's work, where it is frequently cast as repeated attempts (and, usually, failures) to make a tragic history legible in the present.

In addition to the narrative of ruin, the Big Woods stories provide a reasonable facsimile of another hallmark of traditional environmentalism: the ironclad division between humans and nature. In *all* of these stories, the edge of the Big Woods (which retreats steadily from northern Mississippi in "The Old People" to deep in the bottomlands in "Delta Autumn") is described as a "wall" or barrier between the insuperable realms of humanity and wilderness. As young Ike travels to the woods to kill his first deer in "The Old People," he reverently observes "the tremendous gums and cypresses and oaks where no axe save that of the hunter had ever sounded, between the impenetrable walls of cane and brier—the two changing yet constant *walls* just beyond which the wilderness . . . seemed to lean" (168, emphasis mine). In "The Bear," the scene has become somewhat darker, but the rhetoric is the same; Ike now views: "the tall and endless *wall* of dense November woods under the dissolving afternoon and the year's death, somber, impenetrable . . . the surrey moving through the skeleton stalks of cotton and corn in the last of open country, the last trace of man's puny gnawing at the immemorial flank" (184, emphasis mine). And, finally, in "Delta Autumn," another repetition, this one elegaic in tone: "The twin banks marched with wilderness as he remembered it . . . the tall tremendous soaring of oak and gum and ash and hickory which had rung to no axe save the hunter's . . . there was some of it left, although now it was two hundred miles from Jefferson when once it had been thirty" (326). Repeatedly, throughout his life, Ike draws the sorts of hard divisions between "wilderness" and "land" (or, more problematically for Ike in particular, "property") that ecocriticism, since Cronon's seminal essay at least, has set itself against: an anthropocentric, absolutist notion of "nature" as contained in clearly-demarcated sanctified zones.

If our definition of nature is derived from first-wave environmentalism—roughly, "nature is a place far from the industrial city where humans go to experience sublime emotion," then any narrative of southern environmentalism must necessarily be ruinous. And readers of the Big Woods stories have not failed to interpret them in the light of the region's many and repeated environmental failures; Rick Bass, casting his conceptual net somewhat widely, writes "all literature is about loss, and hence, indeed, the South stands waist-deep in literature" (Dallmeyer, *Elemental South* 146). And Ann Abadie, though designating Faulkner as "one of the great harbingers and prophets of Southern environmentalism," nonetheless notes that this particular strain of environmentalism is marked by a great and intractable sense of loss: "the sense of postbellum and early twentieth-century Southern history as a history of environmental degradation was not simply an epiphenomenon but an integral part of Faulkner's declensionary vision of Southern history generally" (Kartiganer & Abadie, *Faulkner and the Natural World* 14–15).[16] If abuse of southern landscapes is intrinsically linked to the abuse of other races and genders by white men (as the ending of "Delta Autumn" implies), if all of this is part of the "epiphenomenon" that gives rise to *Go Down, Moses,* it is difficult to see the novel as anything *but* a story of ruin and failure: not simply the failure of proper land management, but of empathy and ethics much more broadly.[17]

However, I would like to suggest that we, as readers of *Go Down, Moses*, should regard Ike's seemingly intractable conception of wilderness with at least some measure of irony. Faulkner himself pointed us in this direction during a 1956 interview in which he espoused something more akin to contemporary "dirty ecology," to use Patricia Yaeger's phrase, than the apocalyptic despair and vanished "pure" wilderness binary familiar to preservationism: "I don't hold to the idea of a return [to Nature]. . . . We mustn't go back to a condition, an idyllic condition, in which the dream [made us think] we were happy, we were free of trouble and sin. We must take the trouble and sin along with us, and we must cure that trouble and sin as we go" (Meriwether, *Lion in the Garden* 131). And, in a 1952 interview in which he emphasized the "deep indestructible bond between man and his environment," it is worth noting that he went on to clarify that by "environment" he meant "a common acceptance of the world, a common view of life, and a common morality" (*Lion in the Garden* 72). Faulkner was, of course, a notoriously poor interviewee, and here seems to directly contradict the notion of even ideological diversity across the South as a region, but I take his statement to intimate an environmental ideal that incorporates ethics and human behavior rather than relying upon an absolutist notion of untouched "wilderness." More significantly, his insistence that "we must cure that trouble and sin as we go" flies in the face of the narrative of irreparable ruin, suggesting alternatives to the tragic narrative. Is it possible that the Big Woods stories could be read as evidence of southern environmental *resilience*?

It is worth noting that, in "The Old People," the environmental ethos that Sam hands down to Ike is fundamentally incomplete; thus, in addition to Ike's lessons and morals, he gains an understanding of the tragic history that Sam relates as ultimately a discursive phenomenon. In the small but subtle gaps between Ike's interpretation of the world and the narrator's embellishments upon those interpretations, the tragic arc of *Go Down, Moses's* narrative is revealed as a series of attempts at making sense of loss rather than as simple aggrievement. Ultimately, the key moment at which Sam reveals his history to Ike is not an act of remembrance, but confabulation: "The boy would just wait and then listen and Sam would begin, talking about the old days and the People whom he had not had time to ever know and so could not remember (he did not remember ever having seen his father's face), and in place of whom the other race into which his blood had run supplied him with no substitute" (162). The parenthetical clauses I take to be commentary on the narrator's part; Sam cannot articulate memories that he does not possess, and thus is able to delineate the edges of his lack but not its specific quality. Ike, whether he understands it in the moment or not, here learns that loss walks hand-in-hand with *bricolage*. To return to Faulkner's own statement on nature, Ike is learning to "cure" his own "trouble and sin" as he goes.

Looking at *Go Down, Moses* in this regard exposes the striking quantity of Ike's reflections on the wilderness that are ultimately interpretations shaped to fit a tragic mold rather than judgments passed by the text itself—ironically, error lies in taking Ike's pronouncements at face value. It is easy to overlook this because our first introduction to the titular character of "The Bear" is in a voice that appears authorial, designating Old Ben as an "anachronism" out of an "old dead time" that is "too big for the dogs which tried to bay it, for the horses which tried to ride it down, for the men and the bullets they fired into it; too big for the very country which was its constricting scope" (183). Old Ben manifests in the text as a relic, a superfluous and ultimately doomed creature whose correlate out of mythology is not the hero who suffers trauma or the beasts who inflict it, but the reluctant and improbable survivor, "Old Priam reft of his old wife and outlived all his sons" (183). It is unlikely that Old Ben himself, as a bear, conceives of himself in such terms; rather, this is an instance of an aspect of the biotic community being shaped to fit a particular narrative arc by Ike, who would grow into the old man watching the Delta wilderness "not being conquered, destroyed, so much as retreating since its purpose was served now and its time an outmoded time" (326). The periodic, subtle narrative flash-forwards (such as when the narrator remarks that a particular simile would not occur to Ike until "years later, after he had grown to a man and seen the sea") emphasize this confabulative process (185). When the young Ike gazes on Lion's paw-print in the mud outside Major de Spain's stable, he finds it baffling; only after the events of the story are long past do the print and Sam Fathers' reaction to it make sense to him:

> Later, a man, the boy realized what it had been, and that Sam had known all the time what had made the tracks. It had been foreknowledge in Sam's face that morning. *And he was glad,* he told himself. *He was old. He had no children, no people, none of his blood anywhere above earth that he would ever meet again. And even if he were to, he could not have touched it, spoken to it, because for seventy years now he had had to be a negro. It was almost over now and he was glad.* (203)[18]

What is phrased as revelation here is in fact a surprisingly elaborate process of discursive formation on Ike's part—over a period of many years, he concludes that, in this moment, Sam possesses knowledge of the future (including his own death), an understanding of both Lion's existence and his textual function, and, indeed, a vision of the entire tragic story arc that Ike has forged.[19] It is necessary for Ike's crafted narrative of the Big Woods's inevitable ruin that a "fatality" lurk within all of these events, which he compares to "the last act on a set stage," and he, the witness, being "humble and proud that he had been found worthy to be a part of it" (214). If all of the events of the story are "fated" to happen, ruin is inevitable; Ike can only be a witness to their unfolding.

However, melodramatic accounts of southern "fates" in Faulkner's fiction generally say more about those who lay claim to suffering under such a curse than about some intrinsic character of the social or natural environment. The repeated insistence of the Compson family in *The Sound and the Fury* that they are doomed to decline on account of a familial curse, for instance, is predominantly indicative of the family's desire to *have* a grand, tragic ending rather than the more likely series of myopic and petty errors. And what Ike realizes, by the time the trilogy reaches "Delta Autumn," is that his lifetime of bemoaning the tragic loss of the Big Woods and his long endeavor to exempt himself from the patterns of exploitation and misuse that he recognizes in his family have succeeded in improving neither the actual condition of the wilderness nor the destructive behaviors of humans toward each other that abet such ecological loss. Witnessing the doom of the Big Woods permits the tragic narrative to play out, but does nothing to alter that narrative. Environmental depletion in "Delta Autumn" is no longer the series of sharp shocks that it was in "The Bear"—violent deaths and catastrophic transformations of familiar landscapes—but a steady, bathetic decline. At the beginning of the story, Ike notes that, in contrast to the mule-drawn wagons of the past, "now they went in cars, driving faster and faster every year because the roads were better and they had farther and farther to drive, the territory in which game still existed drawing yearly inward as his life was drawing inward" (319). Here, Ike's own declining faculties (his own death, unlike the sudden tragic end of Old Ben and Sam Fathers, constituting a gradual loss in parts) mirror the slow retreat of the woods, implying that this mundane declensionary narrative may be more fitting than a grand, tragic end for the landscape. Similarly, at the end of the story, his realization that the McCaslin scions, despite his past denunciations, seem to still be making the same exploitive and incestuous errors as their predecessors have over the course of their entire lineage (in his encounter with Roth Edmonds's distant Beauchamp cousin and mistress and her child), suggests that his fervent self-exemption from his McCaslin heritage was also misguided. In one of his final comments in "Delta Autumn," Ike implicitly renounces the tragic narrative that has so preoccupied his life in favor of a much more flexible conception of human error: "no wonder the ruined woods I used to know dont cry for retribution! he thought: The people who have destroyed it will accomplish its revenge."[20] Here, Ike seems to realize that the interplay of retributive moral and primal forces that his earlier pronouncements were predicated upon is an ultimately symbolic means of reacting to actual environmental loss. In place of the "curses" and "dispossession" that characterized "The Bear," in "Delta Autumn" Ike comes to recognize the seemingly chaotic and mundane constellation of human missteps that gradually result in environmental crisis.

In the end, Ike realizes that his acceptance of ruin—the "doomed" woods, the "anachronistic" bear—as a fundamental truism of southern landscapes has blinded him to the possibility of resilience. For environmentalism narrowly conceived, the trilogy is a tragedy, a narrative of "man conquering nature," as an endlessly antagonistic set of undergraduate essays in my classes proclaim. For readers who can see past the narrative of ruin, however, the Big Woods stories are a cautionary tale, suggesting that the logical endpoint of too-deep investment in tragic narrative environmentalism is, essentially, paralysis. Philip Weinstein finds in Faulkner's view of the environment "something grimmer than the benign causes we currently group together under the notion of ecology," less a celebration of the natural world than an "atavistic sense for the inertial, for impersonal forces immune to individual will and likely at any moment to torpedo the progressive reach of individual projects" (Urgo & Abadie, *Faulkner and the Ecology of the South* 26). Ike's cognitive reluctance (one might say, inability) to come to terms with the destruction of the wilderness *without* the intervening interface of ruin is analogous to the logistical difficulties that contemporary environmentalists encounter when attempting to address issues such as climate change. Timothy Clark writes that, while "ecocriticism evolved primarily to address local and easily identifiable outrages and injustices," climate change is "a global catastrophe arising from innumerable mostly innocent individual actions," and thus "eludes inherited ways of thinking" (11). Could it be that Ike McCaslin's repeated insistence upon the tragic arc of the Big Woods constitutes one of these "inherited ways of thinking"? And that, by the end of the trilogy of stories, he comes to realize—too late, perhaps—that he should instead have focused on his "innumerable mostly innocent individual actions"?

Ruin is seductive. It tries to convince environmentalists such as Ike Mc-Caslin that their actions are inconsequential, that there is little or nothing they can do to avert the apocalypse, that all of this was "fated" to happen. More-over, and paradoxically, it subtly stokes the ego, making us believe that we are the chosen few occupying a special, unprecedented time in history, wit-nessing the prophesied end of the planet. By contrast, resilience is difficult—difficult to identify, difficult to predict, difficult to put into narrative form. Yet that is precisely what southern authors are called upon to perform; the alter-native is the closing scene of "Delta Autumn"—an abandoned woman and her child, a dead doe on the bracken. It is tempting to attempt to do away with the narrative of ruin entirely, to dismiss it as defeatism and fatalism, to orient environmental action in the South toward the future rather than lingering on the past, but, as we will see in the following section, ruin has its uses as well.

———

Twelve older white men and one woman of color pose for a photograph with a rolling pasture as backdrop. She accepts a glass of bourbon from one of them in the same manner that one imagines Persephone accepting pomegranate seeds. She feels, and says so, that she is in "blackface" for the purposes of the photo, and reminds the men that her father is white and comes from the country. "You don't hate the South?" they ask her, echoing the final line of Faulkner's *Absalom, Absalom!*, "you don't hate it?" The men are the Fugitive-Agrarians, the backdrop is a painted stage concealing the skyscrapers of At-lanta, and the speaker, deep in a dream, is the poet Natasha Trethewey.

In "Pastoral," from *Native Guard* (2006), Trethewey attempts to navigate her unique position vis-à-vis the monolith of southern literature. She both sees through the many limitations of the Agrarians—their cultivation of an unrealistic vision of country life, their racial homogeneity and tokenism, for example—and places herself, as a poet who actively chronicles southern land-scapes, among them. The elder writers, to their credit, seem to understand how out-of-place she seems in this company—they have, in fact, scripted her anticipated response: Quentin Compson's manic, conflicted insistence at the end of *Absalom, Absalom!* that he doesn't hate the South. Quentin, like Ike McCaslin, is attempting to form the patterns of the past into a discernible narrative, and reaches a similarly tragic conclusion. In "Pastoral," Trethewey finds herself inscribed into the role of these Faulknerian protagonists—the body of southern literature, Faulkner included, insists that she is a tragic figure and that the South should be for her a tragic region, a place that she would deeply like to forsake.[21]

The narrative of tragedy, of ruin, has been told many times before in the South. It continues to be told in the photographs of destroyed neighborhoods following major hurricanes, the disastrous effects of oil and chemical spills, the towns whose factories are lured to the region by low land prices and taxes, and in countless other stories and images unfolding on a day-to-day basis. For that reason, like Trethewey in "Pastoral," the region can appear at times to be essentially scripted to perform a tragic environmental role. But Trethewey realizes that this is an untenable position, whether in regard to her own career or the region overall and, unlike the Faulknerian characters who impose themselves upon her, goes searching for an alternative to the narrative of ruin.

Native Guard is divided into three sections, each very different in composition. The first bears a strong resemblance to confessional poetry, discussing in intimate terms her mother's death at the hands of her stepfather when the poet was a teenager. The second departs radically from the form and content of the first—these poems deal with history and war, from the early twentieth-century cotton boom to the Civil Rights era, and include the book's longest poem, "Native Guard," an epistolary account of the Louisiana Native Guards, an all-Black regiment in the Civil War. The third section blends the approach of the first two, intermingling incidents from Trethewey's memories with stories out of southern history that she did not witness—the Civil War, for instance, or the height of the cotton economy. Only one poem exists outside this tripartite structure—the first in the volume, "Theories of Time and Space" (a title that evokes notions of relativity), which places both the self and the natural world in flux. "You can get there from here, though / there's no going home," the speaker notes, surveying the Gulf coast near Ship Island, Mississippi.[22] This particular section of the coast, vital to Trethewey's work as a whole, represents a convergence of human and natural rights violations; the speaker's quest to Ship Island involves not only an encounter with the abysmal treatment of the Native Guards by both Union and Confederate soldiers, but also the fundamental neglect afforded to nonhuman nature. The speaker "cross[es] over / the man-made beach, 26 miles of sand / dumped on the mangrove swamp—buried / terrain of the past," a structure that both symbolizes how the past is buried—the speaker excavates the still relatively unknown story of the Native Guard—and how poor southern environmental policy endangers the region today (1). Mangroves significantly reduce flooding and storm surge during hurricanes, though not if they have been engulfed in sand.[23] The remainder of *Native Guard* bears out the promises of "Theories of Time and Space" to describe a region fundamentally destabilized by racial violence and environmental mismanagement alike.

Poetic form in *Native Guard* serves as one means by which the text attempts to encode this lack of stability into meaningful patterns, to give shape to a lack. In doing so, it mirrors the insidious inscription into a tragic narrative advanced by "Pastoral" and "Miscegenation," both of which are squeezed into a restrictive form; "Pastoral" is a sonnet, a famously minimalistic poem, but "Miscegenation" cranks up the dial even further by using only two rhymes ("name" and "same" as well as the identical rhyme "Mississippi," an end-word repeated eight times over the course of the poem). This emphasis on form is also the case in "Graveyard Blues," a frequently anthologized poem from the first section of the book that mimics a 12-bar blues structure, beginning with four tercets, each consisting of a rhyming triplet. The poem concludes with a rhyming couplet, the device so characteristic of the traditional English sonnet, bringing the entire length of the poem to fourteen lines—the length necessitated by that form. The final lines, "I walk now among names of the dead: / My mother's name, stone pillow for my head," additionally invoke the ending of Langston Hughes's well-known "The Weary Blues" (1926)—"He slept like a rock or a man that's dead."[24] The blues, the English sonnet, the work of the country's best-known African American poet—all collide in this poem to create a strong sense of repetition and constriction, of the weight of all of these previous forms pressing down upon the poet in the same way that her mother's funeral (the subject of the poem) exerts pressure on Trethewey's memory. As in "Pastoral," the poet both understands and is able to masterfully manipulate past literary structures while simultaneously being confined by them. Grief, in "Graveyard Blues," becomes a tragic pattern, one that has been articulated many times in poetry and song before.

It becomes clear, as *Native Guard* progresses, that southern environmental history exerts a similarly deterministic pull to that of literary tradition toward restrictive tragic narratives for Trethewey. "Scenes from a Documentary History of Mississippi" opens with "King Cotton, 1907," an account of President Theodore Roosevelt's visit to Vicksburg on a tour of the South during that year. The poem takes the form of a villanelle, a rigid and repetitive form that includes only two rhymes repeated in a pattern over the course of nineteen lines. The villanelle is frequently deployed to evince or toy with a sense of inevitability or predictability; a form that creates this many demands on the poet leaves little room for variation.[25] And Trethewey notes that, even in this scene of celebration, history teaches us that doom is—inevitably—around the corner: "This is two years before the South's countermarch— / the great bolls of cotton, risen up from the ground, / infested with boll weevils—a plague, biblical, all around" (21). The devastation of the Deep South's cotton industry by the boll weevil in 1909 is, of course, one of the first examples on any list of postbellum natural disasters brought on by human misuse of the environment—in this case, a farming monoculture that is easily toppled by pests or disease. Such an occurrence can easily be slotted into the narrative of ruin surrounding the South; motivated by greed, or consumed by hubris, or simply ignorant, humans essentially devastate their environment. Meanwhile, the rest of the nation marches proudly onward, content to leave the region to its tragic fate: "Now, negro children ride the bales, clothes stiff with starch. / From up high, in the photograph, they wave flags down / for the President who will walk through the arch, bound / for the future, his back to us" (21). From this perspective, the poems in *Native Guard*, through their deployment of rigid traditional poetic forms, suggest an inviolable pattern of ruination carried out by humans against both nonhuman nature and themselves. As readers of (among others) Faulkner, we expect this.

However, as I have alluded to earlier, Trethewey is not content to accept the tragic narrative that the region and its authors have seemingly written her into. Rather, the patterns of ruin that proliferate in the first two sections of the book become the necessary preamble for a striking portrait of resilience in the third section. In contrast to the tightly controlled traditional forms of the first two sections, many poems in the final section transition to free verse with irregular line breaks and stanzaic patterns. Consider the first few lines of "Providence":

What's left is footage: the hours before
        Camille, 1969—hurricane
                parties, palm trees leaning
in the wind,
        fronds blown back,

a woman's hair. Then after:
   the vacant lots,
   boats washed ashore, a swamp

where graves had been (42).

"Providence," like many poems in *Native Guard*, recycles many of the images of the poems that preceded it, adopting the ekphrastic approach to history of "Scenes from a Documentary History of Mississippi," reinvoking the "swamp" buried beneath the artificial beach of "Theories of Time and Space," and returning to the cemetery of "Graveyard Blues." Yet "Providence" carries much less of the tragic tone of those poems, instead describing the frantic process by which Trethewey (then only three years old) and her family attempted to weather Hurricane Camille, "moving between rooms / emptying pots filled with rain" (42). While the earlier poems in *Native Guard* frequently settle upon the intractability of history, the enormity of loss, and vanished environments, "Providence" and the four poems that follow it instead view such losses as occasions for the transformation of tragedy and death into new forms of life, from the ants that colonize the speaker's grave in "Monument" to the fish that swim amidst the sunken bones of the Native Guard at Ship Island in "Elegy for the Native Guards."[26] These are, in essence, poems of resilience, though that resilience does not emerge from a closer study of history, or a more intense application of poetic form—the previous poems suggest that such an approach, if not being a zero-sum game, at the very least leads the reader in circles. Rather, resilience, in Trethewey's southern landscapes, comes from unpredictable and potentially destructive sources: a hurricane, or an infestation of pests.

Though the first line of *Native Guard* ends with the words "you can't go home again," the final poem in the volume, "South," does explicitly that:

               . . . I returned

to land's end, the swath of coast
   clear cut and buried in sand:

mangrove, live oak, gulfweed
   razed and replaced by thin palms—

palmettos—symbols of victory
    or defiance, over and over

marking this vanquished land (45).

"South" shares the irregular line breaks and lack of rhyme and meter of "Providence," though its stanzaic pattern and formatting is far more easily parsed. As such, it appears almost as a mediation between the less confined and structured mood of that poem and the more rigidly arranged poems of the first two sections. To be sure, Trethewey is here discussing a portion of the coast that has, for all intents and purposes, been "ruined," its native landscape fundamentally altered and "buried" in the same manner as the mangrove swamp in "Theories of Time and Space." However, here the poet's eye does not take in a wasteland, but a thriving environment marked by the indestructible (as any gardener in a subtropical climate knows) palmetto, its stubborn growth indicating "victory / or defiance" rather than loss. In other words, an environment that could easily be phrased as ruined (and, earlier in the volume, frequently is) instead emerges as a symbol of resilience. No less resilient is the speaker herself; the poem and the volume as a whole conclude with the lines "I return / to Mississippi, state that made a crime / of me—mulatto, half-breed—native / in my native land, this place they'll bury me" (46). Here, Trethewey both acknowledges the infractions the region has perpetrated against her (when she was born, her parents' marriage was indeed illegal under longstanding Mississippi antimiscegenation laws) and refuses to relinquish her ownership of the place.

What both "Theories of Time and Space" and "South," the two pieces that bookend *Native Guard*, share is the knowledge that, to cite the former poem, "everywhere you go will be somewhere / you've never been" (1). Home, the place that the speaker of "South" is "native" to, is a moving target, an ever-changing Heraclitan principle. Though personal and regional history conspire to destroy the speaker's sense that the South is indeed her "native" soil, she instead realizes that the concept of home being "destroyed" is itself a fallacy; there is only change, transformation, and resilience. The tragic narrative of the South, for Trethewey, must produce a new (painful, assuredly, and frequently despairing) version of the place rather than simply leave the region in ruins. Moreover, the tragic narrative—what history and memory give the speaker of these poems—is an utterly necessary component of the resilience that emerges.

———

The number of days that had elapsed since hostilities had ceased in the South could still be counted in three digits when John Muir trekked across the region. Everywhere he went, the scars of war were visible, from plantation owners who had sabotaged their own fields as an act of defiance to whole towns and cities desperately attempting to rebuild. Yet, with his characteristic optimism, he compared the imminent regrowth of the region to the reforestation of woodlands by young trees: "happy, unscarred, and unclouded youth is growing up around the aged, half-consumed, and fallen parents, who bear in sad measure the ineffaceable marks of the farthest-reaching and most infernal of all civilized calamities" (84). This is decidedly not what happens to Faulkner's Big Woods, where the landscape bears irreparable scars and its defenders are paralyzed by beholding what they perceive as its inevitable loss. Trethewey suggests that both perspectives are necessary: we must take account of the seemingly incalculable losses inherent in southern history in terms of human and nonhuman nature, but not mistake ruination for an endpoint. On the contrary, ruin depends on resilient readers to make sense of its narratives, and resilience requires ruin in order to face the future of the region, as complex and problematic as it might be.

TWO

Resilient Routes

Infrastructure and Loss in Eudora Welty
and Flannery O'Connor

Through travel I first became aware of the outside world;
it was through travel that I found my own introspective
way into becoming a part of it.
— EUDORA WELTY,
   One Writer's Beginnings

THE OPENING SHOTS OF THE FILM feature a pair of disembodied hands slowly turning over a variety of artifacts—shards of well-worn pottery, a bullet casing, an array of discarded cicada shells. A rusted, flattened bottlecap. A bird's skull, picked clean by time. A single red-plastic pitted die. These are objects that the viewer has likely not studied closely or at length, but the slow pacing and the tight camera angle force contemplation. Nor do they easily fit into conceptual categories; clearly mass-produced items follow objects that could be scavenged from a forest floor, and ancient relics are placed alongside bits and pieces that could be pulled from the viewer's own recycling bin.

Part of the disorientation that results from viewing the first few minutes of Robert Persons's 2011 *General Orders No. 9* is due to its presentation of the effects, rather than the causes, of the environmental history that it is about to chronicle. The tone of this initial scene is archaeological—the artifacts are presented, examined from a variety of angles, and placed, each in turn, inside a clean wooden display case that lingers in the background—but what confused history produced these disparate fragments? The film cuts to the title card, then to an assortment of explorer's maps of the southeast lacking many significant

FIG. I. A country road in *General Orders No. 9*. Author's screen capture.

features and the familiar dividing lines of state boundaries, now returning to the beginning of the historical narrative. Persons's title references Robert E. Lee's famous farewell address disbanding the Confederate army, and the film itself borrows something of the tone—though less of the content—of that missive: pride mingled with dejection and tempered with a healthy dose of anxiety toward the future. Its seventy-two-minute length falls roughly into three distinct segments, the first being a valedictory and romanticized account of the pre-industrial South, focusing on the middle South and Georgia in particular. This section of the film is marked by slow, lavish shots of southern landscapes: farms at sunrise, the weathered concrete pilings of bridges, forest creeks, cemeteries, and other rural vistas, accompanied by ambient string and choral music (fig. I).[1] The second section effects a reversal, moving from the dirt roads of the country to the tangled interstates of the city (easily identified as Atlanta from a map near the beginning of the segment). The lush colors of the first section become washed out, the peaceful natural setting is replaced with unflattering long shots of parking garages, convention centers, and traffic-choked highways, and the comforting soundtrack turns to harsh, screeching electronic music. Finally, the third segment returns to the methodology of the first, though the mood has become elegiac rather than triumphal; the long shots of landscape return, though they are interspersed with images of antique collectibles and archaeological finds, among other evidence of vanished cultures, and the shots tend more toward a blend of human and nonhuman nature. Throughout the entire film, a narrator (William Davidson) sporadically recites an imagistic prose poem chronicling the history and future of the land being depicted.[2]

FIG. 2. Atlanta industrial district in *General Orders No. 9.*
Author's screen capture.

On a very basic level, *General Orders No. 9* presents an argument that any reader of southern literature or student of southern history will immediately recognize: a romanticized vision of the pre-industrial South with an emphasis on rural areas and agriculture contrasted with a cynical, ruined vision of the modern South's centers of population and industry.[3] The film portrays the rural South poetically as "a protected zone where catfish are in bloom, where Uncle Remus came of age . . . it has its own symbols and its own sovereign," implying strong patterns of local affiliation.[4] The combination of the reverent narration, lavish images, and soothing soundtrack in the film's first section endeavors to construct a sense of place for the region that the following section works to disassemble. "The city is Terminus," the narrator intones over a black-and-white series of shots of barren cinderblock hallways and parking garages, referencing the original name for Atlanta. "It's the absence of ideas, of order. . . . The city is not a place. It's a thing. It has none of the marks of a place and all those of a machine." The film's cityscapes, initially presented in washed-out color, become steadily more drained of hue and shade as the film goes on, eventually transitioning into line drawings and computer-generated building models. Here, too, the message seems clear: the further into the city the film progresses, the more divorced it is from the ideals of human harmony with nature constructed earlier in the work (fig. 2).

General Orders No. 9 fits squarely into the category of what Andrew Murphy calls "antimodern environmental declinism," more a conceptual than a practical ideology insofar as it "represents less a specific response to specific environmental ills than one part of a wider discontent that has repeatedly evoked past golden ages and present degeneration" (80). In other words, the declinism that Murphy discusses precludes itself from dictating specific policy choices or actionable behaviors, instead inspiring a sense of fatalism. Environmental decline is construed to be as inevitable as industrialization or more advanced informational systems, and as irrevocable as new scientific inventions. Allan Dafoe writes of the concept of "technological determinism," the idea that "technological change could be, in some sense, an out-of-control history-shaping process" that "seeme[s] to develop autonomously, following an internal technical logic, and profoundly shape[s] society in ways that were not intended by anyone" (1048). In such a configuration, human capacity to direct the course that development takes and preserve familiar landscape is effaced. Dafoe writes that a deterministic perspective "does not allow the possibility of any human agency and does not refer to the vast majority of perspectives that take the effects of technology seriously" (1052). Given the South's long history of depriving its residents of agency (frequently along racial and class-based lines), it stands to reason that the slow coercion of nonhuman nature to the service of modernity could be phrased as something about which nothing can be done, a pattern that fits easily into the familiar narrative of ruin.

Where *General Orders No. 9* departs from the typical southern ruin-narrative, however, is its location of the point of inflection between the region's environmental potential and its subsequent squandering of that potential. Turning aside from the more popular practice of placing the roots of the South's ecological transformation in Reconstruction and the years immediately following, the film instead focuses on the mid-twentieth century and the construction of interstate highways.[5] Early in the film, the viewer is introduced to southern roadways by a black-and-white graphic of an unnamed Georgia county upon which public thoroughfares are superimposed like veins or tree roots. "Deer trail becomes Indian trail becomes county road," intones the narrator, positing a (problematically) seamless transition between the use of roadways by indigenous animals, indigenous people, and white settlers. As more roads appear on the map, a point of convergence in the center of the county becomes evident: the town, the county seat. "The roads of the county meet like the spokes of a wheel," the narration notes. "It appears as a world entire, as a wheel upon the earth" (fig. 3). The film finds in this configuration a sense of celestial order; having the road system radiate centrifugally from

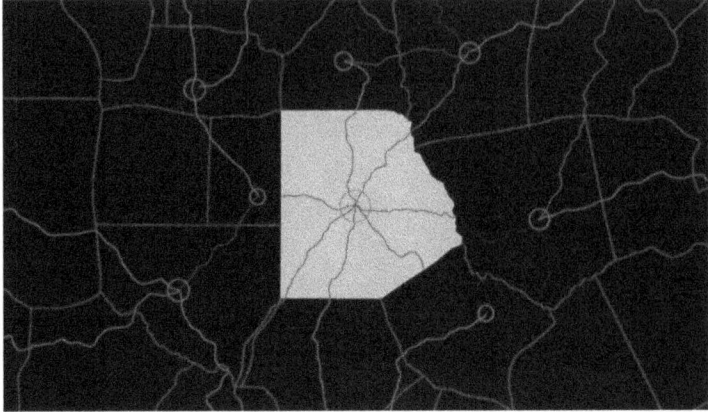

FIG. 3. "Spokes on a wheel" country road configuration from *General Orders No. 9*. Author's screen capture.

the county seat inherently makes sense.[6] "It's a pattern. A pattern of point and periphery, star and satellite," the narrator continues: "here, there is a sense of order, from above and below, from within and without. This shall be the centerpost of the world." Southern roads in the pre-automotive era, the film suggests, evince a logic that connects humans and nature, and the surrounding land with urban centers.

However, in *General Orders No. 9*, the interstate highway system is entirely opposed to the county roads that preceded it, sundering humans from the environments that they inhabit and deadening the natural beauty of southern regions. Over a lugubrious montage of faceless southern interstates, the narrator flatly states: "the interstate does not serve—it possesses," and, "it has the power to make the land invisible to our attention." The film seems opposed to the interstate on general principle, but more specifically as a means of organizing and ordering the metropolises it connects, as opposed to the more organic small-town structure of county roads leading toward a central hub. In opposition to the "spokes on a wheel" that symbolized the transit structure of small southern towns, the perimeter inscribed by the interstate is "a wheel, haphazardly drawn." The interstate "seems to be an emblem of the whole, an image that suggests a center," the narrator claims as the screen fills with an image of I-285, the ring road surrounding Atlanta, an oblong, irregular silhouette. In comparison with the sparse, orderly county roads that the film has already presented, the interstate does indeed seem to be a serpentine parody of the orderly, wheel-like arrangement of southern roads, yet the critique runs

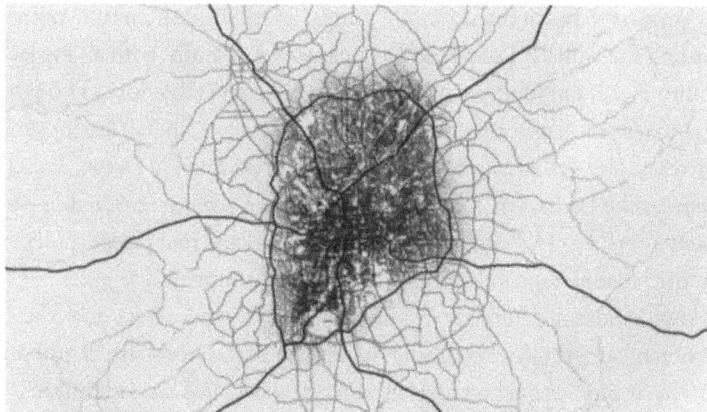

FIG. 4. Aerial view of Atlanta metropolitan area in *General Orders No. 9*.
Author's screen capture.

deeper than this. With the image of the I-285 perimeter still dominating the scene, the film fills in the vast network of city roads encompassed by the ring road like a spider constructing a web, creating a crenelated, ovoid, cancerous mass of darkness (fig. 4). This "image that suggests a center," the narration states over ominous synthesized music, "leads the eye to what must be the city's heart. But it's a false center . . . and a map of what comes next." In the image, the interstates intersecting with I-285 darken and thicken, now representing veins and arteries feeding into a human heart. The interstate system, the film suggests, is more than simply an eyesore, more than a deadening force acting on southern landscapes—it turns the city into a diseased organ, a system that *should* have order and significance, but does not.

General Orders No. 9's anxiety concerning mobility and the commercial development and environmental depletion that attend it might be read as neo-Agrarian—the film tends, broadly, to valorize rural agriculture and condemn urban industry—but its arguments skew environmentally rather than culturally. The film praises stasis and inertia and is suspicious of mobility; when there is any motion at all in the early shots it selects, that motion is invariably languid—a light rainfall on a slow-moving creek, for instance, or the wind in a pasture. The following shots set in Atlanta, by contrast, are a farraginous blur of cars, trains, planes, and industrial equipment busily toiling over anthills of slag. If the region could have just *stayed put*, the film seems to imply, and not sought to test the boundaries of its circumscribed communities, it might have retained some vestige of its idyllic rural character. *General Orders No. 9*

51

is, or appears to be on the surface of things, another southern ruin-narrative, regarding the vanished dirt-road landscape of the South, with all the lack of mobility that it entailed, as a complete and irrecoverable loss. Though the film tends to emphasize urban rather than rural centers, the argument superficially resembles Faulkner's lament for the Big Woods in *Go Down, Moses*—a change to the landscape that was "fated" (there was no reasonable way to prevent interstates from stretching into the South) and that places southerners in an irrevocably tragic relationship to their environment.

From a more measured standpoint, however, what effect does the construction of superhighways during the middle of the twentieth century have upon the South's cherished notions of regionalism and local identity? What are the consequences, both literary and environmental, of rapidly hurtling across landscapes that a few years earlier needed to be traversed slowly and laboriously? How do we extract resilience from the ruins that *General Orders No. 9* surveys?

I would like to address these questions through reference to two roads, the Natchez Trace and I-55, and the separate ways in which these roads foster mobility in and into the South. Their point of convergence is Jackson, Mississippi, the lifelong home of Eudora Welty. The Trace crosses only two interstates, I-55 and I-20, over its entire length, both just outside Jackson, making the southern capital the locus of the old and the new, the haunted Trace and the modern city.[7] Welty's work thus offers an unparalleled example of how regionalism responds to mobility, and how older environmental ideas become displaced, literally and figuratively. By placing Welty's writing alongside that of Flannery O'Connor, an author who has just as frequently (and just as erroneously) been cast in the mold of the inertial, provincial southern writer, I hope to show how, through reference to a range of different landscapes, the place reacts to the "ruin" of roads.

———

"Should one decide to draw up a map of Eudora Welty's fictional countryside," writes Ann Masserand, "one might safely assert that a road would run through it" (1). It is very likely that, as is the case for so much of Welty's fiction, Masserand's hypothetical road would be named the Natchez Trace. In such celebrated stories as "The Wide Net," "A Worn Path," "A Still Moment," and, most prominently, *The Robber Bridegroom*, the Trace emerges as the most storied and significant of Welty's roads, a place of living legend where vernacular southern stories bump elbows with classic myths. Each of these works reinscribes the mystic elements of the thoroughfare in subtly different ways: the forest and its inhabitants become monstrous obstacles in "A Worn Path," "A Still Moment" brings together three living legends of American history, and "The Wide Net," as Nancy Anne Cluck has argued, structures itself around classical patterns of heroism, testing, and reward.[8] All of these encounters unfold against the backdrop of the Trace.

The Trace was, for Welty, a distinctly southern answer to the myth-saturated landscapes of the Old World, an avenue for elevating regional cultures to legendary status. *The Robber Bridegroom* (1942) uses both folktale fabulism (birds and disembodied heads have the power of speech, magical disguises are donned and shed, the laws of physics are regularly bent) and environmental cues to portray the Trace as replete with legendary significance.[9] Perhaps a single example will suffice: the hurried flight that accompanies the abduction and rape of the innocent Rosamond by Jamie Lockhart.

> Birds flew up like sparks from a flint. Nearer and nearer they came to the river, to the highest point on the bluff. A foam of gold leaves filled the willow trees. Taut as a string stretched over the ridge, the path ran higher and higher. Rosamond's head fell back, till only the treetops glittered in her eyes, which held them like two mirrors. So the sun mounted the morning cloud, and lighted the bluff and then the valley, which opened and showed the river, shining beneath another river of mist, winding and all the colors of flowers. (65)

Though, strictly speaking, there is nothing "magical" happening in this passage, the superabundance of luminous language, which it shares with the description of Natchez in the book's initial scene and Clement's account of the wilderness in the novella's closing chapters, broadcasts the mystical valences of the landscape. The trees "glitter" and "foam" with leaves, matching the "sparks" of the birds and the "shining," multihued river. The setting is suffused with light, even in the predawn hours, creating a scene that seems alchemical, transforming mundane features into objects of significance. The environment gives an impression of motion, yet the horse, rider, and abductee remain still—the portrayal invokes the rape of Europa, commonly represented in art as a moment of frozen movement, deepening the mythic resonances of Welty's description.

The above is one instance of many from *The Robber Bridegroom*—throughout the novella, the Trace appears repeatedly as a road that signifies more than simply its route and contours, evincing some vestiges of its history of Native occupation and use, piracy, villainy, and murder, as well as some indescribable fabulist quality added by Welty, a synthesis of American folk legend and European fairy tales. This multifaceted mystic quality of the Trace is borne out in Welty's other writing on the highway as well. Victor H. Thompson notes, in a 1973 article, that Welty's representation of Dow, Murrell, and Audubon in another story set on the Trace, "A Still Moment," while remaining remarkably true to its sources (which are the journals of the three men involved), lends supernatural relevance to mundane events. "The horse stops in Dow's account because an Indian seized it," Thompson writes. "In Welty's account, 'it stopped at a touch'—as if a magic spell had been cast. In Dow's account, the Indians merely surround the horse. In Welty's account, '[They] made a closing circle'—a magic circle" (Thompson 75). Welty herself, in a 1971 letter, claimed that "A Still Moment" had its genesis in the notion that these three "conflicting visions of the world (and eternity) could converge . . . some kind of wonder or divinity is really *there* at such a moment . . . some original wonder is still there, buried however deep under whatever human destructiveness" (33). Magic, divinity, wonder—in Welty's Natchez Trace stories, these terms proliferate, suggesting idiosyncratic epic origins for provincial southern landscapes.

Regardless of the Trace's distinct links to both a romanticized American antiquity and specific regional cultures, however, the road has always served the nationalizing imperatives of American capitalism and transit. In its early days, William C. Davis argues in *A Path through the Wilderness* (1995), the Trace "offered the promise of access to vast new territory, a pathway to empire" (11). Davis sees the Trace as a tool for the gradual establishment of ties of exchange and travel between the North and the South that eventually contributed to early nineteenth-century nation-building. "Only with the coming of sustained communication and trade with their new American compatriots would [early communities] finally, in time, feel a single loyalty, and with the organization of the territory and the further opening of opportunity there for new settlers and entrepreneurs from the United States, that increased level of contact could come" (13). Even Roane F. Byrnes, the prominent Natchez businesswoman whose relentless efforts resulted in the creation of the modern Natchez Trace Parkway, insisted upon the value not of the road's historical or aesthetic virtues, but its economic potential. In a 1937 speech, she proclaimed: "Tourists will pour over [the parkway] by the tens of thousands, just as they do in Yellowstone and all other great National Parks. And Natchez is to be the southern terminus of this road, which bears its name. There is no way to compute what this will mean to us—Natchez will be more famous than she ever was—even in antebellum days" (Leach 110).

When Mike Fink, moonlighting as a postman in *The Robber Bridegroom*, is menaced by the grandfather of all alligators lumbering down the Trace, our tendency is to regard the encounter as the meeting of two legendary characters in a setting worthy of the tallest of American vernacular tales. However, in doing so we may forget the mail pouch he carries, a material marker of the vital necessity of communication in the early republic (Jefferson designated the Trace as a post road in 1801, making it the earliest federally funded interstate road). Similarly, Clement Musgrove falls easily (though rarely perfectly) into the archetype of the naïve, quixotic hero familiar to fable and myth, though he is also, we are told, a prominent farmer and businessman. In truth, the legends of land pirates and wandering spirits that made the Trace a locus for Welty's fabulism were enabled by commerce—the necessity of moving material goods and money across the South. Rather than existing in a nostalgic era before the dawn of the automobile, mass media, and urbanization, *The Robber Bridegroom* marks the Trace as subtly yet indelibly implicated in the rise of all of these elements.[10] The romance that Welty grants to the Trace stems from both the benefit of nearly two hundred years of hindsight and the desire to see vernacular American figures elevated to the status of myth—it is easy to overlook, from the portrayal of the Trace in her novels and short stories, that, entirely independent of its mythical significance, it is also a *road*, and one that served a vital function in the foundation of the South as a region and the United States as a nation.

Though recent scholarship has focused heavily upon migration and emigration of people and culture into and out of the South, especially in the twentieth and early twenty-first centuries, it seldom pauses to consider the physical avenues by which this movement occurs. To this end, it may be worthwhile to contemplate the development of southern infrastructure—by what routes does the rise of car culture make inroads in the South? What is the state of southern roadways when Welty pens her mythic (and frequently nostalgic) tales of the Trace? In 1900, there were a total of twenty automobiles in Mississippi and no federally sponsored highways to Florida, Tennessee, or the

Carolinas. Transportation was largely managed on a county-by-county basis, meaning that the vast majority of public roads were in abysmal condition. In addition, the dominant pattern of roads was the "spokes on a wheel" configuration referenced in *General Orders No. 9*, in which roads led into towns from adjoining farms and departed centrifugally from them, but only intermittently connected towns to each other—most intercity transit was accomplished via railroad. The sole contiguous highway leading from the North to the South was the Dixie Highway, running from Michigan's Upper Peninsula across the southeast, eventually terminating in Miami. The Dixie Highway was laboriously constructed during the 1910s in large part to enable access to cheap real estate in Florida (leading to the infamous Florida land boom of the 1920s), but it was also pressed into service as a hauling road, especially during the First World War.[11] When Welty began her literary career in the early 1940s, the network of roads in Mississippi had scarcely evolved from its rural heritage.

Traveling from one southern town to another by car—to say nothing of attempting to cross state lines themselves—in the middle decades of the twentieth century entailed a roundabout and frequently torturous course through the country, the same process that Welty describes in *One Writer's Beginnings*. "That kind of travel," she writes of the elaborate process of wayfinding and doubling back, "made you conscious of borders; you rode ready for them. Crossing a river, crossing a county line, crossing a state line—especially crossing the line you couldn't see but knew was there, between the South and the North—you could draw a breath and feel the difference."[12] Roads in the premodern South order space, separating it into city and country, *heimlich* and *unheimlich* zones, and permit those borders to be crossed, exceeded, overcome. For Welty, the Trace—which in her fiction doubtlessly bears some imprint of those winding country roads—serves as both a means of mythologizing southern identity and delineating the means by which that identity is connected to others around the region and nation. Also in *One Writer's Beginnings*, Welty describes the process of passing through small southern communities on family road trips to Ohio and West Virginia:

> You could see a town lying ahead in its whole, as definitely formed as a plate on a table. And your road entered and ran straight through the heart of it; you could see it all laid out for your passage through. Towns, like people, had clear identities and your imagination could go out to meet them. . . . Nothing was blurred, and in passing along Main Street,

slowed down from twenty-five to twenty miles an hour, you didn't miss anything on either side. Going somewhere "through the country" acquainted you with the whole way there and back. (46)

There is, I would surmise, some element of nostalgia at work here—Welty's account of passing directly through and absorbing some of the local flavor of the communities along her route is familiar to anyone who has spent time traversing state routes and county roads in the South, but perhaps less so to the driver on the interstate system, whose route will approach many small towns, but only pass directly through a motley assortment of motels and truck stops on the outskirts. The construction of ring roads, such as I-220 in Jackson or I-440 in Nashville, permitted (and, in fact, encouraged) motorists to circumvent the heart of the city in favor of more indirect routes through the outskirts—for the traveler passing around cities by way of these thoroughfares, a southern city strongly echoes a northern one; any indication of regional distinction is effectively erased by the infrastructure, with only local-flavor billboards and bumper stickers self-consciously marking the region's identity.

What seems to be consistent about Welty's various apprehensions of her early travel experiences is the presence of boundaries, be they city limits, geographical features such as mountains and rivers, or even divisions between large and complex sociopolitical regions (the North and the South). The joy that Welty finds in travel stems from the legibility of these boundaries, whether they are sensed directly or more affectively. And yet, even early in the history of southern roadbuilding enterprises, the ostensible aim of the new roads was to break down many of these boundaries. Tammy Ingram notes, in *Dixie Highway* (2014), that "The *New York Times* dubbed [the titular road] 'the Dixie Peaceway' and declared the route 'a memorial . . . symbolical of the accord between brethren which shall never again be broken'" (Ingram 43). John S. Cohen, then-editor of the *Atlanta Journal*, was even more overt in his boosterism, declaring that the Dixie Highway symbolized "'the elimination of the final barrier' between North and South" (Ingram 40). When we broaden our historical scope to include the construction of the interstate highway system in the wake of the Dixie Highway, we discover further attempts to supersede Welty's notion of regional boundaries. Rather than being contrived to support small communities or agricultural economies (as was the case with the preceding "spokes on a wheel" configuration), the interstate had its origins in issues of national defense and industry; in 1955, President Eisenhower called for the creation of the system of roads with an appeal to nationalism: "Our unity as a nation is sustained by free communication of thought and by easy transportation of people and goods. The ceaseless flow of information throughout the Republic is matched by individual and commercial movement over a vast system of interconnected highways crisscrossing the country and joining at our national borders with friendly neighbors to the north and south" ("Special Message," n.p.). Such idealistic rhetoric somewhat cloaks what some have noted as the most pressing call for the construction of interstates: as a means of quickly evacuating large cities in the event of a Soviet nuclear attack.

It is not difficult to see such large infrastructure projects as diametrically opposed to the sleepy, winding roads of the rural South. Elsewhere in Welty's writing, we see a similar suspicion toward the speed and scale of the interstate system. When Laurel Hand returns to Mount Salus to see her father buried in *The Optimist's Daughter*, she is disturbed at night by "traffic on some new highway, a sound like the buzzing of one angry fly against a windowpane, over and over" (57). The cacophony of the new interstate is juxtaposed with the idyllic evening sounds of her parents reading aloud to each other that Laurel recalls from her childhood: "the two beloved reading voices came rising in turn up the stairs every night to reach her . . . she cared for her own books, but she cared more for theirs, which meant their voices" (57). Later, during the funeral itself, the interstate intrudes more overtly upon what would otherwise be a sentimental moment, drowning out the entirety of the ceremony: "Laurel failed to hear what came from [Dr. Bolt's] lips. She might not even have heard the high school band. Sounds from the highway rolled in upon her with the rise and fall of eternal ocean waves. They were as deafening as grief. Windshields flashed before her eyes like lights through tears" (92). Here, technological and industrial development quite literally obscures more intimate, emotional moments; though "tears" are invoked in the above excerpt, this happens only through analogy, implying that the passage (and noise) of interstate traffic has somehow stifled Laurel's natural affective reactions to trauma. Ironically, a system of infrastructure intended to enable a greater range of human movement and experience here serves instead as a barrier, a space of insulation between the self and its emotions, associations, and memories.

In addressing the alienation that, for her characters, frequently accompanies existence in an increasingly mobile, increasingly manufactured and disposable region, Welty frequently turned to vegetative symbolism to indicate the contrast between older, more holistic concepts of nature and how those concepts are repackaged and resold in the modern day. In "Music from Spain," for instance, Eugene MacLain suffers a bout of homesickness whilst strolling the streets of San Francisco: "Now, too late when the city opened out so softly in beauty and to such distances, it awoke a longing for that careless, patched land of Mississippi winter, trees in their rusty wrappers, slow-grown trees taking their time. . . . Eugene looked askance at a flower seller: where had the seasons gone? Too cheap, bewilderingly massed together, the summerlike, winterlike, springlike flowers tied up in bunches made him glance disparately at the old man marking down the price on a jug of tulips" (399). The contrast is stark between the Mississippi woods, which fulfill neither an economic nor an aesthetic function, and the flowers, which are explicitly intended to satisfy both. The mere setting of San Francisco, where the seasons seem to vanish and pedestrians are in constant risk of being obliterated by the streetcars that enable the city to function, seems to stand in opposition to the solidity in memory of Mississippi. The tulips that Eugene observes in this scene are both literally rootless and, as the discounted price would seem to indicate, close to death. Similarly, in "The Wanderers," Virgie lugubriously remembers that, before the nearby road was repurposed as a logging route, her mother "used to set out yonder and sell muscadines, see out there? There's where she got rid of all her plums, the early and late, blackberries and dewberries, and the little peanuts you boil. Now the road runs the wrong way" (435).[13] One way—though not necessarily the best way—to read such instances in Welty's fiction is essentially to regard the southerners described therein as victimized by commercial development, with the road as catalyst and symbol of that metamorphosis. Routes replace, and frequently get in the way of, roots.

To this end, popular wisdom holds that southern regions have historically been suspicious of the automobile insofar as it represented, in Lizabeth Cohen's words, "wholesale participation in a mainstream culture built around mass consumption."[14] Car culture, so the argument goes, claims to offer convenience, promote the economy, and modernize rural areas by connecting them to nearby cities, but in fact accomplishes the opposite: rapid transit becomes impossible on traffic-choked thoroughfares, and funneling drivers through certain selected routes encourages the flow of commerce along those routes, strangling smaller businesses in remote and rural areas. When we look back at the public reaction in the South to first the intrusion of the automobile onto roads that had previously seen only foot and carriage traffic and, later, to the large-scale construction of interstate highways, we see a distinct *opposition* to the notion of connectivity. Ingram takes note of the fact that, during the dawn of the motor age, southern farmers "resisted by refusing to move their horses and wagons to the side of the road in order to allow cars to pass. Others [scattered] tacks and glass in the roads to puncture tires or [strung] rope or barbed wire across the road. In South Carolina, one frustrated farmer even fired his pistol at a car that was attempting to pass his horse-drawn wagon" (24–25). A 1958 editorial in the *Jackson Clarion-Ledger* suggests that this hostility was born in part from the ways in which reliable public roads encouraged the intermingling of urban and rural culture: "The automobile is a double-bitted ax chopping away at the land on which the country's food and fiber are produced. It takes city people into the country to live, and then, because their automobiles get jammed up in the city, it brings factories, commercial institutions and recreation areas out to them, at additional cost to cropland" ("Wide Open Spaces").[15] Ann Brigham contends, in *American Road Narratives*, that the titular stories are "plotted around unsettling processes: the crossing of borders, the courting and conquering of distance, the reinvention of identity, and the access, negotiation, and disruption of spaces" (8). Yet public reaction to the construction of interstate highways in Mississippi, rather than evincing a willingness or enthusiasm for the possibility of greater urban-rural interchange and contact with other regional and national cultures, seems to indicate a preference for keeping the boundaries locals were familiar with in place.[16] Just as Ellie Morgan in Welty's "The Key" feels "some nameless apprehension rising and overflowing within her at the thought of travel . . . as if there had been a death," the construction of the interstate highways was, for many Mississippians, an unwanted, even threatening change in the accustomed rhythms of life.[17]

––––––

In conjunction with the suspicion evinced by Welty and her fellow Mississippians toward the implications of the new southern highways, it may be instructive to contemplate the work of another female southern author active during the mid-twentieth century, the bulk of which seems to express something of the same resistance to infrastructural improvements: the stories of Flannery O'Connor, who composed her major works in Milledgeville, Georgia, somewhat further from the burgeoning interstate system, but no less invested in its steady spread. O'Connor, like Welty, has frequently been cast as a proto-environmentalist southern writer, with critics noting how her relative lack of overt biocentric messages is balanced by her acute awareness of changes in the environment around her, such as the devastation of local cotton crops by the boll weevil or the damming of the Oconee River in 1952. The latter incident serves as the basis for "A View of the Woods" (1957), O'Connor's most overtly environmentalist work. The two main characters, Mark Fortune and his granddaughter, Mary Fortune Pitts, are allegorically juxtaposed in terms that are difficult to nuance; the elder Fortune has dreams of his denuded country plot attracting "a paved highway in front of his house with plenty of new-model cars on it. . . . He wanted to see a gas station, a motel, a drive-in picture-show within easy distance. . . . There was talk of paving the road that ran in front of the Fortune place. There was talk of an eventual town. He thought this should be called Fortune, Georgia" (*Every-thing That Rises* 57–58). However, Mary protests the sale of the land for development on the basis that it will ruin the titular "view of the woods." Her recalcitrance frustrates Fortune, who himself can see the woods only as what they appear to be: "woods—not a mountain, not a waterfall, not any kind of planted bush or flower, just woods. The sunlight was woven through them at that particular time of the afternoon so that every thin pine trunk stood out in all its nakedness. A pine trunk is a pine trunk, he said to himself, and anybody that wants to see one don't have to go far in this neighborhood" (*Everything That Rises* 70).[18]

In this story, which Mark S. Graybill calls "O'Connor's most fulsome, sustained meditation on man's destruction of the environment," major issues raised by infrastructural modernization in the mid-twentieth-century South come to the fore (11). O'Connor explicitly invokes major human alterations of the landscape (the new interest in Fortune's plot comes from the damming of a nearby river, creating a new marine leisure space) with a particular emphasis on roads, which, as with Welty, tend to proliferate in O'Connor's work. In a series of short stories roughly coincident with the construction of the interstate highway system (I-75, the route closest to O'Connor's home in Milledgeville, was completed in 1957—the same year that "A View of the Woods" was published), in fact, she repeatedly juxtaposes the modern, paved highway with the dirt or country road—while the former encompasses modern, civilized, secular life, the latter leads toward more primal ideals of salvation or damnation. In "A Good Man Is Hard to Find," for instance, the highway dazzles the doomed travelers with images of order and beauty: "She cautioned Bailey that the speed limit was fifty-five miles an hour. . . . She pointed out interesting details of the scenery: Stone Mountain; the blue granite that in some places came up to both sides of the highway; the brilliant red clay banks slightly streaked with purple; and the various crops that made rows of green lace-work on the ground. The trees were full of silver-white sunlight and the meanest of them sparkled" (*Good Man* 3–4). By contrast, the instant that the car departs from the highway and begins to follow an unpaved road, the scene becomes akin to the biblical wilderness, a howling wasteland with "sudden washes in it and sharp curves on dangerous embankments" through which the protagonists must travel anxiously: "All at once they would be on a hill, looking down over the blue tops of trees for miles around, then the next minute, they would be in a red depression with the dust-coated trees looking down on them" (*Good Man* 10–11). The moment of enlightenment and divine inspiration (and suffering) only comes for the characters in this story, as in O'Connor's work more broadly, once they leave the illusions and artifice of the well-traveled road behind. Like Welty's Natchez Trace, the unpaved road in O'Connor's writing seems to represent a departure from the rationalist gospel of modernism and toward an older, mythic time.

By contrast, modern transportation systems, particularly the highway, appear in O'Connor's work as ultimately deceptive, concealing true suffering and true knowledge beneath a composed veneer, as the scenery alongside the highway in "A Good Man Is Hard to Find" does. Nowhere is the simulacrum more total, however, than in *Wise Blood* (1952), in which the highway (seemingly *literally*) goes nowhere—the faster Hazel Motes drives his car, the less progress he makes.

> [H]e went over a viaduct and found the highway. He began going very fast. The highway was ragged with filling stations and trailer camps and roadhouses. After a while there were stretches where red gulleys dropped off on either side of the road and behind them there were patches of field buttoned together with 666 posts. The sky leaked over all of it and then it began to leak into the car . . . he had the feeling that everything he saw was a broken-off piece of some giant blank thing that he had forgotten had happened to him. (70)

The landscape here is indistinct, flattened; no one piece of scenery emerges long enough to be described in detail, and the landmarks instead are persistently referred to in multiples, giving an impression of unreality, all extant places smeared into one by the velocity of the highway.[19] Later in the novel, as Hazel attempts to leave town once and for all, he discovers that he, in fact, cannot: "He drove very fast out onto the highway, but once he had gone a few miles, he had the sense that he was not gaining ground. Shacks and filling stations and road camps and 666 signs passed him . . . he had the sense that the road was really slipping back under him. He had known all along that there was no more country but he didn't know that there was not another city" (209).

Critics such as Olivia McGuire, reading the car as "the unmistakable symbol of American prosperity in the 1950s," have interpreted Hazel's desire for the Essex as congruent with his desire for "a place 'to be' and a simultaneous means of escape. . . . [The car] is the only spiritual, emotional home he will accept, and it can deliver him from confronting reality whenever he wants it to, or so he believes" (519). As McGuire's final phrase implies, Hazel's attribution of these significances to his car is ultimately futile—it makes a poor "spiritual, emotional home" and cannot absolve him of his responsibilities in a given place simply by carrying him away. As Monica Miller writes: "the car here at once represents the promise of travel as well as its ultimate futility. . . . While the automobile may allow you to change your physical location, they do not provide any permanent escape from the problems of life. . . . No matter where you go, Jesus will have you in the end" (88). Like other deeply flawed O'Connor characters, Hazel uses something artificial as a prosthetic for something genuine, attempting to convince himself of an equivalence between them. In *Wise Blood*, the car that Hazel drives and the highways he attempts to flee upon serve as modern simulacra for much older and deeper issues.

However, there is evidence to suggest that O'Connor's engagement with the transforming face of transportation in the South was not simply a convenient vehicle for allegory. Even in her early life, she was immersed in the discourse of movement and mobility. A joking letter from her father, dated February 13, 1939 (in the fourteenth year of her life), addressing her as "Lord Flannery O'Connor" promises her a "Valentine's Day tribute," hoping that "your lordship will buy a new automobile with it (as long as it is not a Nash)" ("Unpublished Letter," n.p.). And, though O'Connor is subject to the same fetishizing of place and region as seemingly every southern author, her correspondence reveals a distinct lack of praise for her home. A letter to John J. Sullivan, a friend of her college days, dated April 30, 1945 (shortly after she received a scholarship from the University of Iowa), notes snidely that "if life in Iowa is as vivid and exciting as in M'ville, I will doubtless collapse of complete exhaustion at the age of 104" ("Unpublished Letter," n.p.). A more detailed account of her connection to place, as articulated in a July 8, 1952, letter to Robert D. Franklin, reads: "Most of the time I live in a place called Milledgeville, Georgia, a town made up almost exclusively of nice to not-so-nice old ladies with dead fore and aftbrains, who all bought themselves a copy of WISE BLOOD and now feel that the publisher should give them back their money" ("Unpublished Letter," n.p.). The cynical undertone to these pronouncements indicates that O'Connor was fully aware of the *expected* close bond between southerners and their environment, but saw that stereotype as an opportunity for satire (and, one expects, symbolism) in her work rather than as a genuine source of inspiration.

From very early in her career, O'Connor staunchly resisted the stereotype of harmonious rural life in untouched natural settings. Prior to the more clearly skeptical parables of agrarian hubris, envy, and incompetence in, for example, "Greenleaf" and "The Displaced Person," we can find in an undated work (likely emanating from her years at Iowa) titled "The Agriculturalist" a savage critique of the bond between southerners and their environment. "The agriculturalist," she writes, "never lives on his farm. It is his policy to buy his little graveyard for hard earned dollars at least a hundred miles from all civilization, where it can be reached only by a road that would scarcely do justice to the engineering ability of a tribe of mentally deficient Hooperhaw indians" ("The Agriculturalist," n.p., n.d.). Here, the ostensible purpose of the farm is sacrificed in the name of remoteness—the poor quality of the road (so abominable, in fact, that it warrants a racist aside) acts in service of its true role, which is to remain inaccessible. The landscape in "The Agriculturalist" is put to use as a parody of southern pastoralism, since the title character spends his leisure time in a farcical commune with nature: "each weekend . . . with his threadbare tires and last gasoline ticket, he may be seen speeding merrily up this Hell's Pass to take intimate council with the beauties of nature, and thereby to revive again his wilting spirits" (n.p., n.d.). The words, of course, drip with sarcasm, but it is worth noting that O'Connor uses the concept of travel to a secluded rural retreat with full awareness of its relevance to Romantic visions of nature. The country is where we are *supposed* to escape and "revive" our "spirits," O'Connor suggests, but it does not serve this function in the present day; something has been lost.

We can also find, elsewhere in O'Connor's early and unpublished writing, intimations of an environmental ruin-narrative. In an untitled and undated (though likely from her days at Iowa), short story, parts of which would eventually become incorporated in "The Crop," the central character, Mrs. Winthrop, feels that "the world . . . was growing every day more unsuited to [her]." She recalls her childhood, when there were "low green fields and pleasant hills where there were now concrete cotton-warehouses, aluminum plants, abatoirs [sic], and breweries." While she is able to remember a time when the warehouse district was simply a "low green field . . . speckled with violets and wild asters," these are soon replaced by industrial structures, albeit structures that serve a less offensive, harmoniously rustic purpose: "quaint, wooden buildings that were dark inside and smelled of pine and cotton bales" (3). These, however, are torn down in turn and replaced by concrete structures, "fire-proof and incredibly ugly" (3). The sense of environmental loss here is at least partially subservient to the loss of *social* cohesion that Mrs. Winthrop feels—she reflects: "Peoples [sic] minds in those days were concerned with living the good life, providing for the remains of their families after their own deaths, and certain social functions providing healthy outlets for any energy left over living the good life from day to day. Oh the life then had been like a well-balanced meal. Mrs. Winthrop disliked the word, delicattessin [sic], but now life was like a continuous trip from one delicattessin to another" (n.p.). The loss of her remembered environment is, for Mrs. Winthrop, another symptom of a much more general and wide-reaching assortment of negative changes in the world, lending a sense of largely aesthetic degradation to the passage of time. Mrs. Winthrop's environmentalism, if it can be so called, is centered on causes, not effects—the loss of the green fields of her childhood is a symptom of a much larger societal ailment.

Critics have frequently seen in O'Connor's suspicion toward modernity, as well as in her more specific critique of commercial development in the South in "A View of the Woods," the rudiments of a preservationist ethos. Henry Edmondson, for example, claims that "O'Connor warns that there will always be limits to progress, and, even more to the point, that there is a 'view of the woods' that cannot and should not be eradicated by science and technology" (200). Such readings tend to view the story, as I have hinted earlier, in broadly allegorical terms. John Roos puts the opposition between the viewpoints of the two main characters succinctly: "[Fortune] does not understand what there can be that cannot be substituted, or exchanged, or measured. Mary Fortune, on the other hand, must place some value on the view of the woods from the porch that is incommensurable with other goods" (176). Mary, Roos writes, is an emblem of environmentalist hope, "the hope that there is something beyond use, something that is permanent and unchanging" (178). While Mary is capable of seeing or witnessing the intangible value within seemingly mundane landscapes, whatever value that might be (hope, aesthetic appreciation, biodiversity, divine immanence—the specific character of her capability varies between readers), Fortune is concerned only with profits, prestige, and progress, and thus, as Graybill writes, "misses the forest for the trees" (13). From this perspective, "A View of the Woods" essentially becomes a preservationist parable or object-lesson, with Mary, Fortune, and the woods all playing distinctly defined roles.

O'Connor's strongly dualistic division between the paved and unpaved roads, and, implicitly, between nature and culture, as well as the pervasive schism between the condemned and the redeemed in her fiction as a whole, lend themselves to a fairly binary conception of the "natural" as essentially congruent with the "premodern." Though, as Timothy Vande Brake points out, there can be little question that she savagely attacks American consumer culture during the 1950s, insisting that the "seductions" of postwar commercialism "[lead] only to emptiness and betrayal," her critique tends to gravitate toward the same poles as *General Orders No. 9*—a clear division between sinners and saints and, by extension, untouched versus ruined landscapes, with the same road marking the distinction (28).[20] Christine Flanagan, in a somewhat despondent afterword to a 2017 essay on O'Connor's depiction of various pieces of industrial and agricultural machinery, notes: "Flannery O'Connor's farm, Andalusia, is still an oasis . . . but its 500 acres of farmland and woods are now surrounded by hotels, strip malls, and car dealerships. Down the highway in both directions, Fortune, Georgia, has arrived" (29). It is the word "oasis" that resonates here—a living, fertile, beautiful spot of comfort amid a vile and hostile wasteland. A small patch of soil along a dirt road might be saved, but the surrounding highway is pure desolation.

———

Is there an alternative to the dualistic ruin-narrative of the South's industrialized, yet still relatively isolated, landscape being steadily banished by the spread of interstate automotive travel? Eudora Welty herself would have heard—perhaps even seen—evidence of the construction of I-55 from her house in Jackson (approximately 2000 feet away) in the year of 1957 onward, and this intrusion no doubt works its way into *The Optimist's Daughter* and her other later work. However, I believe that her mild condemnation of the new superhighways stretching across the South only tells part of the story. The interstate becomes in her work, paradoxically, both a means of rapid travel around, over, and near various regional communities and a means of cementing the individual cultures and histories that those regions contain. Despite the bent toward nationalist unity and border-crossing that ushered in the age of the interstate, in Welty's work we find that the accessibility of free mass transit serves to reinforce, rather than break, regional identity.[21] Though the nationalist fantasy of the interstate highway system anticipates a burgeoning homogeneity among disparate communities, in fact it may provide the mobility and means for those communities to further entrench and isolate themselves. These communities, moreover, may be geographical or cultural in their delineations (i.e., towns), but frequently entail race- and class-based segregation. Even very recently, Clayton Nall argues, "highways facilitated urban-suburban partisan sorting by enabling whites and middle- and upper-income citizens to move from declining cities into single-family residential neighborhoods along suburban freeways. A key result has been ongoing partisan residential sorting and associated geographic polarization, especially in the South."[22] In other words, infrastructure that seemed designed to foster connectivity and diversity, especially in urban areas, can permit residents to more easily segregate themselves along racial, political, and economic lines.

However, in Welty's fiction, the process of developing identity and partitioning the self from the world at large, a process enabled by travel (as this chapter's epigraph suggests), need not assume such negative tones. Though travel in Welty's work, as I have noted already, frequently is inspired by or leads to trauma, she generally figures that trauma as a painful necessity for the development of her characters. To take an extreme example: after being abandoned by her lover Floyd in "At the Landing," Jenny undertakes what is implied to be one of her only extended trips away from home to find him. After the death of her grandfather, she is liberated from her hermetic existence: "It was not caution or distrust that was in herself, it was only a sense of journey, of something that might happen. She herself did not know what might lie ahead, she had never seen herself. She looked outward with the sense of rightful space and time within her, which must be traversed before she could be known at all. And what she would reveal in the end was not herself, but the way of the traveler" (*Collected Stories* 284). In her pursuit of Floyd, Jenny is determined to gain "the next wisdom," realizing that she "[knows] very little" and is "lost in wonder again" (*Collected Stories* 254). And what she immediately beholds upon going in search of Floyd is a landscape that recalls those of *The Robber Bridegroom* in its blend of the sublime and the surreal: "The red eyes of the altheas were closing, and the lizards ran on the wall. The last lily buds hung green and glittering, pendulant in the heat. The crape-myrtle trees were beginning to fill with light for they drank the last of it every day, and gave off their white and flame in the evening that filled with the throb of cicadas. There was an old mimosa closing in the ravine—the ancient fern, as old as life, the tree that shrank from the touch, grotesque in its tenderness" (*Collected Stories* 254). Much of the imagery here alludes to Jenny's impending abduction and violent rape at the hands of the fishermen, though (as in Jamie's abduction of Rosamond in *The Robber Bridegroom*) the more sinister aspects of the scene—the "red eyes" of the flowers attended by scurrying reptiles, the oppressive "throb" of the heat, the wilting, grotesque mimosa—are balanced by a profusion of light hues and gentle aromas.[23] What is immediately evident is that this is a moment of contact between not only Jenny's cloistered worldview and the harshness of life outside of her home, but between more amorphous and transcendent forces of good and evil—a conflict enabled by Jenny's embrace of "a sense of journey" and the "way of the traveler."

The same could be said of Welty's attitude toward the culture of mass transit and the interstate system as a whole; she seemed to regard it as, considered on its own terms, a development that disrupted natural, habitual modes of life, yet ultimately necessary to foster convenient transportation—much as the bifurcated images of motion manifest themselves in her fiction: a painful, yet revelatory, development. Though itinerant motorists and their various travails occupy a prominent position in many of Welty's short stories, notably "The Hitch-Hikers" and "Death of a Traveling Salesman," her closest adherence to the above model of the bifurcated nature of the travel narrative is likely "No Place for You, My Love," first published in the *New Yorker* in 1952 and subsequently reprinted in *The Bride of Innisfallen* (1955). Travel consumes the majority of the narrative, as two unnamed strangers voyage through the maze of bayous south of New Orleans on a lark, discovering along the way a vast expanse of jungle, a ramshackle restaurant, a faint romantic encounter, and an immense multitude of reptiles and crustaceans. In some sense, "No Place for You" is a love story, chronicling the rediscovery of erotic potential by two protagonists consumed by romantic inertia and ennui—the time they share at Baba's, at the end of the road in Venice, Louisiana, is phrased as a respite and release from weariness: "Surely even those immune from the world, for the time being, need the touch of one another, or all is lost. Their arms encircling each other, their bodies circling the odorous, just-nailed-down floor, they were, at last, imperviousness in motion" (42). As the travelers perform their dance, they become "impervious" to everything around them: the reeking wood, the chaos and squalor that surrounds them, and the precariousness of their respective positions. The change to a wholly foreign locale, enabled by the polished concrete road they travel to reach Venice, offers the travelers an escape from their entrenched lives.

Yet, if the road offers freedom and agency to the protagonists, it also supplies anxiety, fear, and alienation. Their voyage rapidly becomes an encounter with a vast and immitigable strangeness; the travelers' transition from the city to the jungle is marked by the appearance of alien beings: "More and more crayfish and other shell creatures littered their path, scuttling or dragging. These little samples, little jokes of creation, persisted and sometimes perished, the more of them the deeper down the road went. Terrapins and turtles came up steadily over the horizons of the ditches. Back there in the margins were worse—crawling hides you could not penetrate with bullets or quite believe, grins that had come down from the primeval mud" (38). The crawling creatures, as if summoned by the presence of the travelers, teem over the margins of the levee, matched by the insects that assault them whenever the protective membrane of the car's windows is removed. The environment's sinister, deceptive nature only becomes more pronounced as the pair travels further south: "they were driving through greater waste down here, through fewer and even more insignificant towns . . . in the vast open, sometimes boats moved inch by inch through what appeared endless meadows of rubbery flowers" (40). The artifice of the "rubbery" flowers and their unnerving surroundings is in no way banished by the moment of consummation that the travelers find at Baba's—even on the return voyage, the place is "a strange land, amphibious . . . more than it was like any likeness, it was South" (43). The place itself becomes not a location on a map, but a direction, a bearing to travel upon. Though the protagonists of "No Place for You" seem to find, however briefly, a respite from their stultifying day-to-day lives, said refuge, as the title of the story suggests, is fundamentally unstable, built on swamp

and sand. Such is the reality of travel in Welty's work, simultaneously convey-
ing both the fundamental, unsettling strangeness of contact with the unknown
and the potential for expansion, rediscovery, and passion.

Conventional wisdom holds that the narratives of attachment to place,
regional rootedness, and connection with the landscape that proliferate in
southern literature are always threatened by developments, whether social or
infrastructural, that promote mobility, technological progress, and alienation.
I would suggest that these developments in fact serve the opposite function in
Welty's work; her sense of regionalism, and the sense of self and identity that
accompany that belief, is enabled and supported by modernization. Recent
criticism has endeavored to liberate Welty from the stereotype of the "prim,
provincial, sheltered, sequestered spinster whose 'cramped' and 'sheltered'
life was spent 'in the quiet of a house in a quiet Mississippi town,'" as David
McWhirter has put it (69). But I would like to take this tendency a step further and urge us to examine how Welty's writing stems from mobility rather
than stasis, cosmopolitanism rather than regional identity politics. Though the
state of existence in far southern Louisiana that the two travelers in "No Place
for You" encounter appears to them wholly foreign and disconcerting, the
story closes with the realization, on the part of the unnamed male protagonist,
that the "original meaning" of the "shriek and horror and unholy smother" of
the subway he remembers in fact carries significances of "the lilt and expectation of love" (44). Welty's choice of the subway, the quintessential symbol
of modernity and urban mass transit, as the final image of "No Place for You"
suggests the confluence of the major concerns of both Romantic ideals of self-
discovery and Modernist fascination with speed and efficiency—the issues
are not dualistic, but symbiotic.

Both O'Connor and Welty offer powerful responses to the cultural and
environmental impact of the major highways that began to spiderweb the
South during their careers. In ferreting out the environmentalist messages
that inhere in their major works, however, criticism must necessarily retrace
its steps and revisit some of its primary premises—making authors such as
Welty and O'Connor more mobile and environmentally attuned than we had
previously thought necessitates a revision of where these same authors stand
on syllabi and in the critical tradition. In *Sacred Groves and Ravaged Gardens*
(1985), for instance, Louise Westing contrasts the representation of nature
in Welty's and O'Connor's works: "The gardens, bayous, rivers, and forests
of Eudora Welty's Mississippi world quiver with the very life forces of her

fiction. Unlike the natural world of O'Connor's stories, which seems to function only as rigidly stylized setting for grim dramas as classically restrained as Greek tragedy, Welty's nature is varied, shimmering with its own myriad life apart from human concerns. . . . The pattern of meadow and wood in Flannery O'Connor's fiction is much more specialized, gathering tremendous sacramental significance, with woods protecting vulnerable pastures from invasion" (6). Westing reads O'Connor's vision of nature as essentially comprised of nothing but allegory, a "rigidly stylized setting" rather than some version of an actual landscape, while Welty's fiction for her portrays nature as essentially a fairy-tale realm sundered from the world of humans.[24] No doubt there is some truth to each of these interpretations; certainly, this encapsulation resonates with many of the critical perspectives we have come across over the length of this chapter. Yet in order to view either of these authors as having something important, even vital, to say about environmentalism in the South, we must necessarily move away from overly binaristic conceptions of the function of nature in their work.

Like southern landscapes themselves, the works of both O'Connor and Welty are irreducible to ideas of simple moral or ecological value—rather than suggesting how their accounts diverge, then, I would prefer to regard them as means of triangulating or converging upon a set of common technological and infrastructural changes to the environment of the South. Welty, too, returned to the idea of confluence at the end of both *The Optimist's Daughter* and *One Writer's Beginnings*, both works emanating from a time after the old Trace had been paved and I-55 roared a half mile from her door. Contrasting starkly with the less favorable accounts of mass transit in Mount Salus earlier in the novel, Laurel's dreamlike memory of viewing the confluence of the Ohio and Mississippi Rivers by train induces a rapturous harmony in which the dead return to life and reach communion with the living: "They themselves were a part of the confluence. Their own joint act of faith had brought them here at the very moment and matched its occurrence, and proceeded as it proceeded. Direction itself was made beautiful, momentous" (160). When we recall Welty's refiguration of place as direction in "No Place for You," we realize that motion and travel themselves, the same mobility enabled by the interstate system, have displaced regional stability as the site of affective connection and affiliation in her work. And the final scene of *The Optimist's Daughter*, significantly, depicts Laurel in frenzied motion, rushing to catch a car to the airport while meditating on the flexibility and portability of memory, that "somnabulist" that "come[s] back in its wounds from across the world" (179). The confluence of individualistic, romanticized memory and impersonal mechanized motion works a strange alchemy upon the final pages of the novel, offering Laurel freedom from both the stultifying insularity of a single viewpoint and the homogeneity of a universalized identity. Where the humming interstate crosses the haunted Trace, where we might expect to find opposition and conflict, there is instead a metamorphosis, a liberation.

———

If there is one concept on which the emancipationist ideas in Welty's fiction and O'Connor's more declensionary view can agree, it would likely be that the widespread construction of highways and interstates amounts to nothing short of a transformation for the region. As with so many of the other environmental sea changes brought upon the South, it is perhaps most tempting to regard this change as "destruction," a "blight," to borrow a term from the rezoning practices that attended the construction of interstate highways, on the previously pristine landscape. Yet, as both of these authors' works indicate, the mobilization of the South does not eradicate its environmental potential so much as it opens new avenues for growth. Even *General Orders No. 9* realizes that "though our surroundings have become detestable," resilience is still possible: "This place has not yet perished because, in April, you can still feel it, that something is pushing against the surface of things," the narrator intones as the sun-washed pastures of the film's first twenty minutes give way to more pensive, mist-shrouded copses. Even if the film is unwilling to ascribe transcendental environmental significance to anything within the Atlanta city limits, at the very least it concedes that life does go on there. The narrative of resilience depends absolutely upon that of ruin in each of these sources in turn, making of it a dwelling place, a pulpit, or a horizon.

THREE

Of Yams and Canned Pasta

Southern Foodways as Discourse
in Toni Morrison and Fannie Flagg

AT AROUND THE MIDPOINT of the novel, the title character of Ralph Ellison's *Invisible Man* (1952), suffering an identity crisis in the midst of a Harlem
winter, encounters a vendor selling hot roasted yams. Remembering the tuber
as a staple of his childhood, he orders one and prepares to eat it:

> I broke [the yam], seeing the sugary pulp steaming in the cold. 'Hold
> it over here,' he said. He took a crock from a rack on the side of the
> wagon. 'Right here.' I held it, watching him pour a spoonful of melted
> butter over the yam and the butter seeping in. 'Thanks.' 'You welcome.
> And I'll tell you something.' 'What's that?' I said. 'If that ain't the best
> eating you had in a long time, I give you your money back.' 'You don't
> have to convince me,' I said. 'I can look at it and see it's good.' 'You
> right, but everything what looks good ain't necessarily good,' he said.
> 'But these is.' I took a bite, finding it as sweet and hot as any I'd ever
> had, and was overcome with such a surge of homesickness that I turned
> away to keep my control. I walked along, munching the yam, just as
> suddenly overcome by an intense feeling of freedom—simply because
> I was eating while walking along the street. It was exhilarating. I no
> longer had to worry about who saw me or about what was proper. To
> hell with all that, and as sweet as the yam actually was, it became like
> nectar with the thought. If only someone who had known me at school
> or at home would come along and see me now. How shocked they'd be!
> (264–65)

The Invisible Man, who by this point in the narrative is no stranger to the gap between appearances and reality, is reminded by the yam salesman of this schism—taste, the man sagely implies, must be the final word in separating the false from the true. And, in fact, at the taste of the yam, the invisible man discovers a new sense of self-integrity and pride in his origins—consuming yams, and chitterlings and hog maws, represents for him a marker of the bond between himself and his region of origin, a sloughing-off of the coldness and artificiality of the city. Significantly, as a prelude to the yam scene, Ellison walks the character through a street filled with cheaply manufactured images of artificiality; he spies "two brashly painted plaster images of Mary and Jesus surrounded by dream books, love powders, God-Is-Love signs, money-drawing oil and plastic dice" followed by "a window decorated with switches of wiry false hair [and] ointments guaranteed to produce the miracle of whitening black skin" (263). In contrast to these false temptations, the yam offers a "surge of homesickness" accompanied by "an intense feeling of freedom," as the invisible man feels himself liberated from the pretentions placed on him by the city.

The immutability of taste—and, to a large extent, smell—has been disproportionately embedded in literature. Eyes are easily deceived; sounds and words are unreliable and easily misheard; to rely on tactile sensations is to be as misguided as a blindfolded child fumbling with raw noodles in a bowl at Halloween. Yet taste and smell—the only two senses directly associated with consumption—override any attempts at subterfuge. Like the yam enjoyed by the Invisible Man, the primacy of taste short-circuits postmodern complexities of being in favor of simpler platitudes: "home," for instance, or "place," or even "the environment." Though it is commonly used as a simple vehicle for nostalgia or inclusion within a (real or imagined) community, as the yam seems to signify in *Invisible Man*, taste can also serve as a proto-environmentalist evocation of sentiment. Characters displaced from their home regions and deprived of familiar (dominantly rural) landscapes by their residence in far-off cities can access something of the nostalgic *terroir* of those regions and, implicitly, realize that they were always more connected to those environments than they ever knew. Though the city in *Invisible Man* speaks the language of ruin—characters cut off from their origins and imprisoned in a plastic underworld—taste posits a pastoral cure for those ailments.

This idea (or fantasy) of an environmental ethos stemming from sensation and other ephemera that do not necessitate a fully formed aesthetic, philosophical, or intellectual armature underlies many, if not most, major works of southern environmental writing. For the purposes of this chapter, I term this move toward an essentialized relationship between southerners and landscape "visceral environmentalism," a concern with the natural world stemming from affect rather than intellect, the guts rather than the brain. Scott Slovic has used the term "visceral" in reference to the work of Faulkner and other southern writers to indicate a "gut-level sense of connectedness to the world," in essence a variety of sensory imagism that sharpens the reader's awareness of the environment both within and outside of the text (Urgo & Abadie 120). Yet Slovic's visceralism involves "a moral and political valence—a purpose inclusive of and exceeding luxuriation," cultivating place-based awareness and, ultimately, ecological sensitivity (120). However, I am more interested in the means by which, in southern literature in particular, visceral description tends to override (if not simply circumvent) complex issues of environmental significance.[1] I see the visceral turn as essentially a reaction to both the problematics of southern environmental history and as a gesture toward compensating for the narrative of ruin—an attempt to reify southernness while paradoxically eliding the very elements that have historically defined it. The South has always had a weak environmental tradition but a strong *culinary* tradition, so the argument goes, and, approached from a certain angle, the latter can be deployed to bolster the former. I contend that the *actual* narrative of environmental resilience that emerges from a survey of southern foodways is less idealistic than a pure, visceral return to one's origins: rather, food in southern literature indicates a complex, oftentimes vexed relationship between humans and their environments.

————

Though traditional southern dietary habits draw upon a vast network of intersecting culinary traditions dating back centuries, widespread academic interest in southern food as a distinctly regional cuisine may only be as old as John Egerton's *Southern Food* (1993), a collage of snippets of history, encounters with prominent southern dishes, and descriptions of significant restaurants in the region. Egerton opens with the assertion that "the South, for better or worse, has all but lost its identity as a separate place, and its checkered past now belongs to myth and memory, but its food survives" and that "a meal in the South can still be an esthetic wonder, a sensory delight, even a mystical experience" (3). Egerton's linkage of traditional southern cooking to mysticism is twinned by his fetishization of the origins of these same foodstuffs:

"The South's food heritage is filled with clues to the character and personality of the region itself. The heritage originated in nature, in sun and earth and water. . . . From the beginning, Southerners, like most Americans, were close to the soil. Their lives revolved around the seasons" (35). In tasting southern food, Egerton claims, we experience a veritable transubstantiation of that food into the elements of its composition—a "closeness" to the soil and seasons that we (implicitly) associate with the South as a region. Southern food, Egerton suggests, can invoke a more authentic and complete portrait of southern history and identity than narrative accounts could ever hope to. Significantly, Egerton casts southern life in a pastoral mode that resists modern patterns of migration and technology, implying that the southern table captures an authenticity contradictory to notions of environmental ruin.

In the light of the latter-day popularity of local, organic foods and an emphasis on small rather than large-scale production, culinary trends in southern foodways have moved toward heirloom varietals, artisanal growers, and sustainable methods. In *Southern Provisions* (2015), David Shields chronicles and comments upon the drive to discover and revive traditional ingredients of southern cuisine, freeing them from the stranglehold of pesticides and pollution. Suspicious of the tendency toward fetishizing and romanticizing southern foods, Shields nonetheless takes the opportunity to praise the virtues of indigenous, rare varieties of South Carolina rice. "We could all savor the faint hazelnut delicacy, the luxuriant melting wholesomeness of Carolina Gold," he writes, "and we all wondered at those tales of Charleston hotel chefs of the Reconstruction era who could identify which stretch of which river where a plate of gold rice had been nourished. They could, they claimed, *taste* the water and the soil in the rice" (16–17). Shields invokes the culinary concept of *terroir*— the "taste of place" detectable in certain distinctively produced foods—to fuse sensory and historical data. Bernard Herman in a describes this process as food producing "narratives of place and experience" and "captur[ing] a consciousness of association and belonging," in essence, positive connections between southerners and their environment (37). Through sensory and affective description, Shields both invokes and collapses history—the Carolina Gold becomes simultaneously an artifact and a contemporary visceral experience.

Academia has, over the last decade, tended to regard southern foodways as a sort of universal key to the complex set of environmental, social, sexual, and racial histories that define the region; interpreting southern food, these studies suggest, gives us privileged access to a wide spectrum of regional identity. Marcie Cohen Ferris, in *The Edible South* (2014), reads southern food as a multifaceted, though distinctly bifurcated, signifier: "In food lies the harsh dynamics of racism, sexism, class struggle, and ecological exploitation that have long defined the South; yet there, too, resides family, a strong connection to place, conviviality, creativity, and flavor" (1). Wendy Atkins-Sayre and Ashli Quesinberry Stokes suggest that "embracing Southern food and drink is a way to take on [the] challenge of honoring positive elements of Southern history without glorifying or ignoring its past mistakes. . . . Given the diversity of its roots, Southern food provides opportunities for dialogues and experiences shared across cultural, racial, and socioeconomic lines. Food, perhaps more than anything else, provides a common ground and opens up possibilities for crossing barriers" ("Crafting the Cornbread Nation" 80–81). What these studies seem to share is the insistence upon food being the key to understanding a set of (generally positive) affiliations between humans and nature. One of the most direct routes to understanding how southerners occupied, managed, and ultimately *used* their landscapes would seem to be to study, know, and consume traditionally southern foods.[2] However, I believe that these accounts should be taken less as indicators of any authentic character inherent in southern environmentalism than as statements of what the authors—and, potentially, their readers—*want* southern foodways to represent: an apolitical, positive communion between southerners and their landscape.[3] Southern environmental history contains few enough instances of such cooperation, creating a ruinous lacuna that food and its origins hasten to fill.

Thus, the question in regards to the visceral turn toward southern foodways may not be how authentic a vision of southern environmental philosophy it represents, but the extent to which scholars *create* that authenticity. Lily Kelting, for instance, compellingly asks whether the fetishization of agricultural and labor history that accompanies paeans to southern foodways can potentially coexist with the inclusive, progressive ideals of the region today: "Can Southern food have it both ways—renewal and return? Does looking backwards towards an idealized agrarian past as a model for a new Southern multicultural utopia render the labor of food production stylized and therefore erased?" (365–66). Similarly, Stokes and Atkins-Sayre caution that celebratory accounts of southern foodways risk "proposing a postracial take on the South, blending all experiences into one" (*Consuming Identity* 74).[4] While "historical," "traditional," or "heirloom" ingredients and recipes frequently bear the aura of authenticity, such descriptors frequently elide the

oppressive conditions of race, class, and gender that produced those foodstuffs. The same might be said of southern environmental policy vis-à-vis
foodways: modern-day valedictions of inventive, forward-thinking ingredients, producers and chefs can obscure the centuries of poor environmental
stewardship that preceded them. It may be more valuable, as Scott Romine
suggests in "Where Is Southern Literature?" (2002), to regard "authentic"
southern culture as "a condition of pure textuality impervious to material,
ideological, or even cultural content," a postmodern construction rather than
a definite set of criteria. "This, I take it, is the way certain persons eat grits,"
Romine writes (Monteith and Jones 37). Romine focuses on southern food as
a means of producing, rather than reinforcing, southern affiliation, deflating
the appeals to authenticity invoked above.

When we discuss visceral appeals to southern foodways, then, we are in
truth dealing with how literature and other media construe affective connections to landscape as distinctively southern, independent of any actual historical evidence or circumstance. In contemplating such questions, we frequently
turn to literature as a record and articulation of affective connections between
humans and landscape, and, in southern literature, such bonds appear only
relatively recently. Definite origin points for visceral environmentalism are
difficult to locate, but by the turn of the twentieth century the South's agricultural origins, legacy of slavery, and subsequent struggle to reinvent itself
had begun to produce narratives of southerners' ostensibly mystical bond
with their foods. Charles Chesnutt's well-known short story "The Goophered
Grapevine," (1899) in many ways deals with the fundamental question of
how the postbellum South wished to define and represent its culinary and
environmental concerns, particularly as compared to other regions. In "The
Goophered Grapevine," northern entrepreneurs John and Annie consider
purchasing a vineyard in North Carolina because they are told that the "climate and soil were all that could be asked for, and land could be bought for
a mere song" (1). The vineyard turns out to be inhabited by the avuncular
former slave Julius, who relates a tall tale of the previous owner's attempts
to curb the theft of his grapes by first magically poisoning the vintage, then
turning an unfortunate slave into a human grapevine.

In Uncle Julius's (admittedly unreliable) account, the relationships between humans and landscape are *literally* mystical, arising from a variety of
West African spiritualism enabled by Aunt Peggy, the obeah-woman. They
are also distinctly racialized: the slaves on Master Dugal's plantation not only

suffer the effects of Aunt Peggy's incantations, but look on in horror as Dugal, on the advice of a northern horticulturalist, uproots the grapevines and douses them in toxic chemicals. Soon, Dugal's poor environmental practices bring about the ruin of the plantation, and when John and Annie arrive they find that his "shiftless cultivation" has "well-nigh exhausted the soil" (2). Yet even the transplanted couple (who seem on the whole to be better-attuned to the needs of the land) see the plantation only in terms of potential profit; they shrug off Julius's tale as an idle fantasy and restore the farm's yield in short order. While Julius manufactures and distributes local-color scenes for the delectation of the northerners, John and Annie manufacture and distribute grapes destined for the same market: "The vineyard . . . is referred to by the local press as a striking illustration of the opportunities open to Northern capital in the development of Southern industries. The luscious scuppernong holds first rank among our grapes," John proclaims near the end of the piece, "and our income from grapes packed and shipped to the Northern markets is quite considerable" (13). Foods that carry complex racial, geographical, spiritual, and narrative codes in Julius's story become, at the close of John's story, simple commercial window-dressing. Though Chesnutt certainly postulates a visceral connection between humans and their environment, that connection is racially and regionally insoluble; when exported across such boundaries, it loses its significance and power.

Chesnutt's methodology in "The Goophered Grapevine" is proto-environmentalist insofar as it does not necessarily issue a call for awareness of southern environmental issues, though it does denote a variety of means— traditional and affective, modern and impersonal—by which people of differing races and origins apprehend the southern landscape. "The Goophered Grapevine" is also remarkable in an ecocritical sense in that food (the muscadine) acts as catalyst for *both* of these means of interacting with nature. However, "The Goophered Grapevine" by no means invokes the sort of harmonious cooperation with the environment that later Agrarian and still later food writing would attribute to the region. The former owner of the land's poor treatment of the soil and his slaves alike create a landscape ripe for little beyond further exploitation—which the blithe northern newcomers readily visit upon it. Meanwhile, the characters who *do* seem to have an understanding of the environment's unique characteristics—the slaves on Dugal's plantation who behold their master's blighting of the soil—are alternately tormented by Dugal himself and treated as objects of amusement by the vineyard's inheritors. The scuppernong, in a word, is fraught; one can hardly imagine John, Annie, or Julius himself consuming one with the same nostalgic transport that the Invisible Man experiences when devouring his yam.

———

Is it possible for southern food to conjure the visceral environmentalism attributed to it by contemporary food writers while still taking account of the (oftentimes ruinous) circumstances of its production? A contrary narrative to the exploitation of Chesnutt's plantation might be that of the development of "soul food," which overtly links categories of racial and emotional belonging and spirituality to diet. Adrian Miller, in *Soul Food* (2013), traces usage of the term to the late 1950s and early 1960s in the United States, concurrent with the rise of soul music. In invoking the soul, Miller contends, black cooks and artists sought to connote something unique and indivisible about racial history and lifestyle. Coincidentally, what came to be known as "soul food" was commonly eaten both within the home and at large Sunday church picnics, a tradition that Frederick Douglass Opie traces back to the antebellum era in *Hog and Hominy* (2008). The continuation of this tradition, especially during the Great Migration, permitted the preservation of a sense of community and belonging in many black populations. In addition, consuming certain foods—Miller takes note of fried chicken and fish, cake, sweet potato pie, red drinks, and watermelon—in a setting that was simultaneously religious and public caused those foods to become associated with black spirituality, frequently in negative ways.[5]

Such is the brief history and etymology of soul food, but what visceral significances does it carry for southern literature and culture? Laretta Henderson attempts a formal definition in "*Ebonyjr!* and 'Soul Food'" (2007), reaching several conclusions: "Scholars define soul food in terms of three attributes: a connection to Africa and the diet of enslaved blacks, something inherent in the black body, and a tool to define a black identity" (82). From Henderson's standpoint, soul food both helps to constitute and is itself constituted by African American identity, and as such, like Chesnutt's muscadines, is racially indivisible. Opie arrives at "multiple definitions" of what "soul" might signify: "Soul is the product of a cultural mixture of various African tribes and kingdoms. Soul is the style of rural folk culture. Soul is black spirituality and experiential wisdom. And soul is putting a premium on suffering, endurance, and surviving with dignity . . ." (xi). Elsewhere in *Hog and Hominy*, Opie refines these definitions to some extent: "Soul is a hunch about what is good in a racist society that defines most cultural productions associated with black folk as inferior. . . . It served black people as a necessary collective consciousness" (129). Opie accounts for the wealth of connotations accompanying the term by noting that "soul" is, ultimately, "all wrapped up in feelings . . . an art form that comes from immersion in a black community and an intimate relationship with the southern experience" (136–37). In soul food, as I have noted earlier, we have clear and legible patterns of affect between southerners and their traditional foodways, but the link between those subjects and their landscape is conspicuously absent; none of these definitions attempt to make the case for soul food invoking the southern environment in a positive sense. In other words, soul food seems to invoke imagined rather than environmental communities, communities that explicitly transcend geographical boundaries and are not linked to specific landscapes. Certainly such a realization problematizes the visceral environmentalism that seems to frequently inform accounts of southern foodways; foods strongly associated with the region are centered in identity rather than the environment.

It is evident that, owing to widely differing associations with both landscape and taste, in addition to the race- and class-based valences of certain foods and preparations, simply appropriating visceral experiences of "traditional" southern foods as a means of countering the longstanding narrative of ruin in the South is a fragile assertion at best. Such experiences are too deeply individuated to be reworked into large claims about the region, its people, or its food. We see this in the work of Wendell Berry, the Kentuckian farmer-poet, revered in environmentalist circles for his powerful focus on restoring basic, uncomplicated human/nature relationships. In *Farming: A Hand Book* (1971), Berry (evidently speaking from his own experience) is straightforward in his argument that long agricultural experience leads to visceral affiliations. He writes, in the poem "The Man Born to Farming," that to the titular subject "the soil is a divine drug"; and, in "Prayers and Sayings of the Mad Farmer," portrays the process of cultivation as evincing a Zen-like unity between the self and the environment: "Having cared for the plans / my mind is one with the air. / Hungry and trusting, / my mind is one with the earth. / Eating the fruit, / my body is one with the earth" (31, 68). Where Berry diverges from some of the more expansive accounts of visceral environmentalism, however, is in his insistence that the attachment of humans to landscape always happens on an individual rather than a collective basis; there is no assertion here that southerners in particular encounter the environment more simply and directly, or even that agricultural laborers do. Rather, the sort of visceral affection that Berry details is reserved for individuals for whom said labor is itself transformative. He writes, "The *real* products of any year's work are the farmer's mind and the cropland itself," implying that personal revelation is more important than actual agricultural production (69). Moreover, Berry implies elsewhere in *Farming* that historical concerns are ultimately subordinate to personal and subjective realizations.

Berry's contention holds relevance for the current status of southern foodways, which today is in the paradoxical—though not necessarily untenable and certainly not unprofitable—position of desiring both visceral authenticity and modern trendiness. Contemporary locavore chefs and critics seek to push against both southern ecological and culinary history, reversing the narrative of ruin. Jane Black, writing for the *Washington Post*, speaks in rapturous terms of Travis Milton, a rising star in the Virginia food scene. After describing his armful of tattoos—many of them depicting heirloom vegetables—she relates the ink to Milton's philosophy as a whole: "Behind the Technicolor vegetables is a cloud of black. 'It shows all the beautiful things coming out of coal country,' Milton says. 'It's not me wearing my heart on my sleeve. It's my plan for Appalachia'" (n.p.). From a visceral standpoint, the connections articulated by Milton and other localist chefs seek to provide a counternarrative to the stories of poverty, monotony, and malnutrition familiar to southern culture and history, to suggest that there are aesthetically and culinarily pleasing elements buried underneath the veneer of environmental depletion and the dominance of fast food. Similarly, Marcie Cohen Ferris finds in the story of Ben and Vivian Howard's efforts to open a farm-to-table restaurant in rural eastern North Carolina the inspiring message of how "the power of place, personal relationships, hard work, and locally produced and procured seasonal foods tell a southern story," and that "with education, experience, and exposure to artisanship, seasonality, and flavor, hope persists that Southerners will reject processed commodity food in favor of their true culinary inheritance" (329). The "true heritage" of the South, Ferris implies, is not necessarily contained in the region's historical record of poverty and convenience foods, but in "the power of place," among other things. Here we see a turn toward visceralism in the linkage of southern subjects to southern landscapes through the medium of food, oftentimes in a manner that either elides or challenges historical, economical, and racial narratives.

The southern appeal to "tradition," and especially traditional foodways, as rehabilitative counters to the ruination wreaked upon the region by processed convenience food is common enough to serve as a shared subtext in the region's fictions. Toni Morrison's *Home* (2012) tells the story of Frank Money, a Korean war veteran from the town of Lotus, Georgia, who returns to his hometown to rescue his sister Ycidra ("Cee") from the clutches of the sinister Dr. Beauregard Scott in Atlanta, who has been performing ghoulish genetic experiments upon her. Frank's gradual progress toward rehabilitation is mirrored by the changes in both his diet and his interpretation of the environment around him. He initially recalls: "*I have eaten trash in jail, Korea, hospitals, at table, and from certain garbage cans. Nothing, however, compares to the leftovers at food pantries . . . a tin plate of dry, hard cheese already showing green, pickled pigs' feet—its vinegar soaking stale biscuits*" (40, italics in original). In fact, processed and discarded foods are central to his traumatic war memories, as he recalls murdering a Korean girl on a trash heap: "*She wasn't picky. Anything not metal, glass, or paper was food to her. She relied not on her eyes but on her fingertips alone to find nourishment. K-ration refuse, scraps from packages sent with love from Mom full of crumbling brownies, cookies, fruit. An orange, soft now and blackened with rot, lies just beyond her fingers*" (95). After Frank shoots her, "*only the hand remain[ed] in the trash, clutching its treasure, a spotted, rotting orange*" (95). In addition to the general centrality of food throughout the volume, as in many of Morrison's novels, mass-produced and artificially flavored foods are construed as unhealthful for both the body and spirit in *Home*. Allison Carruth links these dietary prejudices to Morrison's larger critique of consumerism "for reifying goods and thus eschewing their environmental and social histories" (600). Emma Parker also writes that sugar and sugary foods in Morrison's work serve as "signifier[s] of race and gender power structures in her texts . . . sugar has a seductive appeal, but sugar satisfies desire only temporarily" as opposed to "highlight[ing] the nourishing values of a black cultural heritage" (614, 615). In *Home*, processed and "trash" foods become inextricable from painful histories, a trauma that must be addressed for Frank's healing to begin.[6]

Frank Money is first seen in the novel at a West Coast mental institution following his tour of duty in Korea. He has received a note imploring him to return to Lotus for the sake of his sister Cee's life, though he is both penniless and reluctant to revisit his hometown: "He hated Lotus. Its unforgiving population, its isolation, and especially its indifference to the future were tolerable only if his buddies were there with him" (15–16). Frank contemplates his hostility toward Lotus whilst eating soda crackers and drinking hot salted water given to him by church volunteers; before he is sent off on his journey to Georgia, he is also given cheese, bologna, and oranges—a simple selection of processed, portable foods. As Frank gradually approaches his hometown, however, food begins to signify community over alienation and environmental affinity over artificiality. This begins at a cafe called Booker's in Chicago, where Frank is seen "scooping up navy beans and buttering corn bread" (29). Snippets of dialogue at Booker's suggest a diasporic black population brought together by common culinary experience:

"You ever eat dandelions?"
"In soup, they good."
"Hog guts. They call it something fancy now, but butchers used
to throw them out or give them to us. Feet too. Necks. All offal." (29)

The invocation of a differing terminology for historical and contemporary offal in this passage suggests a schism between traditional and commercial appropriation of the same food—Morrison implies that even historical significances ostensibly buried can be rehabilitated. The unnamed conversants' observation that the dish is "call[ed] something fancy now" also shows an awareness of the revival of culinary interest in offal and traditional African American foodstuffs by the (oftentimes white) foodie community. And, in time, Frank begins to recall how traditional foodstuffs signified a sense of community in Lotus during his childhood: "If someone had an abundance of peppers or collards, they insisted Ida take them. There was okra, fish fresh from the creek, a bushel of corn, all kinds of food that should not go to waste" (46). Food, if not the cause of Frank's reconnection with his home, is at least a signifier that indicates the renewal of those ties.

Conversely, Cee's ensnarement by the evil Atlanta eugenicist Dr. Scott is construed as explicitly unnatural, and marked by the consumption of processed, sweetened foods. Immediately after arriving at Dr. Scott's office, she is given a glass of root beer by Mrs. Scott and ushered into "a living room that seemed to her more beautiful than a movie theater. Cool air, plum-colored velvet furniture, filtered light through heavy lace curtains. Mrs. Scott, her

hands resting on a tiny pillow, her ankles crossed, nodded and, with a fore-
finger, invited Cee to sit" (59). Dr. Scott's experiments wreak irreparable
damage on Cee's reproductive organs, and in this scene the living room appears as a diseased womblike enclosure, putting forth a false image of safety
and hospitality. When Frank carries her out Dr. Scott's door, however, and
back toward the healing hands of the group of women in Lotus, natural imagery proliferates: "Some dogwood blossoms, drooping in the heat, fell as
Sarah shut the door. . . . Frank [took her] to the bus stop and waited for what
seemed like an eternity. He passed the time counting the fruit trees in almost
all the yards—pear, cherry, apple, and fig" (113). The fecundity of the natural
world in this scene contrasts sharply with the barrenness of Dr. Scott's endeavor (Cee is, ironically, rendered sterile by his gynecological experiments),
and, when Frank and Cee finally return to Lotus, they are welcomed by both
images of harmony in the natural world and a profusion of traditional foods:
"Every yard and backyard sported flowers protecting vegetables from disease
and predators—marigolds, nasturtiums, dahlias. Crimson, purple, pink, and
China blue. Had these trees always been this deep, deep green? . . . This
feeling of safety and goodwill, [Frank] knew, was exaggerated, but savoring
it was real. He convinced himself that somewhere nearby pork ribs sizzled on
a yard grill and inside the house there was potato salad and coleslaw and early
sweet peas too" (118). In short, Morrison's *Home* suggests that food can be
emblematic of both trauma (in its recollection of Frank's painful history) and
community (in its reinstatement of broken bonds). Though Cee is elsewhere
described as "indifferent to food," during one of the novel's final scenes, after
a partial recovery under the care of the Lotus community, she proclaims "I
ain't going nowhere, Miss Ethel. This is where I belong" whilst smearing
blackberry jam on biscuits, and Frank notices how healthy she looks as she
boils cabbage with ham hocks (83, 126). However, for Morrison, food tends to
symbolically fall into binary categories: that which is *manufactured*, invoking
only late-capitalist alienation and despair in nightmarish urban environments,
and that which is *made*, which signifies cooperation, tradition, and community in pastoral small towns.

    Home is not a novel explicitly "about" food in the manner of, say, John
Lancaster's *The Debt to Pleasure* (1996) or Ruth Ozeki's *My Year of Meats*
(1998), in which particular dishes and preparations drive the plot of the book
itself. Rather, it is a novel in which food is ever-present in the background as
a signifier, continuously establishing and reinforcing a set of attitudes toward

characters and the environments that contain them. Its deployment of food as a trope is entirely consistent with the ruin-narrative of southern foodways—processed and mass-produced food, especially of the sugary and fattening variety, accompanies a displacement from characters' "natural" environment, a betrayal of their origins and tradition. Simple and healthy foods, however, mean rehabilitation, regrowth, and return to communities. This is the narrative that we expect from much southern literature, and though it appears to be an optimistic one—the most elemental form of food-based catharsis involves a character consuming a fondly remembered dish—it is also strongly exclusive, with little middle ground between righteousness and ruin. The symbolism of *Home* is not distant from the frequency, in the southern ruin-narrative, of simple human errors directed toward the environment being responsible for the region's downfall. In Morrison's work, poor dietary choices simply stand in for greed, viciousness, or overambition: root beer instead of crude oil, bologna instead of the factory farm.

———

Frank Money does not pine for the landscapes, vegetation, or geography of Lotus, Georgia, at any point during Morrison's *Home;* rather, it is the cuisine and its accompanying values of family, community, and authenticity that stir his imagination. Similarly, recent southern ecocriticism has resisted the troublesome attachment to "land," "soil," or "place," all distinctions that tend to fragment deeply along racial and political lines, preferring the ostensibly neutral, big-tent approach of food studies. Only in the last few years has the field begun to acknowledge that cuisines are anything *but* neutral, and that the prejudice against widely consumed processed food in favor of fetishized artisan foodstuffs may have its shortcomings. Zackary Vernon, in 2014, found it "perplexing" that agrarianism had become "not only a buzz word in contemporary environmental, agricultural, and food studies, but also a popular label for the theoretical framework underpinning sustainable and organic agricultural techniques," given its exceedingly problematic and inconsistent moral framework.[7] Vernon suggests that straightforward celebrations of southern agrarianism cannot be morally neutral, and he is suspicious of attempts to lionize it. Other scholars discussing southern foodways have followed suit. David Shields makes it clear in *Southern Provisions* that his intent is not to romanticize, or even to argue for the distinctiveness of, local cuisines or ingredients: "In no way can Southern food claim a distinct and organic character on the basis of [nineteenth-century agricultural] developments. Growers, marketers, and food preparers in the southern states embraced all of the innovations of plant breeding, selling, baking, and cooking that transformed practice throughout the United States and Europe" (28). Similarly, Elizabeth Engelhardt seeks to demystify southern foodways in "Appalachian Chicken and Waffles: Countering Southern Food Fetishism" (2015), claiming that any holistic conception of southern cuisine needs to take account of both historical circumstances and modern developments, both heirloom vegetables and industrial foodways. "Local and processed food may be difficult to study simultaneously," Engelhardt writes, "but this is how people actually eat, historically and into the present. From this perspective, the Appalachian chicken might come from a grandmother's cast iron, or it might be a frozen chicken finger dinner. . . . We should look to the combinations actual eaters make in their daily lives, recounting all of it: the foods from home, factories, and afar" (79). Engelhardt advocates a synthetic view of southern foodways—a fusion of traditional ingredients and means of preparation with mass-produced, heavily processed convenience foods.

Engelhardt's position, from the perspective of the traditionalist foodways scholar, looks like ruin: the surrender of Ferris's "true heritage" to foods that, by definition, are unmoored in space and time. Visceral environmentalism carries a prejudice for foods that are derived firsthand from the soil, or at least raised upon a particular patch of earth; the Invisible Man's evocative yam is powerful as a symbol not simply because it carries a long cultural heritage but because it is literally embedded in the soil of a particular place; its excavation and consumption is analogous to the Invisible Man's recovery of buried aspects of his personality. By contrast, processed foods available in large quantities, having traveled great distances, would seem to indicate rootlessness. But, given our understanding of the deeply individuated nature of visceral appeals to the environment, the prejudice for unprocessed, "traditional" foodstuffs seems misplaced, designed to correct the perceived ruination of southern diets. A resilient approach to southern foodways acknowledges traditional foods and their communitarian (and, in some cases, place-based) affiliations, but also understands "tradition" as an inclusive rather than exclusive category, permitting attachments to southern environments to be arbitrated on an individual basis. And, as with other contemporary narratives of southern environmental resilience, these ideas originate from unexpected places.

One such unexpected place (from the perspective of an academic audience, to be sure) may be Fannie Flagg's 1987 *Fried Green Tomatoes at the Whistle-Stop Cafe*, which remains perhaps the most popular representation of southern food in any medium—it could be argued, in fact, that the appearance of the novel six years prior (and the film two years prior) to Egerton's landmark *Southern Food* contributed very significantly to popular conceptions of what constitutes Southern cuisine. That being said, the titular dish appears surprisingly infrequently, perhaps a half-dozen times over the course of the four-hundred-page novel. Heavily processed and, frequently, branded food products are far more common in the novel than any distinctively southern dishes. The frame narrative of Flagg's novel is a series of vignettes that the aging Ninny Threadgoode tells the depressed housewife Evelyn Couch in a nursing home. Each of Evelyn's many meetings with Ninny is marked by the women sharing a different food product, a bewildering list that includes candy bars, Hostess Snow Balls, Coca-Cola, pimento cheese, chocolate-covered peanuts and cherries, ginger snaps, Raisinettes, Nilla wafers, ice cream, Hershey bars, Cracker Jacks, corn chips, brownies, Golden Flake potato chips, Fig Newtons, and Honey Buns. Though Ninny relishes the processed snacks that Evelyn brings, she longs for the more traditional homemade dishes she recalls being prepared at her family's cafe. In the nursing home, she claims, "you cain't smell anything they've got cooking out here, and you cain't get a thing that's fried. Everything here is boiled up, with not a piece of salt on it! I wouldn't give you a plugged nickel for anything boiled, would you?" (5). Throughout the novel, Ninny and Evelyn both consume a stupefying quantity of empty calories (at one point they split a five-pound block of fudge) and long for more nourishing fare.

Given Evelyn's severe depression, unsatisfying domestic life, and poor health at the beginning of the novel, it is tempting to regard her devastating dietary habits as symbolic of her personal struggles in something of the same manner as we see in Morrison's *Home*. As her relationship with Ninny deepens and her knowledge of the past and traditional southern foodways expands, her physical and mental health correspondingly improve. Inspired by Ninny's stories of the strong women in her lineage, she begins to eschew the "cookies and cakes and white breads" in the grocery store, passing over "aisle three, canned goods, where she had spent most of her shopping life" in favor of skinless chicken breasts, broccoli, and sparkling water (233). The emotional climax of the novel comes when Evelyn brings Ninny, instead of the processed snacks that have thus far defined their relationship, a homemade plate of food in the nursing home: "The old woman was waiting, and Evelyn made her close her eyes while she unwrapped the plate and undid the lid on the jar of iced tea with mint. 'Okay. You can look now.' When Mrs. Threadgoode saw what she had on her plate, she clapped her hands, as excited as a child on Christmas. There before her was a plate of perfectly fried green tomatoes and fresh cream-white corn, six slices of bacon, with a bowl of baby lima beans on the side and four huge light and fluffy buttermilk biscuits" (354). In this scene, food becomes a means of addressing Ninny's nostalgia—Evelyn treats her as if she were still a child as she serves her the foods that feature prominently in her stories. And a by-the-numbers denouement follows this moment of culinary communion; Ninny passes away in the nursing home, having successfully passed down her stories and symbolically returned to the past, while Evelyn begins to benefit from professional nutritional and psychiatric aid.

On closer examination, however, *Fried Green Tomatoes* is more attentive to some of the ironies and problematic aspects of southern foodways than this simple outline might suggest. The book is not unaware, for instance, that the "traditional" foods Ninny remembers originate from a very different historical and racial history than her own. Moreover, in the first few paragraphs of the novel, an account of the original opening of the Whistle-Stop Cafe makes it clear that the claims made on possession of its cuisine by the white residents of the town are facile and, in fact, laughable: "Idgie [Threadgoode] says that for people who know her not to worry about getting poisoned, she is not cooking. All the cooking is being done by two colored women, Sipsey and Onzell, and the barbecue is being cooked by Big George, who is Onzell's husband" (1). Idgie's culinary incompetence and reliance upon black labor to produce the dishes that Ninny remembers with such fondness are open secrets among the family, and Ninny criticizes Evelyn for patronizing Ollie's and The Golden Rule, two historically white Birmingham barbecue restaurants: "Well, they're all right, but I don't care what you say, colored people can make barbecue better than anybody in the whole world," to which Evelyn responds: "They can do most everything better. I wish I was black" (300). This exchange occurs a scant few pages after Ninny spontaneously proclaims "I don't care a thing in the world about going to Cuba," expressing a preference for Florida instead (298). The inconsistency between Ninny's ostensible idolization of black culture and her simultaneous hostility toward American locales construed as foreign (not coincidentally, southern barbecue itself is thought to

have its origins in the Caribbean) creates a distinct irony that is mirrored by
her more general naïveté toward culinary history overall.[8] Flagg uses Ninny's
narrow culinary scope to create humor in several instances, as when Evelyn
brings an order from Taco Bell to one of their meetings: "Mrs. Threadgoode
was fascinated. 'This is the first foreign food I've ever had except for Franco-
American spaghetti, and I like it.' She looked at her taco. 'This is about the
size of a Chrystal burger, isn't it?'" (92).[9] In short, if Flagg's novel establishes
"traditional" southern foodways as an *ur*-text and lodestone over the length of
its plot, it also disassembles the concepts of authenticity and cultural integrity
that such a guiding principle would seem to rely upon.

Moreover, Flagg's novel is, however inadvertently, involved in producing
certain foods as southern based on the author's own culinary history rather
than the more commonly cited factors for determining a dish's regional identity. Though fried green tomatoes would seem to draw on the region's history
of poverty and convenience foods, as well as the use of animal fats for frying
(a recipe, quaintly given in the voice of one of the novel's characters, at the
end of the novel recommends bacon drippings), the latter-day popularity of
the dish on menus across the region and its strong association with southern
locales seems to have resulted from, rather than anteceded, the novel's publication. Robert F. Moss, author of the unambiguously titled *The Fried Green
Tomato Swindle*, finds that "fried green tomatoes are by no means a Southern dish at all. By all accounts, they entered the American culinary scene in
the Northeast and Midwest, perhaps with a link to Jewish immigrants, and
from there moved onto the menus of the home-economics school of cooking
teachers" (4). With a note of hostility, Moss challenges the regional affiliation
of the dish as a whole: "I am not going to question Fannie Flagg's memory
and suggest that the Irondale Cafe wasn't serving fried green tomatoes as far
back as the 1930s. But, if it was, they were likely serving not an old Southern
recipe but something the cook may have found in a syndicated newspaper
column or a general-interest, national cookbook" (5). Moss's tone here is
likely as instructive as the fruits of his research, since the reviled mediums
of the "syndicated newspaper column" and the "general-interest, national
cookbook," not to mention the whole realm of "the home-economics school
of cooking teachers," would seem to compare unfavorably with the genuine
"old southern" recipes. From Moss's perspective, the lack of a historical or
genetic pedigree for the dish transforms its appearance in Flagg's novel into
a flight of fancy or, as his title indicates, a "swindle."

Yet, as I have hinted already, it is hardly difficult to point out the holes in Flagg's characters' knowledge of southern foodways, as well as culinary history in general. Nor is it challenging to deride their catastrophically un-healthy diets or their overly sentimental perspectives on cooking, eating, and family life as a whole. However, none of these flaws changes the fact that, as a result of *Fried Green Tomatoes*, fried green tomatoes themselves are now a staple item on the menu of countless restaurants specializing in "traditional southern" cuisine. To return to Engelhardt's argument, it may be worthwhile to reconsider what is meant by "traditional" cuisine, and the connections to place, environment, and family that participating in such a culinary tradition might entail.[10] Food types might seem at first to occupy the same roles in Flagg's novel as we see in *Home;* both texts are, after all, about a physical or spiritual homecoming accompanied by a newfound appreciation for "pure" southern foodstuffs over processed and manufactured fare. However, while Morrison insists upon the regenerative potential of foods with an established history and communitarian function, Flagg makes the individual the arbiter of what "traditional" southern foodways look like, and this category may (and does) include varied, contradictory, and troublesome food choices.

———

The Invisible Man, upon finishing his first yam and experiencing the pro-foundly novel reclamation of his own identity that follows, is so enthused that he orders another round. "I can see you one of those old-fashioned yam eaters," the salesman comments. "They're my birthmark," the Invisible Man responds, "I yam what I am!" (266). The notion of laying claim to one's "birthmark," or an intrinsic, indelible aspect of one's personality and being, through the consumption of traditional foods is a familiar one, yet something is off here. The Invisible Man transitions rapidly from a statement of nativist pride to a cartoon catchphrase, implying that the former may not be entirely free of irony. And, in the exchange that follows, the nostalgic, communitarian function of food is further deconstructed: "'Then you must be from South Car'lina,' he said with a grin. 'South Carolina nothing, where I come from we really go for yams'" (266). The yam seller posits a simple correspondence between the Invisible Man's home location and his dietary preference, but the Invisible Man himself denies this—consuming the yam is for him a marker of racial identity, but not necessarily regional or political identity. Thus, though it is easy to construe the yam scene as a literal and metaphorical return to the

Invisible Man's "roots," in reality those origins are far too complex and obfuscated to be summoned by a simple tuber.[11] Food does not represent the easy alliance between the consumer and their home region that texts frequently seek to invoke. Rather, it simply reveals that such affiliations develop along the lines of individual ideation instead of primal connections construed as "natural."

Southern food studies is a tantalizing field of study for ecocriticism in several regards. First, it seeks to counteract the narrative of environmental ruin so common to environmental accounts of the region: even if the South's environmental tradition has always been weak, its culinary traditions—implying strong connections to the landscape, the seasons, and native flora and fauna—have been and remain strong. Second, it provides a method for talking past the profound political and racial schisms that have shaped southern environmental usage—no matter what race, class, and gender identifiers southern subjects adopt and what those distinctions imply about differing attitudes toward the environment, food is a universal constant. Finally, food studies captures the public imagination in ways that, say, literary criticism does not; if southerners care about how their food is produced and where it comes from, they implicitly care about the environment—thus, at long last, bringing environmental issues in the South to center stage. All of these potentialities are notably rehabilitative, seeking to counteract, or at least compensate for, the ruin-narrative that claims no clearly delineated and no distinctively southern environmentalist ethos. And, as I have noted in previous chapters, ruin is not useless. On the contrary, the drive to research, recover, and recirculate traditional southern foodways has uncovered buried ways of living, changed dietary habits and trends, revived interest in Black history—perhaps changed the face of the modern South as we know it today. But ruin—straightforward narratives of disappearance and revival, rise and fall—never tells the full story.

A simple WorldCat search for peer-reviewed articles on Toni Morrison's work produces over 20,000 results, including 8,402 articles and nearly as many full-length books and dissertations. A similar search for Fannie Flagg produces less than 650, with a mere 35 peer-reviewed articles. Over 277,000 readers on Goodreads have rated *Fried Green Tomatoes,* while *Home* clocks in at a shade over 20,000. According to this (rather unscientific) methodology, Flagg's popular readership outpaces Morrison's by more than tenfold, while thirty times more academic readers are interested in Morrison's work. There are many reasons for this disparity, not least of which is a vastly different target audience for each respective author. I would contend that the tale of recovering and rehabilitating vanished histories (or cuisines), one of Morrison's *leitmotifs* and, as we have seen, a keystone in crafting narratives of ruin and recovery in southern food writing, is clearly more engaging for an academic audience than Flagg's mild-mannered portrait of middle-class ennui. However, it should also be evident that the experience, both personal and culinary, of Evelyn Couch is significantly closer to the ways in which the vast majority of southerners live and dine than that of Frank Money or Cee. As such, Flagg's perspective seems to—intentionally or ironically—elide the racial, historical, and environmental trappings of southern foods, and chaotically embrace and celebrate hand-prepared and heavily processed foodstuffs alike. Its characters' loose grip on history permits a contrary narrative—a position often overlooked by food writing that insists upon authenticity and pedigrees.

Visceral environmentalism depends on an appeal to the uniformity of taste—a shared set of associations linking concepts of home, place, belonging, return, revival, rehabilitation. What Berry derives from long hours of farm labor may inspire a more holistic knowledge of botany, biology, and horticulture than what Morrison's characters get from a well-made pan of cornbread or pot of collard greens, or what Flagg's characters absorb from a can of Buffalo Rock or bag of Golden Flake potato chips, but all follow the same essential route of accessing an understanding of the environment through sensory experience. We, therefore, must take the appeal to visceral environmentalism for what it is—not a return to the primitive affective roots of humans' relationship with their environments, but as a movement that reacts to and depends upon modern development. The fantasized connection between southerners and their landscapes, like the fetishization of the southern diet into a contemporary cuisine, depends upon our existence in a world mediated by industry and technology—the very forces that so frequently inspire a hunger for tradition.[12] In this sense, both Morrison's and Flagg's perspectives are necessary, just as ruin and resilience are symbiotically joined in southern environmentalism.

As the world pushes on into the Anthropocene, it has become increasingly impossible to separate concern for human welfare from environmental issues. The locus of environmental thought and action is shifting ever-further from the images of untouched wildernesses empty of any human presence that energized second-wave environmentalism and toward what Rob Nixon calls, in *Slow Violence and the Environmentalism of the Poor* (2011), "vernacular landscapes," regions "shaped by the affective, historically textured maps that communities have devised over generations, maps replete with names and routes, maps alive to significant ecological and surface geological features" (17). These are the landscapes, both historical and contemporary, that have defined the South, and southern writers have long realized, as Christopher Rieger says of Marjorie Kinnan Rawlings's work, that "nature as a network of relations in which humans participate [is] more accurate than a Newtonian, mechanistic view that deepens the divide between nature and humans by assuming an ideal of scientific detachment" (56). What visceral environmentalism can contribute to contemporary environmental thought is not the hoary and romantic notion that southerners are deeply, elementally connected to their landscapes, but that centuries of human inhabitation, use, and abuse of those landscapes produce concepts of environmental stewardship that are inextricable from messy histories, economies, and racial divisions. Moreover, such a history must not preclude the alienation of humans from those landscapes and their consequent integration of manufactured and artificial products into their lives, diets, and memories. It is this mélange of ruin, resilience, and above all the acknowledgment that environmental history demands a synthetic approach to humans and their landscapes, that visceral environmentalism brings to the table.

FOUR

Leaving the Ruins

Mobility and Southern Disaster-Narratives in
Zora Neale Hurston, William Faulkner,
and *Beasts of the Southern Wild*

IN THE FIRST SEASON OF HBO's dramatic series *Treme* (2010–11), Creighton Bernette (John Goodman), an author and professor of English at Tulane living amidst the ruins of Katrina, is haunted by the Mississippi Flood of 1927. Gradually, circumstances reveal that he is working (and has been, largely fruitlessly, for the past six years) on a historical novel based on the flood. After Katrina ravages New Orleans, Bernette takes to recording enraged You-Tube videos lambasting the poor urban planning, disastrous relief efforts, and continued ignorance on the part of the American public toward the ongoing marginalization of New Orleans. His screeds delight both his Internet viewership and his publishers, who attempt to convince him that a volume of prose scripts of his YouTube complaints would be far better received than the novel. No, he insists, the book must be about the 1927 flood. The script paints him as sympathetic but stubborn, fixated on the past while the present crumbles about him. What does the 1927 flood, the show ironically asks, have to do with *modern* disasters (Bernette claims that his prospective novel "speaks to the present situation only as metaphor")? Why can't Bernette simply let go of his historical niche concerns and write something *relevant?* Though the series does not acknowledge it directly, Bernette *is*, or wants to be, writing about the present; the flood of 1927 and Hurricane Katrina fit into a longstanding pattern of human disasters in the South, brought on by social and planning failures and exacerbated by political mishandling.

It is easy to read the litany of natural disasters in the South as a compilation of the region's failures of environmental oversight—to see mirrored in the overreliance on the levee system on the Mississippi as described by Faulkner in "Old Man" (1939) and the failure of the dikes and canals surrounding Lake Okeechobee in Hurston's *Their Eyes Were Watching God* (1937) the more recent breaking of the levees surrounding New Orleans during Hurricane Katrina. It is scarcely more difficult to note the inherent environmental racism that defined each of these moments of disaster, from the flooding of low-lying and lower-class rural areas and the forcible conscription of Black labor to deal with the aftereffects of both the flood of 1927 and the Okeechobee Hurricane of 1928 to the flooding of the Ninth Ward during Katrina. History ruinously repeats itself, Bernette reminds us. The South continues making the same racial and environmental mistakes over and over again—and these are not separate issues, but part of the same complex of oppression and ignorance. No wonder his YouTube outbursts are so ridden with profanities.

I have written earlier in this volume of the South's desire for a "nature poet," with the implication that the traditional location of the aesthetic sublime in unspoiled wilderness areas is incompatible with the histories of ruin that tend to dominate southern literature. Rather, southern literature must, as a first principle, take account of the fundamental alteration of landscapes from their "unspoiled" originals and the centuries of misuse of both human and nonhuman nature that inhere in those landscapes. No works of southern literature more succinctly represent the confluence of all these factors than disaster-narratives, accounts of natural disasters compounded by human failures and the network of compensatory and explanatory reactions that follow them. Brad Richard has proposed that such large and multifaceted disasters as Katrina require a "poetics of disaster" to be adequately apprehended, entailing an intimate understanding of not only "the bellicose and paranoid Zeitgeist of the post-9/11 world, but also the ecological and economic histories of the Gulf Coast, the histories of race in America, and many other factors."[1] In a manner of speaking, all southern nature writing, by necessity, is such a disaster-narrative—it is incumbent upon such texts to deploy the same rhetoric of representation and the same strategies of dealing with the aftermath of disasters.

The southern disaster-narrative, the text that represents not only the destruction of southern landscapes by natural forces and the chaos that results, but also views both the destruction and the chaos that follows as symptomatic of much more long-lived and distinctively southern errors, represents the most tightly entwined coexistence of the dual entities of ruin and resilience that define the southern ecotext. There are no clearer examples in the body of southern literature of the southern subject, freighted with all of the prejudices, inequalities, and tensions that define their character, being confronted with the destruction of a familiar environment and coming to terms with the necessity of survival despite this ruination. In *Beyond Katrina* (2010), for example, Natasha Trethewey notes that, along the Gulf Coast as well as in Hegel's philosophy, "when we turn to survey the past . . . the first thing we see is nothing but ruins." Moreover, the ruins that Trethewey contemplates near Gulfport, Mississippi simultaneously encompass current (caused by Katrina) and historical (caused by Camille) destruction: "As I contemplate the development of the coast, looking at old photographs of once new buildings," Trethewey writes, "I see beneath them, as if a palimpsest, the destruction wrought by Katrina" (51). Yet, catalyzed by the percussive force of disasters, narratives of ruin and resilience coexist for Trethewey. At one point, she restrains herself from correcting one of her interviewee's romanticized accounts of rebuilding, reminding herself that "a preferred narrative is one of the common bond between people in a time of crisis. This is the way collective, cultural memory works, full of omissions, partial remembering, and purposeful forgetting" (20). If Trethewey acknowledges, on one hand, the procession of natural disasters, compounded and exacerbated by decades of overdevelopment and weak environmental policy, that have afflicted the Gulf Coast as an intrinsic aspect of its character that have inspired irrecoverable losses, she sees on the other hand the messy, chaotic, human processes that accompany recovery from those disasters as equally necessary.

Ruin, as we have seen, is at root a fairly uncomplicated narrative, regarding transformations in southern environments as "gains" or "losses," the former brought on by heroic (though rare) acts of environmentalism and the latter resulting from simple patterns of human greed, myopia, and cruelty. Yet recent critical work by Martyn Bone, Scott Romine, Leigh Anne Duck, and James Peacock, among many others, has insisted that the South (if it exists at all) must be reconceived as more malleable, problematic, varied, and contradictory than historical studies frequently make it.[2] The necessity of this change, these authors assert, is at least partially due to the metamorphosing of southerners themselves—more mobile, less reactionary, connected to the world at large rather than excluding it. All of these readings could be said to efface the narratives of provincialism, isolation, backwardness, and unity embodied by the period of early to mid-twentieth century southern criticism emanating from the Agrarian school and its scions.[3] As literary accounts of the three southern disasters I study here (the flood of 1927, the Okeechobee Hurricane of 1928, and Hurricane Katrina) indicate, however, if the transformation of distinctively southern landscapes figured as "home" constitutes ruin, that ruination must be twinned with more complex and resilient ways of navigating the relationship between the self and the environment. In short, the disaster-narrative would seem to defeat notions of "home" and "place" when those home places are submerged beneath floodwaters or washed out to sea. Yet resilience emerges from ruin in unexpected ways, and the vision of the region that rises up out of the flood is nothing less than an entirely new and strange landscape.

———

The romanticizing of southerners' relationship with their landscape is a familiar trope in early criticism from and concerning the region, but environmental history tells a tale in which the actions of southern subjects, even when their claims of attachment are taken at face value, seem distinctly at odds with how the land was actually treated.[4] In *This Land, This South* (1996), Albert E. Cowdrey claims that the South "tended to exalt, sometimes with a special anarchic heedlessness, the contemporary American standard of exploitation without limit" (83). The question of how the region could maintain an insistence upon the importance of place, belonging, and rootedness while simultaneously enabling environmental policies that could charitably be described as "insufficient" is one of the central ironies of southern environmentalism. I would contend that, if we wish to arrive at an understanding of the value (if any) of appeals to regionalism balanced against environmental depletion in the South, we must examine nonhegemonic narratives of people and groups who have perennially been passed over by ideas of regional association: migrants, itinerants, the poor, and prisoners, to name a few. With this in mind, I would like to proceed to the first of my examples of these groups responding to disasters that fundamentally change the environments that they call home: the final act of Hurston's *Their Eyes Were Watching God*.

"Oh down in de Everglades round Clewiston and Belle Glade where dey raise all dat cane and string-beans and tomatuhs. Folks don't do nothin' down dere but make money and fun and foolishness," Tea Cake effuses to Janie at the opening of the Okeechobee section, positing a model of capitalist gain not unlike those explicated by the aforementioned historians (128). Two sentences later, Janie and Tea Cake have joined a steady stream of itinerant workers come to farm the "muck" around Lake Okeechobee. All that unites the laborers is their motivation; for Janie and Tea Cake, the Everglades represent autonomy and financial security for these migrants. "They came in wagons from way up in Georgia and they came in truck loads from east, west, north, and south. Permanent transients with no attachments and tired looking men with their families and dogs in flivvers. All night, all day, hurrying in to pick beans. Skillets, beds, patched up spare inner tubes all hanging and dangling from the ancient cars on the outside and hopeful humanity, herded and hovered on the inside, chugging on to the muck. People ugly from ignorance and broken from being poor" (131). The exodus here is phrased as migration, motivated, as is so often the case, by poverty. Hurston's narrative eye lingers, as is her custom, on the physical indices of class: patches and fabrication, weathering and rust. The human and material are twinned here across the membrane of the vehicle's glass and metal; the people as much as the domestic flotsam adorning the cars bear the marks of use and re-use. They are, in a word, hampered by what Rob Nixon calls "slow violence," whose "unseen poverty is compounded by the invisibility of the slow violence that permeates so many of their lives" (4). Marginalized and impoverished by generations of legal, social, and economic discrimination, the migrants seize upon even hazardous opportunities for stability and recuperation. In Hurston's narration, even their origins are anonymous—they emanate from any of the cardinal directions (or Georgia).

Nixon argues that the invisibility of the victims of slow violence to the general public is mirrored by that same public's ignorance of the landscapes they occupy, "ecosystems treated as disposable by turbo-capitalism" (4).[5] In *Their Eyes Were Watching God*, Florida is the epitome of a disposable landscape—valuable to the extent that it can be exploited for agriculture, living space, and recreation, but also a *terra incognita*, where Janie and Tea Cake shoot hawks and alligators for amusement while the black earth "cling[s] to bodies and bit[es] the skin like ants" (131).[6] The Everglades section of the novel recasts earlier fissures between the dictates of culture and those of nature (Janie's early sexual desire abutting the imperative toward marriage and childbearing) in the mold of landscape and its inhabitants. The economic and social (for Janie and Tea Cake seem more at home and self-assured in the Everglades than in any of their previous residences) advances that the migrant workers achieve during their time on "the muck" are balanced by their ever-mounting dissociation from the place itself. With deep irony, Hurston creates a schism between the narrative of economic advancement endorsed by her characters and the narrative of impending disaster communicated by the landscape when a group of Seminoles leaves the area, claiming an oncoming hurricane. Tea Cake brushes off their indigenous wisdom contemptuously: "Beans running fine and prices good, so the Indians could be, must be, wrong. You couldn't have a hurricane when you're making seven and eight dollars a day picking beans" (155). The capacity to occupy, work, and obtain a living from the land does not enable Janie and Tea Cake to read correctly the signs given by nature—precisely the opposite.

It is easy to read the destruction of the work camps at Belle Glade in terms of the patterns of infraction and retribution familiar to the southern ruin-narrative; Okeechobee becomes a mythic beast, "muttering and grumbling . . . like a tired mammoth," furious at being confined by mortals, that "give[s] life to lots of things that folks think of as dead and give[s] death to so much that had been living things" in a parody of Christian resurrection (160). Yet such an interpretation effaces the capacity for human agency, the accumulation of which has so consumed Janie's efforts over the course of the novel, reinforcing Nixon's idea of disposable or inconsequential subjects. In contrast to the idea of natural disasters' effects resulting from happenstance (or divine retribution), Nixon makes it clear that the impact of these same disasters is never coincidental or random, but part of a longstanding pattern of structural violence and oversight: "Discrimination predates disaster: in failures to maintain protective infrastructures, failures at pre-emergency hazard mitigation, failures to maintain infrastructure, failures to organize evacuation plans for those who lack private transport, all of which make the poor and racial minorities disproportionately vulnerable to catastrophe" (59). Hurston alludes to this vulnerability on multiple occasions in *Their Eyes Were Watching God.* Janie and Tea Cake's quarters are "so close that only the dyke separated them from great, sprawling Okechobee," the same lake whose threat is ostensibly blunted by engineering projects: "There were the seawalls to chain the senseless monster in his bed" (130, 158). Perhaps unsurprisingly from a literary (or a well-informed historical) standpoint, it is these engineered barriers that ultimately fail, bringing catastrophe to the Belle Glade community.

Janie and Tea Cake remain in Belle Glade as the storm approaches not out of any sense of allegiance to the community, and even less from an ephemeral attachment to place. They are told to leave, in fact, by members of the community. In response to the Bahamian Elias's offer to transport him and Janie off the muck, Tea Cake says: "You ain't seen de bossman go up, is yuh? . . . de white folks ain't gone nowhere. Dey oughta know if it's dangerous" (156). Later, when the storm arrives, Hurston makes this train of thought more overt still: "The folks let the people do the thinking. If the castles thought themselves secure, the cabins needn't worry" (158). In brief, Janie and Tea Cake stay in the Everglades out of an overprivileging of human agency: the capacity of the white overseers to predict disaster, the capacity of man-made edifices to contain the elements, and the belief, fatuously advanced by Tea Cake, that natural forces are subordinate to the agricultural market. The disaster itself exposes all of these beliefs as illusory, founded upon an abdication of personal judgment to a higher (generally, class-based) authority. Without necessarily assigning blame, Hurston reveals the ingrained biases, predilections, and uncertainties inherent in taking a place, and its economic and social structure, for granted.

What I find most interesting about the account of the Okeechobee Hurricane in *Their Eyes Were Watching God* is its rhetoric of disposability—the quarters that Janie and Tea Cake occupy are as flimsy and patched-together as the migrants who come to occupy them. Moreover, in this moment the *concept* of home itself begins to deteriorate. Emerging from their place of shelter, Tea Cake sees "houses without roofs, and roofs without houses. Steel and stone all crushed and crumbled like wood" (169). Belle Glade, the place where the couple found more home and community than they had ever known, has become an *unheimlich* location. During a wrenching postdisaster scene, in what was once an egalitarian settlement where at least a semblance of racial equality was maintained, a ghoulish segregationism now reigns: "Miserable, sullen men, black and white under guard, had to keep on searching for bodies and digging graves. A huge ditch was dug across the white cemetery and a big ditch was opened across the black graveyard. Plenty quick-lime on hand to throw over the bodies as soon as they were received. They had already been unburied too long" (170).[7] The hierarchical race- and class-based values that Tea Cake insists upon are preserved even in desperate circumstances, and the alive seem scarcely better off than the dead. Moreover, the land itself becomes disposable following the hurricane; deprived of their means of making a living in the Everglades, the surviving workers—including Janie and Tea Cake—simply move elsewhere. In contrast to narratives of stability and stasis oftentimes entailed by literature that links the people of the South irrevocably to their landscapes, *Their Eyes Were Watching God* represents this same link as tenuous and able to be swiftly severed.[8]

The ruination effected by the hurricane in *Their Eyes Were Watching God* is swift and complete, as the vivid images that Hurston uses to describe the aftermath of the storm make clear. However, resilience, in this text, does not take the form usually ascribed to survivors of natural disasters—here, there is no description of rebuilding, no appeal to the tenacity and determination of the residents, no heroic or impassioned defense of this remarkable place (one of the survivors, Motor Boat, rides out the storm simply by falling asleep in the upper story of a flooded building, escaping harm simply through random chance). Resilience consists not of endurance, but adaptability—perhaps, in this context, even abandonment. The resilient disaster-narrative that Hurston's novel presents, in which attachment to "place" and "home" runs no deeper than profitability, and in which what could be construed as divine judgment for the sins of humans against the environment in a manner entirely consistent with dominant ideas of ruin is instead an incitement to migrate, constitutes a potent challenge to the idea of the bond between southerners and their landscape and a distinct critique of the stereotype of the determined, attached survivor.

———

Such stereotypes portray southerners as fundamentally bound to their home-places to such an extent that, when faced with the transformations brought on by natural disasters, resilience resembles nothing so much as an intensification of attachment to those places, ruined as they may be. A prominent contemporary example of this trope appears in Benh Zeitlin's 2012 film *Beasts of the Southern Wild*. Set in a faintly postapocalyptic, archipelagic community called, colloquially, the Bathtub (which resembles a hybrid of the Ninth Ward of New Orleans and the slums of Mumbai), the primary action centers around the reaction of the six-year-old Hushpuppy and her father, Wink, to the submersion of the town during a Katrina-esque hurricane. Inspired by the Isle de Jean Charles southwest of New Orleans, the fictional Isle de Charles Doucet (which shares its surname with Hushpuppy and Wink), upon which the Bathtub perches, is situated southwest of Thibodeaux, near what is today the Atchafalaya Delta. This is revealed during a brief glance at a tattered map in Hushpuppy's floating classroom early in the film (fig. 5):

Close inspection reveals the names of parishes, towns, and roads beneath the veneer of blue that surrounds the Bathtub; the map has been painted over, with land that was once solid replaced by sea. "They built the wall that cuts us

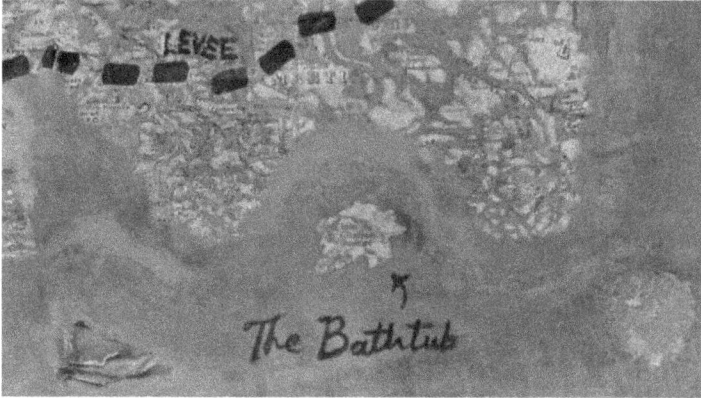

FIG. 5. Map of The Bathtub in *Beasts of the Southern Wild*.
Author's screen capture.

FIG. 6. Aerial view of The Bathtub. Author's screen capture.

off," intones Hushpuppy in a voiceover during the first minutes of the film, while the camera hovers ominously over a ragged collection of shanties on the edge of the Gulf (fig. 6).

Minutes later, continuing her voiceover, Hushpuppy makes the Bathtub-bers' perilous state of existence more overt still: "one day, the storm's gonna blow, the ground's gonna sink, and the water's gonna rise up so high, there ain't gonna be no Bathtub, just a whole bunch of water." The Bathtub is a landscape saturated with slow violence, where the poor (and the rising waters of climate change) are walled off from the rich, cobbling an existence out of the detritus of the "dry world," but perhaps even more evocative than the touchstones of class inequality in *Beasts* is the looming belief—even certainty—that a single disaster will finish the work that slow violence began.

Yet one of the hallmarks of Nixon's slow violence is the disappearance of the poor's safety factor; poverty—and other social factors—compel communities to occupy more hazardous and disaster-prone regions. Beverly Wright estimates that ethnic minorities in the United States comprise the majority of residents living within two miles of major hazardous waste sites. "Neighborhoods in an overwhelming majority of the 44 states with hazardous waste sites have disproportionately high percentages of Hispanics (35 states), African Americans (38 states), and Asians/Pacific Islanders (27 states)," she writes (1). And it must be said that southern Louisiana, the location both of *Beasts of the Southern Wild* and the infamous industrial "Cancer Alley," represents significant grist for the statistical mill. In 1988, a panel appointed by then-governor Buddy Roemer concluded that Louisiana "had the poorest environmental program of any 'highly-industrialized state'" (Bauer 269). The authors of "Two Faces of American Environmentalism" (2006) contend that the grievous damage inflicted upon residents of southern Louisiana by environmental factors can be attributed in large part to legislative failures: the toxic oilfield waste, for example, deposited at Grand Bois (where, in 1994, residents became violently ill immediately after the filling of an open-pit waste site) was exempted from US hazardous waste laws. In addition, Jenkins et al. claim that, in Grand Bois, "the bayou residents' lack of education and their geographic, linguistic, and cultural isolation left them vulnerable to those who came to their region in search of natural resources, including oil, timber, and gas" (Bauer 272). This is an example of southern environmental usage consistent with the narrative of environmental ruin—the South as a region of exploitation and depletion by outsiders, frequently to the detriment of both local residents and the landscape itself.

Against this narrative, literature and film frequently craft tales of resilience predicated on localist attachments to the land, hereditary holding of property, and romanticized depictions of the landscape itself. *Beasts of the Southern Wild* employs all of these tactics. Early in the film, Hushpuppy and Wink, their faces bathed in soft sunlight, float on their makeshift raft near the levee that separates them from a smog-belching industrial park (the screenplay reads "This is the engine that runs the Northern world") (fig. 7).

"Ain't that ugly over there?" Wink asks. "We got the prettiest place on Earth." These early scenes, as well as the pre-storm section of the film as a

FIG. 7. The levee surrounding The Bathtub. Author's screen capture.

whole, seem to bear out Wink's assertion, as the Bathtub's shabby *brico-lage* is lavishly illuminated and fetishized by the camera, providing ample instances of what Patricia Yaeger calls "luminous trash"—discarded objects given new, radiant life through literature and film. "[*Beasts* is] a movie where debris and light vie for screen time," she writes in "*Beasts of the Southern Wild* and Dirty Ecology" (2013). "In the film's opening scenes the screen floods with light when the Bathtub's bright revelry spills over and neons the Cineplex audience." When the storm sinks the Bathtub and the few residents who refuse to leave contemplate their next actions, Wink is adamant: "that's my beautiful place under there," he proclaims. Throughout the film, Wink refuses to hear any arguments, from Hushpuppy or the other Bathtubbers, in favor of leaving his home. Even as the hurricane rages, he stands, furiously discharging a shotgun into the storm clouds, proclaiming "no storm can't beat no Doucet!" Wink's defiance, and the invocation of the surname that ties him to the landscape in overt (linguistic) terms, create a powerful logic of resilience to counteract the marginalization and effacement of the Bathtubbers.

As I mentioned above, this is a familiar, if not wholly expected, narrative, and it is supported to an extent by the accounts and social studies emerging from post-Katrina New Orleans; residents frequently remained in the dev-astated city out of a sense of value-based attachment. Brian C. Theide and David L. Brown, in a 2013 study, find that "strong local connections had a binding effect, lowering the propensity of respondents to evacuate" after Ka-trina (813).[9] Thiede and Brown determine that lower-class Black households were the most likely to remain in the city during the storm, a conclusion corroborated by Lynn Weber and Lori Peek in a 2005 study: "The vast majority," they write, "of those who either chose or were forced to stay behind were African American, poor, elderly, and/or living with a disability" (2). These conclusions seem in line with the deep attachments (implicitly strengthened by class and race) to place as a means of compensating for ethnic, economic, and environmental marginalization in *Beasts of the Southern Wild*—place-based resilience pushes against the narrative of oppression and ruin. Yet the demographic studies emanating from post-Katrina New Orleans offer a simpler explanation than a nebulous sense of filiality toward the landscape: simply put, poor and minority residents of New Orleans disproportionately remained simply because they tended to lack the means to leave. Weber and Peek note that 26 percent of New Orleanian households had no access to an automobile, while Theide and Brown find that "black non-evacuees [were] more than two and a half times more likely to have been unable to evacuate than white non-evacuees" (8, 813).[10]

None of the aforementioned studies speculate about whether, had they possessed the means, potential evacuees without access to transportation would have left or stayed; presumably they have too many unknown quantities to draw such conjecture. However, interviews conducted by Weber and Peek suggest that, while some Katrina survivors maintained the narrative of emplacement and attachment to community, others were more ambivalent. Natasha, a twenty-eight-year-old black mother of two displaced to Houston after the storm, seemed distinctly unattached to the place: "At this point, I still don't believe home is anywhere. . . . I consider wherever I am with my kids as home. . . . It's like Katrina just stripped me of roots. I don't have any roots [in New Orleans] anymore because it's not the same. And I don't have any roots [in Houston]" (164). Another interviewee expressed a seeming contradiction (tinged with ironic humor) of the popular narrative of love for the region: "I think about just before Katrina happened, I always prayed that God would take me out of there so my kids could have a better life. So I came back and said to God, 'You didn't have to do it that drastic'" (224). These accounts deflate the narrative of place-based attachment and love for the region that, I will show, emanate largely from external sources.

In the years following Katrina, the city mounted multiple advertising campaigns to recoup the loss in tourism. Lynnell Thomas writes, in "Roots Run Deep Here" (2009), that these marketing schemes were designed to convince visitors that, "instead of destroying New Orleans's vibrant culture and community, Hurricane Katrina may have enhanced it," presenting "an interracial coalition around New Orleans food, music, art, and ambience" that "jarred with the contemporaneous political battles over rebuilding and economic recovery along racial and class lines" (754–55). Traditionally Black and lower-class areas of the city, among the hardest-hit regions during Katrina, were repurposed by marketers and tour guides as "old, historic neighborhoods . . . in a city that pays especial homage to the past" (757). Even if Naomi Klein is correct in her assertion, in *The Shock Doctrine* (2007), that, in the years following major disasters, residents most want to "reaffirm their relatedness to the places that formed them," she also believes that the "disaster capitalists" who use the process of rebuilding as an opportunity for exploitation have little interest in preserving that sense of "relatedness" (8). Similarly, Kenneth Gould and Tammy Lewis have, in a 2007 article, noted the troublesome trend of "eco-disaster tourism" in the months following Katrina in which tour companies led sightseers through devastated areas of New Orleans to witness the wreckage and suffering. Such endeavors, Gould and Lewis suggest, only exacerbate postdisaster income inequality: "both the attribution of blame for the ecodisaster, and the erasure of racial and class conflict serve the redevelopment agendas of local elites" (196). Though disasters, whether partially or totally anthropogenic, may seem to offer the opportunity to create or reinforce the bond between humans and landscape, this is rarely the result. More frequently, said disasters only cultivate further alienation and oppression.

Like Janie and Tea Cake in the postdisaster Everglades, Hushpuppy and her companions find their once-welcoming home utterly transformed and defamiliarized in the days following the hurricane. After a boisterous scene in which the surviving Bathtubbers drink heavily, devour steamed crabs, and boast of their strength and solidarity, the film moves on to a foraging trip in the waters surrounding the Bathtub. "Two weeks later, everything started to die," Hushpuppy's voiceover laments. In a harsh contrast to the luminous representations of the region from earlier in the film, the survivors now traverse a bleached maze of dead grass, accompanied by melancholy piano music. Around them floats a vast array of damaged and discarded bits of trash and the corpses of animals (fig. 8).

Their faces are marked with disappointment and desperation. Wink pauses to lean into the water and retrieve some item of interest; as soon as his ears are submerged, Hushpuppy turns to her companion and asks whether he intends to leave the Bathtub. A noncommittal sound is her only answer as

FIG. 8. Wink and Hushpuppy scavenge in the flooded Bathtub.
Author's screen capture.

Wink re-emerges. "I heard that," he says sharply to Hushpuppy. What the film's opening phrased as a genuine sense of belonging in and attachment to a particular landscape is here revealed as deeply contingent upon the conditions of the moment. Whatever commitment the residents of the Bathtub feel toward their home cannot overpower the full range of exigencies and suffering entailed by postdisaster life. Resilience has become an issue of mobility rather than attachment.

The concluding scenes of *Beasts of the Southern Wild* depict Hushpuppy coming to terms with Wink's death following the Bathtubbers' forcible evacuation from their ruined home and their daring escape from the hospital to which they are relocated. Hushpuppy's final monologue, delivered while she gazes out to sea at her father's floating funeral pyre, seems to overtly suggest her achievement of an environmental consciousness: "I see that I'm a little piece of a big, big universe, and that makes things right." Yet Hushpuppy's statement does not seem to so much affirm her emplacement in a limited world (the local), but rather her connection to much larger (global) environments. The death of Wink, who has consistently denied any desire voiced either by his daughter or others to leave the Bathtub over the course of the film, is for the Bathtubbers a symbolic liberation from the confines of the local—to survive, they must leave. And the film's closing shot is of Hushpuppy messianically leading the supporting cast along the causeway leading out of the Bathtub (fig. 9).[11]

FIG. 9. Hushpuppy leads the Bathtubbers across a flooded causeway in *Beasts of the Southern Wild*'s final scene. Author's screen capture.

Though *Beasts of the Southern Wild* to some extent treats the hoary notion of the bonds between lower-class southerners and the land with sympathy, that romanticism papers over the pragmatism at the film's heart. Hushpuppy's realization at the film's conclusion does not save the Bathtub from its reclamation by the sea any more than it heals the community torn apart by the disaster. Though the film may gesture toward the homespun stereotype of the emplaced southerner, ultimately it seems to discard the necessity of self-sacrifice for the good of the region.

In the end, it is implied, the Bathtub becomes wholly uninhabitable; Hushpuppy's insights into the globality of environmentalism are, implicitly, the symbolic recompense for losses of home, habitat, and community. This exchange is symbolic because the subjects are necessarily powerless to effect larger environmental change; any presumptive victory or catharsis must be purely on the level of the individual. Sarah McFarland, in a recent essay, recognizes this fundamentally cynical undertone of the film's conclusion, arguing that "*Beasts* leaves readers and viewers aware that it is too late for swamp communities featured there to remain unchanged, much as it is too late for the real residents of Isle de Jean Charles" (Vernon, *Ecocriticism and the Future of Southern Studies* 189–90). McFarland contends that, despite the fact that the Bathtub itself seems to be irrevocably doomed, its residents nonetheless seek to deploy their "important connections to place, people and their ethical-ecological framework that accepts good with bad" against a pernicious political body that "rejects the modes of expression by which the Bathtub's human residents define themselves" (*Ecocriticism and the Future of Southern Studies* 192). The very fact that those residents return to their homes, despite the injunctions of authority figures, is for McFarland a means of resistance. "Migration in apocalyptic fiction is a form of hope," she writes, "however, here we see its rejection—going home instead—as a powerful form of agency and an outright disregard of the very capitalistic, consumeristic, and cultural factors that precipitate climate change in the first place" (*Ecocriticism and the Future of Southern Studies* 193). Though the people abandon the Bathtub at the end of the film, Hushpuppy's displays of resolve in her final pronouncements insist that this is not surrender.

Yet if, as McFarland argues, the ethos of the Bathtubbers is centered around "important connections to place," the final exodus from (and, presumably, eventual literal submersion of) the wellspring of their communal identity has problematic implications for their endurance as a social unit. How do connections to place remain when the place itself becomes (literally and figuratively) absent? Evangelia Kindinger posits that the dominant social structures of other diasporic groups may hold true for refugees of disasters, suggesting that "one unifying feature of most diasporas is the role of the original homeland for the creation and sustainment of diaspora communities." She cites Robin Cohen's work on diasporic identity, to wit, that "all diasporic communities settled outside their natal (or imagined natal) territories, acknowledge that 'the old country'—a notion often buried deep in language, religion, custom, or folklore—always has some claim on their loyalty" (Vernon, *Ecocriticism and the Future of Southern Studies* 175–76). What is perhaps most intriguing about this line of reasoning is the notion of a deeply "buried" set of origins for the relevant group's set of affiliations. In the case of the residents of the Bathtub in the present, such origins are sunken, inaccessible, wholly confined to the realm of ideation. McFarland contends that the catastrophic nature of displacement strengthens survivors' continued attachments to their home regions; separation "facilitates the myth of home" (Vernon, *Ecocriticism and the Future of Southern Studies* 177). However, I would suggest that the conclusion of *Beasts* construes the myth of home as precisely that—a myth, something decidedly constructed, illusory, a set of standards to organize a community around, but not something accessible. Certainly not, in the exodus depicted in its final scenes implies, something worth dying for.

———

In both Hurston's and Zeitlin's works, though the survivors of natural disasters lay claim to close affiliation with local landscapes and communities, the lack of agency afforded them by slow violence that exacerbates the effects of those very disasters mean that resilient responses to environmental ruination necessarily involve migration, the severing of ties to familiar homeplaces. In my final source, Faulkner's "Old Man" (1939), we re-encounter the now-familiar narrative of anthropocentric disaster, defamiliarization, and loss of irreplaceable environments, yet these tropes are apprehended by the story's characters in a wholly different manner. As with the aftermath of the two hurricanes in my previous sources, "Old Man" deals with the difficult process of coming to terms with sudden environmental transformation and loss, as well as the necessity of synthesizing a new narrative of the relationship between a group of people and the land they once occupied. Among critics, "Old Man" occupies a vexed position; while Lawrence Buell believes that the novella represents "Faulkner's strongest presentation of Nature untrammeled," calling Faulkner "one of the great harbingers and prophets of southern environmentalism," critics such as Anthony Hoefer lambaste the ecocritical school (including Buell) for "minimiz[ing] it as a 'gripping narrative of man against flood'—that is, of man in conflict with nature" (Buell 5, 14, Hoefer 543). Perhaps the most equivocal (and, for my purposes, useful) approach to the story comes from Susan Scott Parrish's "Faulkner and the Outer Weather of 1927" (2012) owing to Parrish's observation of "a complex of anthropogenic changes such as wetlands drainage, cotton monoculture, massive deforestation by the timber industry, and the building of ever higher levees to manage the Mississippi and its tributaries" (34). Parrish finds in "Old Man" a precedent to *Go Down, Moses*'s tragic narrative of the ruination of oppressed landscapes and communities. She writes: "[Faulkner's] demonstrated awareness of what 'man' had done shows that he understood the role humans played in turning naturally occurring floods into catastrophic events" (35).

Parrish is correct in asserting the anthropogenic elements that led to the 1927 flood of the Mississippi. Efforts to control and contain the river on a large, engineered scale began as early as 1861, with Captain A. A. Humphreys and Henry Abbott's "Report Upon the Physics and Hydraulics of the Mississippi River"—this report advocated the now-infamous "levees only" policy, which recommended protective berms surrounding the river, but no system of canals or secondary flood protection for the surrounding areas.[12] Such levees, however, carry a host of attendant problems; Klein and Zellmer note that surrounding the river with levees prevented the conveyance of valuable sediments and nutrients to Delta wetlands. This alteration sped land loss in the Delta, as did dredging shipping channels (15–16). Following the flood, federal officials were forced to admit that "the Army Corps of Engineers' approach to flood control had been a 'monumental blunder,' causing a disaster that was 'man-made' rather than natural" (Klein & Zellmer 18).[13] The engineering failures were mimicked by the human errors in dealing with the persistent floodwaters. "Old Man" accurately reflects the conscription of southern convicts and poorly paid minority workers to aid in the relief efforts; these actions, writes Michael Powers, "specifically, and often illegally, reinforced the subjugation of black laborers" (Hartman & Squires 19).

Along with the acknowledgment that "the story of the 1927 flood . . . is not simply a story of nature's force" but a colossal failure of human planning, engineering, race relations, and land ethics, the common thread among critics who write about the flood is the narration of its origins and progress, as well as its attendant recovery efforts, in terms of the evolving relationship between man and nature, the plot of which is the familiar trope of hubris and punishment (Barry 116). While, immediately prior to the disaster, the Army Corps of Engineers boasted that "man had triumphed over nature" and that "the Mississippi River had finally been restricted to its channel," the disastrous effects of the flood and its bungled recovery efforts "altered the underlying theory regarding man's relationship with nature from one of domination to one of accommodation" (Spencer 170, Hartman & Squires 20). Yet this narrative, rather than being a watershed in American land ethics or encouraging wiser use and a greater measure of respect for forces of nature, is only repeated in the disasters that follow the 1927 flood. John Barry notes that, with the loss of sediment created by building levees that blocked seasonal flooding on the Mississippi, South Louisiana began to sink, making it more vulnerable to catastrophic storm surges (118).[14] Environmental policy, it would seem, is more cyclical than linear; repeatedly, major environmental lessons go unlearned.

In short, perennial riparian mismanagement fits easily into the ruin-narrative that we have seen so frequently in southern environmental history, which Faulkner himself seemed to explicate in *Go Down, Moses*. However, while the trilogy of environmental stories in *Go Down, Moses* relied upon the familiar tropes of deep attachment to particular landscapes and the tragedy of those landscapes' destruction, "Old Man" offers a vision of environmental resilience that effectively satirizes such affiliations. While Hurston and Zeitlin suggest that fidelity to landscapes of personal significance must give way to the necessity of mobility in the wake of natural disasters, "Old Man" views the concept of a static "home" itself as comic.[15] As such, it offers a counterweight to the common use of tragedy and ruin to describe natural disasters in the South, as well as a model of resilience that refigures the very notion of the ostensible drag of belonging. The central character of "Old Man" (the tall convict) lives, up until the time of the flood itself, in virtual isolation from his surroundings, barely able to guess that the river lies just beyond the prison's levee. For the entirety of his and his fellow convicts' tenure there, they have "plowed and planted and eaten and slept beneath the shadow of the levee itself, knowing only that there was water beyond it from hearsay and because now and then they heard the whistles of steamboats from beyond it, and during the last week or so had seen the stacks and pilot houses moving along the sky sixty feet above their heads" (85–86). Part of the theme of "Old Man" is the sudden and violent awakening to the presence and force of nature, and the convicts begin in a state of complete ignorance, dissociated from even their immediate surroundings by the penal system. Only when the tall convict first hears the sound of the floodwaters does he first acknowledge the "profound deep whisper" of its movements, though "for seven years now he had run his plow and harrow and planter within the very shadow of the levee on which he now stood" (61). Yet this revelation less grants the tall convict some essential insight into the workings of the landscape than it reveals the myopia of his prior relationship to that landscape—the same ignorance of natural forces, processes, and cycles that produced the aforementioned human blunders in riparian management.

The concept of attachment to landscape which Hurston and Zeitlin gesture toward (yet ultimately repudiate) becomes parodic in Faulkner's story; rather than pining after a romanticized hereditary locale, the tall convict, adrift on floodwaters, fondly remembers his incarceration. Faulkner accomplishes this through reference to a pastoral ideal; the tall convict remembers "home, the place where he had lived almost since childhood, his friends of years whose ways he knew and who knew his ways, the familiar fields where he did work he had learned to do well and to like," an image indistinguishable from the emplaced southerner working the land (123). Yet this image shortly coalesces into "the barracks at night, with screens against the bugs in summer and good stoves in winter and someone to supply the fuel and the food too; the Sunday ball games and the picture shows" (124). The tall convict recalls his imprisonment selectively, given the circumstances, and undoubtedly romanticizes prison life in the Mississippi Delta during the early 1920s, but there is a conscious irony in displacing the site of southern attachment to landscape from the farm, the small town, and the wilderness to the prison, where any genuine cognizance of the surrounding environment is stifled.

I would like to take the argument a step further, however, and examine how the tall convict, once removed from his prison "home," becomes divorced not only from that *particular* place, but the very concept of place in general. The floodwaters upon which he floats dissociate him from identifying any meaningful spatial divisions, any human markers or barriers imposed upon distance. He sees nothing but "trees and water and solitude," himself and the waters "hanging suspended simultaneous and unprogressing in pure time, upon a dreamy desolation" (143). Ahead there is "nothing," and behind only "the outrageous idea of a volume of moving water toppling forward" (144).[16] The concept of place, so crucial to the development of southern literature, here becomes a nonentity, or, in places, a comedic inversion of its former self. Whilst being transported to the levee camp by train, the convicts notice a burning plantation house through the windows: "Juxtaposed to nowhere and neighbored by nothing it stood, a clear steady pyre-like flame rigidly fleeing its own reflection, burning in the dusk above the watery desolation with a quality paradoxical, outrageous and bizarre" (95). Here, Faulkner figuratively burns the myth of the Old South and all of its fantasies of harmonious and rightful land usage; rather than serving as a stable site of habitation and signification, here the house serves as a simulacrum, unmoored from its proper place, incomparable and meaningless, a dead sign. It serves, in short, as an apt symbol for the representation of nature throughout the novella: places that could potentially serve as junctions between humans and nature are drained of significance; their symbolism is blocked. Here, perhaps more so than in any of the texts I have presented in this chapter, the bond between southerners and their land becomes fragile, temporary, the product of convenience and necessity rather than allegiance and honor.

———

What pervades all three of the disaster-narratives I have here presented is a strong sense of the logic of necessity—when placed into situations in which only one option offers the possibility for survival, characters inevitably take that option. Thus Janie and Tea Cake flee the flooded Everglades, the Bath-tubbers abandon their sunken home, and the convict furiously paddles his forsaken canoe. The ruin-narrative in southern literature emphasizes the in-tractability of loss and the tragic transformation of landscapes of significance into landscapes of absence; when characters adhere to this narrative (as Wink does in *Beasts of the Southern Wild*) and insist on maintaining their attach-ment to and residence within locations doubly imperiled by slow violence and the sudden violence of hurricanes and floods, they inflict still greater suffering on themselves and others. The ruin-narrative creates powerful dichotomies of community insiders and outsiders, "us" and "them," and these dichotomies, owing to the presence of slow violence, oftentimes cleave to race and class divisions. Accounts of southern disasters frequently deal with navigating the gap between these traditionalist affiliations and a resilient approach to the catastrophe, which necessitates sudden and rapid change—through extreme hardship in Hurston's novel, with great reluctance and melodrama in *Beasts of the Southern Wild*, and with the bewildered realization, in "Old Man," that the very concept of "home" is unstable. It would be easier, perhaps, and provide a more emotionally satisfying conclusion to the ruin-narrative, to remain. To go down with the ship, so to speak, or to sacrifice oneself in loving homage to a place. But "narrative closure" loses much of its currency when balanced against survival.

By and large, the disaster-narrative lacks closure. The survivors are left in a wholly unfamiliar landscape whether they have remained in their home-places or fled; a repaired and rehabilitated life seems distant, if not wholly inaccessible; cohesive lessons and plans for mitigating such disasters in the future have not yet coalesced. The postdisaster landscape is a realm of spon-taneity and uncertainty—the "great fish-net" of Janie's final revelation, the flooded open road that Hushpuppy walks, and the rambling, ironic recol-lection that concludes Faulkner's story. Rather than falling back upon the familiar Romantic narrative of human interference with natural forces (in these cases, through the construction of inadequate dams/levees) producing a corresponding punishment from capital-N Nature, the resilience that emerges from these disasters demands a more complex and less narratively satisfying set of conclusions. What if, rather than relying upon the tired man/nature duality, we accepted the biocentric edict that the boundary must be dissolved and humankind accepted as part of one inclusive natural category? We would be punished not by the landscape but by means of the landscape—both the infraction and the penalty would be ours. Such a move would preclude the normative conceptions of "nature," "landscape," and even "place" that have been the hallmarks of southern narrative for decades—such terms would be replaced by a new vocabulary of subjectivity, centered about how humans think and act, not toward the land but toward an agglomeration of comparable subjectivities that includes the land. I believe that Hurston, Zeitlin, and Faulkner's work exists in this space—they make no necessary distinction between human problems and natural problems, but suggest that these categories are identical.

FIVE

Glimpses of the Whole

Climate Fiction and Resilience
in the Remnant South

THE MAN AND THE BOY traverse a blank landscape of ruin made blanker by
the prose that describes it. They have no names; the author does not provide
them. The ash of the burnt (but remembered, though only by the man) world
and the condition of the shopping cart that he laboriously pushes forward
consume the novel's foreground. The contours of the landscape itself, and
whatever structures might remain, is synecdochic backdrop, with only rare
and occasional promontories penetrating the perpetual fug of gray: "They
trucked on along the blacktop. Tall clapboard houses. Machinerolled metal
roofs. A log barn in a field with an advertisement in faded ten-foot letters
across the roofslope. See Rock City" (McCarthy 18) (fig. 10).

Any traveler on the interstate within a hundred miles of Rock City in
Chattanooga is likely to be familiar with Cormac McCarthy's allusion, in
The Road, to its highly visible signage, oftentimes occupying entire roof sur-
faces. Yet, while the traveler on Interstate 40 accepts the relentless parade of
billboards and the more rustic yet no less visible barn boards noted by the
novel's protagonists as simply another manifestation of the grim ubiquity of
advertising, the painted barn appears in *The Road* as something remarkable
and unexpected, both because it remains intact and because it *places* the text
in a specific and immutable manner in a particular region of the country.[1]
However, though the Rock City advertisement emerges from the monotonous
fabric of declarative landscape-fragments like a beam of light, promising a
new clarity and directionality, it holds little significance for the protagonists'
journey, and the man (who is the only one who could conceivably know
what Rock City is) does not comment on it. It is never mentioned again in

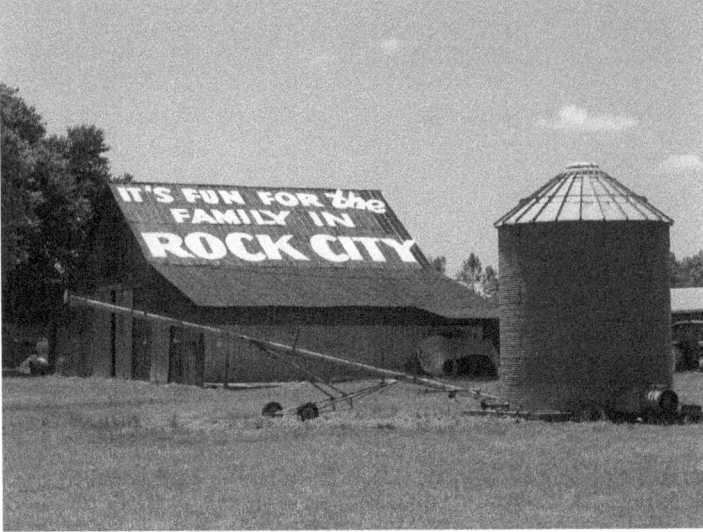

FIG. 10. Advertisement for Rock City near White City, Tennessee,
photo by Brent Moore. https://upload.wikimedia.org/wikipedia/
commons/2/2d/%22Home-made%22_See_Rock_City_Barn.jpg,
Creative Commons License 2.0, unaltered image.

the novel. Rock City exists in *The Road* as a fragment from an earlier time, drifting through the landscape of the text without anything to connect to, a remnant of a southern locale with seemingly no latent significance.

The ultimate end of the southern environmental narrative of ruin is not the loss of its hallowed places per se—the clear-cut Big Woods or the flooded Everglades are still "places" to the extent that they were before their respective catastrophes—but rather the extinction of the human significance of those places. Mike Hulme, in "Four Meanings of Climate Change" (2010), claims that climate change, like other apocalyptic environmental narratives, "really *is* about symbolic loss, a loss to our imaginative capacities rather than a loss of something material and substantive" (52). From this perspective, the irrevocable alteration of southern landscapes is a "tragedy" not necessarily because of the loss of, say, biodiversity, or aesthetically pleasing geographical features, but because of the dehumanization of those landscapes. Elements of the environment—even those as banal as the Rock City advertisement—that once carried meaning, housed memories, and could be read as texts become indecipherable, and that deeply *human* loss is phrased as tragic. *The Road* invokes this sense of tragedy continuously by juxtaposing the dreary present with the luminous past. Adeline Johns-Putra, in a 2016 article, contends that the novel invokes the preapocalyptic environment "not to inspire its narrative with possibility but to haunt it with loss" (526). Instead of a postapocalyptic setting that is replete with fundamentally unknowable places (thus opening spaces of possibility for rehabilitation) Johns-Putra argues, the environment in *The Road* is "known only as what it is not," making it in essence "a non-place" ("My Job Is to Take Care of You," 526). Johns-Putra's "nonplaces," are, of course, still physical locations on the earth, though locations that have little to offer humans; places drained of significance become "nonplaces."

When we contemplate the massive looming environmental catastrophes of the Anthropocene, we are almost compulsively lured to metaphors of loss and tragedy. The retreat of glaciers, the shrinking of green spaces, the extinction of species—we prefer to conceptualize threats to the environment in terms of these losses rather than, say, the unwholesome *gain* of several meters of seawater or extra heat accumulated by the planet. If the rhetoric of loss and ruin that saturates contemporary environmental discourse is preapocalyptic in tone, however, narratives of Anthropocene resilience are postapocalyptic, asking what is *left* rather than what has been *lost*. If disasters, rapid environmental changes, and massive disruptions of existing communities rob places of significance, as I have noted, the work of resilience lies in attempting to stitch those significances back together, to make sense of what remains of the old world. Places irrevocably changed are not necessarily "nonplaces," but fragments, remnants of meaning. Though we frequently phrase this fragmentation as loss, it should perhaps more accurately be called *change*, even if that change is deleterious to humans. If a coffee mug falls from a desk and shatters on the floor, no fragment of its initial structure is lost, only scattered—all that has been lost, per se, is its utility as a receptacle. Literature is one means of pulling those fragments together and guessing at their meaning, and the most profound set of environmental changes of the Anthropocene—the greatest shattering, so to speak—is climate change.[2]

Regarding the transformations inherent in the Anthropocene as "loss" or "change," however, is not necessarily a choice but a dialogue, a conversation between ruin and resilience. In southern climate fiction, it is also a dialogue between the characters' understanding of change (in their awareness of the vastly altered world around them) and the readers' understanding of loss (in their awareness of the gap between the world presented by the fiction and their own). Neither position is entirely adequate to the task of comprehending global environmental change, so the meaning, lesson, or moral of the climate change novel exists only in fragments that the readers and characters both labor to understand—fragments such as the Rock City sign in *The Road*. I would contend that this notion of a "fragmented" or "remnant" South is one of the defining features of the region in the Anthropocene, signifying a significant new transformation. While first-wave studies of southern literature in the early twentieth century regarded the region as essentially a monolith, a frequent object of curiosity, interest, and ridicule, with the publication of Michael Kreyling's *Inventing Southern Literature* in 1998, criticism came to regard southern culture as less something innate than something deliberately produced, and, more to the point, produced by much more fluid and dynamic pathways of race, class, and gender than had been previously thought. During this postsouthern second wave, which perhaps culminated with Scott Romine's *The Real South* in 2008, the distinctiveness and authenticity that the first wave depended upon became, in the era of late capitalism, its inverse: a manufactured, performative, self-aware simulacrum. Over the course of roughly the last decade, however, criticism has, with some hesitation, approached the frontier of discarding "the South" as a signifier that carries any discernible meaning—the 2015 collection *Undead Souths*, for example, seems to imply that the state of the field is almost zombified, shuffling forward without clear signs of either continued vitality or definite perishing. This ontological uncertainty, I would argue, extends to the appearance of the remnant South in climate fiction: a fundamentally fragmented, unparseable series of signifiers in which the interplay between the respective knowledge bases of characters and reader creates a powerful portrait of how narratives of resilience and ruin persist in the Anthropocene.

Perhaps the first and most imposing hurdle that any discussion of climate change must overcome, and the largest cognitive challenge that many cli-fi protagonists face, is the simple difficulty of adequately conceiving of the magnitude and extent of the problem. Dipesh Chakrabarty, in "The Climate of History," asserts that humankind (the small sector of humankind that contains historians most certainly, but also the human species more broadly) tends to take a priori "the assumption that our past, present, and future are connected by a certain continuity of human experience. We normally envisage the future with the help of the same faculty that allows us to picture the past" (197). However, according to Chakrabarty, climate change and the range of futures that it represents constitute a challenge to "not only the ideas about the human that usually sustain the discipline of history but also the analytic strategies that postcolonial and postimperial historians have deployed in the last two decades in response to the postwar scenario of decolonization and globalization" (198). Chakrabarty admits that his own considerable readings in postcolonial and Marxist theory "ha[ve] not really prepared [him] for making sense of this planetary conjuncture within which humanity finds itself today" (199).[3] In a larger sense, the concept of "humanity" itself, Chakrabarty contends, requires sufficient renovation in the era of climate change to bring on new shades of contradictory and paradoxical being. For example, though taking a longer view of the human species *qua* species, that is, as evolutionarily adapted from and intimately linked to nonhuman nature, may open up historiographical and cognitive pathways instrumental to conceive of climate change, Chakrabarty also acknowledges that "we humans never experience ourselves as a species. We can only intellectually comprehend or infer the existence of the human species but never experience it as such. There could be no phenomenology of us as a species" (220). One of the many reasons why critics have perennially found it difficult to discuss climate change in the same manner as other environmental crises is the seemingly impossible position that it imposes upon human subjects. To discuss "the human species" is to flatten a vast spectrum of cultural, geographical, ethnic, and linguistic (to name only a few) differences into a single aphorism—to say nothing of "human history," "human impact on the environment," or the combination of all of these factors, which is what we are being asked to comprehend when discussing climate change.

Faced with such an untenable complexity, we tend to gravitate (in narrative as well as mass media) toward accounts of individuals, families, communities—discrete units of humanity who experience the effects of climate change in distinct and unique ways. Johns-Putra sees in *The Road*, for example, an abdication of fictions of planetary change in favor of micronarratives of human care. In "The Rest Is Silence" (2018), she contends that such a turn stems from the problem of how to "recuperate a nuanced view of human agency that enables humans to engage more fully with the unprecedented crisis now engulfing human and nonhuman organisms and environments" (26). This enhanced engagement provides the backdrop for Johns-Putra's concept of "care," which emerges across the bulk of her writings as "the answer to rampant scientism and ecological crisis," a syllogism that she regards as "so apparently plain that a concept such as 'earthcare,' put forward by

Carolyn Merchant in the 1990s, seems hardly to need explanation" ("Care, Gender" 129). Whether Johns-Putra is correct in her assertion that "love will let us save, survive, or escape an ecologically degraded planet" is perhaps an untestable hypothesis; I am more interested in her contention that climate fiction as a whole performs an "assessment of humanity's collective hubris," frequently concluding that "we simply have not cared enough, and that the way forward lies in caring more" ("Care, Gender" 128). Johns-Putra posits a simple explanation for an immeasurably complex problem; it is likely that "hubris" and its antonym, "care," play large roles in explaining and responding to the vast superstructure of climate change, but this simple dichotomy cannot possibly encompass its entirety. The attribution of such multifaceted environmental threats to simple human failures is a hallmark of the narrative of ruin that proliferates in environmentalist discourse—and which gives only a partial view of human reactions to change.

It is possible to craft a cornucopia of ruin-narratives relating to climate change—the hunger for endless, unrestrained growth that Johns-Putra alludes to, addiction to fossil fuels, campaigns of misinformation and political recalcitrance, and reluctance toward surrendering any of the comforts and privileges that attend a petro-centric lifestyle, to name only a few—though *any single one* of these narratives is ultimately insufficient. Christophe Bonneuil and Jean-Baptise Fressoz, in *The Shock of the Anthropocene* (2016), claim that "we should be suspicious . . . of a grand narrative of the Anthropocene that presents interactions between the human species and the earth system" because such cognitive measures produce "historical explanations that are impoverished or erroneous, comforting the interests of a minority of the planet's population" (71). Ruin is a *narrative* precisely because it attempts a conceptualization of incalculably complex histories, environmental changes, and catastrophes within familiar structures of culpability. To do so is not misguided—climate change would not be anthropogenic if humans were not, ultimately, *to blame* for it—yet the only viable, the only practical, answer to the climate crisis is to place the ruin-narrative in dialogue with resilience, realizing that, while large ethical plot-arcs cannot be ignored, the easy resolutions offered by those narratives are insufficient to the task of comprehending planetary changes. Nor do the (theoretical) lessons learned and admissions of guilt that accompany such explanatory schemes provide a set of directives for survival in a fundamentally altered landscape, a road map for the world to come.

Climate resilience thus resembles, more than anything else, a fiction—the coastal Florida city that hires on teams of engineers to mitigate anticipated flooding and the woodsman who hoards drinking water and freeze-dried meals are both constructing fictions of what will happen next, acting on some admixture of scientific projections, historical observations, and general reckonings of human nature. Cli-fi engages in the same process, though it is the preclimate world itself that has become the fiction, the text that must be dimly read by the novel's characters. At this they seldom succeed; the postclimate backdrop of the text is only granted focus when measured against the (comparatively) pastoral environment that the reader inhabits. Between the two is the vast cognitive gulf that constitutes, if any single element does, the common thread of most climate-change fiction: whatever else the postclimate world might entail, it represents a drastic, unprecedented environmental sea-change, and thus a distinct challenge to comprehension, to say nothing of action. Ian Baucom puts the daunting imaginative labor of envisioning climate futures succinctly in "Moving Centers" (2015): "We seem to be living, already, in the moment of ultrahistory, in the 'end times' between catastrophe and apocalypse, as the past that has made the present now includes not only a political, social, or economic past but, emerging from all of these, a carbon past that appears to have predetermined the ruinous deep future of the planet" (138). Like Chakrabarty, Baucom views a large-scale reconception not only of the relationship between humans and their environment, but also of the very nature (both historical and recent) of human presence on the earth in a sense that approaches Heidegger's holistic "habitation" as an imperative brought on by climate change.[4] Baucom calls humans in the new geological era "radically decomposed, nonontological being[s]," who, consequently, "cannot conceive a new theory of justice or a new form of freedom adequate to that mode."[5] Rather than interpret Baucom's view of Anthropocene subjects being adrift on a sea of ultrahistory as a paralytic ruin-narrative, however, I would suggest that said subjects require fictions in order to compose themselves. Resilience depends on a dialogue between reader and climate-text.

Moreover, despite the radical changes portended (and, indeed, already in progress) by the Anthropocene, and despite the necessity of rethinking what is entailed by human presence on the earth and the application of concepts such as "justice" and "freedom," the forces of cultural and *regional* identity remain crucial. While Chakrabarty and others regard climate change as wholly unprecedented and foretold by no extant histories, it is the complexities of those particular histories' collisions that produce such an ineffable conclusion. Christian Parenti writes, in *Tropic of Chaos* (2011) that excessively tribalistic and dictatorial responses to climate change, though they masquerade as *sui generis* twenty-first-century political phenomena, are in fact "the result of a history—particularly the history of the Global North's use and abuse of the Global South—that has destroyed the institutions and social practices that would allow a different, more productive response" (8). And Rob Latham sees in the frequently expressed paralysis in the face of climate change only an exposure of a lack of agency that has *always* been historically present: "The sense of helplessness—geographic, economic, military, and so on—reinforced by catastrophe scenarios lays bare the underlying anxieties of hegemonic power, its inherent contingency and vulnerability, notwithstanding the purported inevitability of Western 'progress'" (78). Climate change is, perhaps unsurprisingly, imbricated in historical structures of power—power that operates on the global, national, and even regional level. Thus, we can see in the legacy of southern environmentalism—the emphasis on strong states' rights that permit weak environmental policies, the exploitation of resources without consideration of sustainability or public health, and the deregulation and proliferation of toxic industries, to name a few—a ripple effect that radiates from the region to impact the nation, and from there to the world at large. In other words, far from being "just another region" that will be impacted by climate change, more even than being a region that will be *quite severely* impacted by climate change, the South represents a pattern, an archive of the decisions, lifestyles, political persuasions, and deeply individuated histories that led to the edge of the precipice.

For the protagonists of southern climate and postclimate fiction, this archive appears only as a collection of remnants both physical and ephemeral. These may take the form of ruined structures, rusted equipment, and discarded consumer trash or lingering memories, half-formed thoughts, and distant recollections. These characters are engaged in a running battle to comprehend these remnants in the context of the drastically changed world around them; climate-change discourse, as Sylvia Mayer writes in "Exploration of the Controversially Real" (2014), is always concerned with the difficulty in linking large global climate events with local, even individual, behaviors. Mayer calls climate change itself "intangible" insofar as there are distinct difficulties in causally linking individual weather events, for instance, to worldwide phenomena. That challenge, Mayer postulates, is related to "the more general difficulty of linking individual, local experience with processes of global ecological transformation that usually occur over a longer period of time."[6] As the reader of the southern cli-fi novel wrangles with the intangibility of their own experience of climate change, the time-lapsed tales of catastrophe that parade daily down their news feed, they find their cognitive dissonance mirrored back to them by the fictions they consume. The tendency toward ruin, toward regarding one's own experience of climate-change reality as the terrifying and ultimate conclusion of a series of escalating human errors, is nearly irresistible in such a situation. What climate fiction, and southern climate fiction in particular, *can* do in the teeth of this dilemma, through the invocation of remnants of persistent local meaning that the reader makes legible, is square the distance between the reader's lived reality and one particular fiction of the future in which such remnants still carry meaning. Such a process cannot offer comfort, or catharsis, but it may perhaps achieve some measure of clarity that can lead to composure, a kind of resilience.

––––––

Of the fairly small quantity of texts dealing explicitly with southern landscapes vis-a-vis climate change, Barbara Kingsolver's *Flight Behavior* (2012) has received the most critical attention, though the very concept of climate change is not mentioned until past the halfway point of the four-hundred-page novel. The reasoning behind this omission is simple: the protagonist, Dellarobia Turnbow, has been conditioned to be skeptical of the concept by her social circle and the media in the fictional, deeply conservative locale of Feathertown, Tennessee. *Flight Behavior* thus borrows much of its structure from the bildungsroman, as several critics have noted—a naive, perhaps even deeply misguided, protagonist gradually progresses toward enlightenment (or disillusionment) through many false turns. Though she does not attribute the phenomena to climate change, Dellarobia keeps a running commentary on the uncanny climate events visiting Feathertown, noting that "summer's heat had never really arrived, nor the cold in its turn, and everything living now seemed to yearn for sun with the anguish of the unloved. The world of sensible seasons had come undone" (49). Amidst the bizarre weather events, Dellarobia herself feels continually out-of-sorts, contemplating an affair to break up the monotony of her loveless marriage and grant her a reprieve from her demanding children.[7] She becomes unmoored in time; the simple act of stepping outside her house causes her to "struggle a few seconds trying to place the month of the year" (84). Yet, despite Dellarobia's baffled observation that "it felt like no season at all," the concept that she might be experiencing the effects of climate change fails to enter her line of thought. Axel Goodbody, in a 2014 article, suggests that the novel's persistent focus on Dellarobia's limited personal perception of the situation rather than on a broader attention to regional (or global) events is deliberate: "Political and commercial interests are present in the background," Goodbody writes, "but rather than asking the machinations of lobby groups responsible for environmental apathy, or even the media, [Kingsolver] focuses on the everyday worries of people without higher education, bordering on poverty" (Mayer and von Mossner 50). One of the common components of climate change fiction—an emphasis on individual, personal relationships rather than global events—is clearly present in *Flight Behavior*.

Moreover, Kingsolver links this interiority to a strong lack of comprehension and vexed state of being on her protagonist's part. The novel opens with Dellarobia in a turbulent state of mind, laboriously scaling the slopes of an Appalachian knoll in poor weather, clad in fashionable garb unsuited to hiking, with the intent of meeting a potential paramour. Her precarious physical and romantic circumstances consume her train of thought sufficiently to require a moment of quasi-divine revelation to interrupt, and, in a moment reminiscent of O'Connor's sudden insights, she finds that the branches of the trees on the mountain she is climbing are unexpectedly alive with monarch butterflies: "The forest blazed with its own internal flame. 'Jesus,' she said, not calling for help, she and Jesus weren't that close, but putting her voice in the world because nothing else present made sense . . . trees turned to fire, a burning bush. Moses came to mind, and Ezekiel."[8] Like the biblical prophets, Dellarobia later comes to view her initial mental state as "stupid, or blind . . . unreceptive to truth. . . . [She had] shuttered her eyes and looked without seeing" (52). Yet, at this point in the text, Dellarobia has no full-formed conception of what "truth" the profusion of butterflies might hold; climate change, and the vast disruption of existing migratory patterns that it entails, is scarcely a blip on her radar. What the text emphasizes through its repetition of Dellarobia's state of ignorance, however, is the massive upending of her previous priorities that the butterflies' arrival heralds. The scattered, frantic train of thought of the novel's first chapter coalesces into a series of discrete enigmas: why are the butterflies here? Where did they come from, and why? Mysteries proliferate, and the arrival of a group of entomologists tasked with studying the displaced butterflies only raises more questions; Dellarobia finds it impossible to parse their technical verbiage. "Bio-geography, roosts, host plants, overwintering zones, loss of something-communities, devastation. That one she got, devastation" (147). In short, the novel's structure is meteoric, providing a sudden and massive impact (the unexpected arrival of the butterflies) at the outset followed by an extended process of the protagonist attempting to put the pieces together, to understand what has happened, revise her existing set of beliefs and predilections to respond to it, and to prepare herself for what comes next.

Though other critics have focused on Dellarobia's steady assembly of all of the various clues and implications of widespread environmental threats that she witnesses into a single narrative of climate change, I would prefer to read the dominant mode of the novel as *fragmentation*, the replacement of the set of fairly mundane anxieties and discontent that Dellarobia experiences at the beginning of the novel with a far more decentered, multifaceted set of fears. The point of inflection comes with the arrival of the entomologists, who convince Dellarobia that the arrival of the butterflies is one element of a complex web of environmental consequences. Ovid Byron, the fancifully named lead scientist, postulates, in the first mention of climate change in the novel: "We are seeing a bizarre alteration of a previously stable pattern . . . a continental ecosystem breaking down. Most likely, this is due to climate change. Really I can tell you I'm sure of that. Climate change has disrupted this system" (228). From this point onward, Dellarobia is forced to confront "a world where you could count on nothing you'd ever known or trusted," developing a dread of the future far greater than she possessed at the beginning of the novel (325). As she listens to the scientists discuss the global effects of climate change, she awakens to the true scale of the problem: "The elephants in drought-stricken Africa, the polar bears on the melting ice, were 'as good as gone,' they said with infuriating resignation as they worked through what seemed to be an early autopsy on another doomed creature. . . . Dellarobia felt an entirely new form of panic as she watched her son love nature so expectantly, wondering if he might be racing toward a future like some complicated sand castle that was crumbling under the tide. She didn't know how scientists bore such knowledge. People had to manage terrible truths" (247). For perhaps the first time, Dellarobia is forced to process the concept that the uncanny butterflies that have arrived in her hometown and the suffering endured by other organisms across the world are linked; the issue is not simply a swarm of confused insects, but an immense, far-reaching phenomenon. The realization is, at least at first, wholly incomprehensible to her, a set of dissociated data able to be approached only metonymically through the struggles of the butterflies and other organisms.

If *Flight Behavior* fractures and fragments the unitary known into the scattered unknown, however, it is also adamant about *not* reassembling those pieces into a single, easily grasped moral or conclusion; at the end of the novel, Dellarobia remains anxious and fearful, having gained knowledge but lost surety. Sylvia Mayer suggests that the novel as a whole emphasizes "uncertainty and openness," and that even its ending, which involves a dramatic flooding of the region surrounding Feathertown, "can be ambiguously read: either as a sign of destruction, or as a sign of cleansing and renewal" ("Exploration" 31). In the final scene, when the butterflies depart Feathertown for unknown destinations, Kingsolver's imagery mingles trauma, hope, and deep uncertainty: "The shards of a wrecked generation had rested alive like a heartbeat in trees, snow-covered, charged with resistance. Now the sun blinked open on a long impossible time, and here was the exodus. They would gather on other fields and risk other odds, probably no better or worse than hers" (433). In the end, the fate of the insects—like Dellarobia's own future, or that of the human race itself—is deeply unstable. The chaotic effects of climate change work in manners that are impossible to predict and, as in *The Road*, produce fragments that are impossible for the characters to unite into meaningful wholes.

Though *Flight Behavior* by no means suggests a solution to climate change—perhaps the closest it comes is a sanctimonious episode in which Ovid Byron berates a reporter from a local conservative news station for obscuring the truth—its final pages suggest that resilience, which in this case consists of abandoning certainty and progressing forward into a distinctly unknown and unknowable future, is possible only once narratives of ruin (the large planetary losses that attend the butterflies' displacement) are reconciled with local perspectives. In other words, the reader of *Flight Behavior* likely knows vastly more about climate change than Dellarobia does at the beginning of the novel.[9] Though the novel masquerades as a mystery (what are the butterflies doing here?), the core of the plot lies within Dellarobia's ongoing attempt to make sense of climate change itself, which for her has been either a myth or impenetrable scientific jargon. When she finally comprehends what is happening to the monarchs, she phrases the realization in terms that are familiar to her: "'One of God's creatures of this world, meeting its End of Days,' she said after a quiet minute. Not words of science, she knew that, but it was a truth she could feel" (229). Dellarobia explicitly notes that her own means of apprehending the effects of climate change differ significantly from those of the entomologists—they are *not* "words of science." Over the course of the novel, as Dellarobia gradually puts the pieces of the (already solved, by the reader) mystery together, she resolutely does so on her own terms, at her own pace.

When juxtaposed with the reader's own understanding of climate change, the narrative that Dellarobia is reluctant to accept—that the butterflies are responding to large-scale planetary changes—dovetails with contemporary local climatological issues: why are people in the South, the most vulnerable region in the nation to climate change, reluctant to take action? On this front, the knowledge of the novel's protagonist enters into dialogue with that of the reader, and the justification for Dellarobia's protracted set of inner conflicts surrounding climate change comes into focus. Late in the novel, she converses with Julia, Ovid Byron's wife, who informs her that "once you're talking identity, you can't just lecture that out of people. The condescension of outsiders won't diminish it. That just galvanizes it," to which Dellarobia responds: "Christ on the cross. . . . The rebel flag on mudflaps, science illiteracy. That would be us" (395). Dellarobia's response suggests that southerners (including, implicitly, herself) must follow a similarly gradual course to her own in accepting climate change, and that the tardiness of that response is tied up in local associations: the history of southern rebellion and education, among other things. In this moment, briefly, remnants that make little sense on their own (butterflies, Confederate flags, bored southern housewives, unseasonable rain) align into a constellation of meaning when viewed on the other side of the interface of the page. The fragments left behind by the narrative of ruin become, briefly, comprehension.

———

Flight Behavior constitutes what Mayer calls a "risk narrative of anticipation," which distinguishes itself from the "risk narrative of catastrophe" insofar as it deals with the unknown, the uncertain, the yet-to-be ("Exploration" 25). In fact, uniting the fragments of meaning that *Flight Behavior* scatters over its length would seem to be the bailiwick of the dystopian and postapocalyptic novel, in which the ultimate effects of the dire warnings issued by the narrative of anticipation are displayed. As Frank Kermode writes in *The Sense of an Ending*, "an end will bestow upon the whole duration and meaning," and the two postclimate southern novels I am about to discuss suggest potential futures in which the contemporary South and its burgeoning environmental challenges gain legibility only within a wholly shattered landscape.[10] Significantly, both of these texts are oriented toward young adult readers, and both center around young, independent female protagonists. This is not coincidental, however; Greta Gaard has written that young adult literature "seems many steps closer [than typical cli-fi] toward providing an accurate portrayal of climate change causes and interventions" in part due to its involvement of the "poor women, rural women and women of color who are most affected by global climate change effects . . . it is women who are working as grassroots heroes to mitigate and adapt to the results of a global environmental crisis created by the world's elites, largely, white men" (175, 177). Similarly, the authors of a 2007 Australian study of linkages between pedagogy and speculative climate-change fiction conclude that "speculative and aesthetic milieus have the capacity to support children as practitioners capable of producing finely tuned research outputs that are steeped in the culture of the minor, the aberrant, the nomadic, and the geomorphic. Crucial to this argument is the reconsideration of children as researchers, as artists, as writers, as scientists, and as philosophers who are intimately attuned to planetary changes" (Rousell et al., 668). If climate fiction is not too young a genre to have developed a canon, we might observe that, broadly speaking, the hero of the canonical cli-fi novel is a white man, typically a scientist, who must perform great feats of strength and intellect to combat the hazards posed by the changing climate.[11] In contrast, the novels that I will discuss next present far more diverse heroes who, despite their strength and will, are forced into positions of vulnerability and peril, finding themselves forced to react to the fragmentation of their homes and cultures.

Sherri Smith's *Orleans* (2013) opens with a list of fictional hurricanes that struck (or would strike) New Orleans in the second decade of the twenty-first century, assigning various casualty counts to each; from the beginning of the novel, we are firmly in the realm of speculative fiction. The "Declaration of Separation" adopted by Congress that dissolves the states of Florida, Alabama, Georgia, Louisiana, and Texas as political entities, also provided in the first few pages, notes that "the shape of our great nation has been altered irrevocably by Nature, and now Man must follow suit" (7). This "irrevocable alteration" sets the tone for the remainder of *Orleans*, which features a sunken future city (the

"New" is dropped in the novel to create the postclimate "Orleans") beset by plague, walled off from the rest of the (former) state, and roamed by bands of murderous thieves intent on stealing their rivals' blood to mitigate the effects of the disease. The plot of the novel centers on the quest of a teenaged Black girl, Fen de la Guerre, to transport an orphaned infant across the ruined city to safety in the wake of the massacre of her home tribe. She is joined by Daniel, a biologist from outside the wall, who is seeking a cure for the disease afflicting Orleans. Through the character of Daniel the reader perceives much of the transformed landscape of the city independently of the context that Fen could provide. To Daniel, Orleans is an uncanny space, eerily mingling elements of departed human life and riotous nonhuman nature: "They moved into the Garden District, where the city had gone to seed, a cancerous jungle. Lush garden courtyards had burst like tumors, swallowing their outer buildings whole. Entire families had perished in some of those buildings, drowned in their attics or consumed by Fever in their beds. Their remains fed the madly flourishing bougainvillea and morning glory vines, even in early winter. The streets were quiet, waiting. Daniel shuddered. Orleans was a living city of the dead" (162–163). If the Garden District becomes a literal garden in the postclimate world of *Orleans*, it is decidedly not an idyllic one. Rather, nature is described in afflicted terms: the jungle is "cancerous" and the courtyards are devouring "tumors." The profusion of vegetal life leads Daniel to reflect on the city's quasi-undead status, simultaneously harboring life and death.[12] In explaining the city to Daniel, Fen similarly employs uncanny language that emphasizes the thin boundary between the living and the dead: "this ain't always been marshland. There be houses under here, silt and mud on top. Acting like a natural levee for us, but used to be somebody's home. Now it be they crypt. Things inside them houses float up in a rainstorm. Furniture, food bones. You name it" (225). Though the city is merely a remnant of its former self, it remains, paradoxically, vital and continuously growing.

The same could be said of the cultural landscape of *Orleans*, in which familiar landmarks and traditions alike are broken and scattered. Fen, who is old enough to remember the unsunken city, gives snippets of historical data: "what once been a green hill now be a beach dune made of debris—everything from washing machines to refrigerators and old cars been hauled and dumped here . . . But the land gave way when the river rose, and the junk be left behind. Daddy used to say you could give a history of the place just by looking at those layers of trash" (13). Like the houses that double as tombs, the environment of *Orleans* is fabricated from scraps of the preclimate world, which Fen can only recall with nostalgia. She remembers, for example, that the New Orleans residents "could dance like the city, and sing like the city, and love like the city was loved by the sky and the sea. It was the *people* who made the city of New Orleans" (35). Fen's recollection, however, is inadequate to the task of piecing together the assorted remnants of New Orleans's cultural identity that she and Daniel encounter as they make their way across the city. Instead, she regards them as oddities held over from a more complete era, shreds of ritual and performance that lack context. This is most evident when the pair observes a group of revelers dressed in Mardi Gras regalia promenading through the streets. In a rare expository passage, Fen explains what she knows of the tradition to Daniel: "That first year after [Hurricane] Jesus, when it been looking like we dead, that when the first krewe start. Somebody found an old Mardi Gras warehouse or something, and he pull out some costumes and go riding through the streets. Just one man holding up a lantern, saying 'We still here, we still here, thank Lord almighty, we still here' . . . And every year, when the season for storms be over, somebody get out there and take up a torch and find theyselves a horse and do it all over again" (171–173). Fen seems to have an inkling of the procession symbolizing the endurance of traditions and the rehabilitation of a vanished culture, but lacks the necessary context to link the parade to New Orleanian culture; for her, the ritual has taken on a wholly new connotation of survival against harsh environmental conditions. The Mardi Gras celebration has become unmoored in time (as Fen reveals, it happens at the close of hurricane season every year) and memory, drifting in the text as a remnant that the characters cannot fully explain. The reader, however, presumably being acquainted with the tradition, recognizes it within the text as bearing much more historical significance than either character can bestow upon it.

Paul Dobraszczyk has written of the cognitive dissonance experienced by urban residents in the postclimate "sunken city," noting that, though they tend to live "lives we can barely imagine, they nevertheless draw those lives firmly within the orbit of the familiar," as evidenced by the prominent appearance of recognizable landmarks and fragments of the preapocalyptic world (872). In this sense, though climate fictions "project the city forward in time," they also "draw readers back into the world they inhabit in the present, a world that is already set on a future course that they will . . . play a part in bringing into being" (874). The lesson contained in climate fiction, as in all apocalyptic literature, is intended for the reader rather than the characters; while the latter can merely behold ruination, the former possesses the context necessary to identify and understand it, or perhaps even take steps to avoid it. The fragments themselves, the bits of southern landscapes and cultures that surface sporadically throughout *Orleans*, are placed in the uncanny position of signifying meaning without possessing it, a troubled epistemological position that Gerry Canavan attempts to articulate in a 2014 volume: "'When we contemplate ruins,' Christopher Woodward writes, 'we contemplate our own future'; the apocalypse is thereby transformed into a memory, an event that is yet to come but which has also somehow, paradoxically, already happened" (11–12). If the characters in *Orleans* are tasked with the difficult proposition of survival in the hostile city, the reader is similarly required to derive insights and intelligence about their own, undrowned, world from the text's ruins.

———

The final novel that I would like to discuss, Omar El Akkad's *American War* (2017), opens with precisely the same images of ruination that Canavan discusses. Benjamin Chestnut, the nephew of protagonist Sarat Chestnut, insists in the book's opening frame-narrative that "this isn't a story about war. It's about ruin," and, fittingly, the novel takes place well after the conclusion of its titular conflict, a second Civil War fought over fossil fuels, banned in the northern states but still used in the South (6). Benjamin assumes the mantle of the text's historian, sorrowfully reflecting on the fact that "an entire region decided to wage war again, to sever itself from the Union rather than stop using that illicit fuel responsible for so much of the country's misfortune" (18). Benjamin's summary simplifies the matter somewhat, however; more than simple recalcitrance, the South's decision to secede is motivated by economic depression brought on by the decay of the oil economy in Texas and Louisiana and the massive infrastructural problems incurred by large-scale migration away from the drowned coast (South Louisiana is entirely gone, and Florida reduced to a scattered archipelago).[13] What remains of these vanished locales is, as in *Orleans*, an uncanny assemblage of fragments that contain only illegible memories of the past:

> For decades, the governments of the state and the country spent billions trying to save lower Louisiana from the encroaching seas—building hundreds of miles of seawalls, levees, raised causeways, and even,

toward the end, floating towns. . . . All that remained now were the entrails of that long-subsumed world and the futile efforts to preserve it: thin strips of asphalt that disappeared at high tide, ghost towns propped on man-made hills, crumbling bridges that nosedived into the water. Scattered among the islands that remained, these things stood as ruins and like all ruins were in their own way grotesque, a transgression against the passage of time (55).

El Akkad's description of the over-engineered solutions to the rising ocean are entirely consistent with flood and riparian management in South Louisiana as detailed in the previous chapter, and similarly motivated by the "optimistic notion that with enough concrete and dirt and pride and money the low country could be saved" (55). However, it is the description of the ruins themselves that is most striking about this passage; El Akkad's figurative language moves through several different tenors over the course of only a few sentences, enhancing the impression of disorientation and fragmentation that the ruins evoke. Organic metaphors—the "entrails" of the submerged buildings"—mix with antique "ghost towns" and speculative "floating towns," all contributing to the "grotesque" character of the place.

American War treats the topic of southernness and its cultural remnants in a significantly broader sense than *Orleans*, despite Benjamin's assertion that these "impotent trinkets of rebellion, touchstones of a ruined and ruinous past" are better forgotten (3). Early in the text, while her family resides at a refugee camp near Memphis, Sarat apprentices herself to an older man named Albert Gaines, one of the few keepers of southern history in the postwar world, who unravels "the old mythology of her people," revealing ". . . the South of Spanish moss and palmetto fronds . . . of whole pigs smoked whole days and of peaches and pecans and key lime pie. [Sarat] gorged on it all, delighted not only that such a world existed but that she held to it some ancestral claim . . . He said that her country once occupied the most fertile land in all of the world; mother of sugar and mother of cotton and mother of corn" (135). The environmental and culinary realm presented in this passage is overtly nostalgic, and even as Gaines sets the idyllic scene, the text dismisses much of his speech as "pleasant fantasy." Though the reader likely can identify the Arcadian region of plenty that Gaines describes as a fabrication, Sarat lacks the necessary context to doubt his words; for her, the prewar South becomes an idealized, "ancestral claim." Gaines's speech also trades in the literary over-emphasis on taste as a vehicle of visceral associations, as noted in an earlier chapter, with its invocation of "whole pigs smoked whole days," "peaches," "pecans," "key lime pie," "sugar," and "corn." Furthermore, Sarat does not simply receive these details, she "gorge[s]" on them, a verb that is usually reserved for eating. It is only much later in her life, after becoming thoroughly disenchanted with the southern cause, that she begins to doubt this affiliation. As the plot of the novel unspools, an escalating cycle of violence perpetrated against and by Sarat and her family leaves her embittered, unwilling to choose a side in an ongoing conflict (the guerilla warfare enacted by southern partisans against the northern army) that she increasingly regards as having no moral victor. Eventually, her desire for revenge leads to her volunteering to release a toxic virus at a ceremony commemorating the cessation of hostilities between the factions, an action that, the book informs us, leads to more than 100 million casualties.

American War, though it gestures toward many of the didactic environmental messages of postapocalyptic literature and postclimate fiction, is ultimately more concerned with the ethics of suffering and torture than the overuse and depletion of fossil fuels that headlines the conflict.[14] Sarat, by the end of the novel, simply wishes to inflict as much damage on as many people as possible, regardless of their political or environmental affiliation; after being praised by a southern general for her impending act of nihilistic patriotism, she responds: "Fuck the South. . . . Fuck the South and everything it stands for" (313). The book strongly implies, from Benjamin's assertion in its initial pages that the story is about "ruin" rather than "war," that there are no definitive moral imperatives that characters in such extreme circumstances can follow; though Sarat spends her early life believing in the cause and liberation of the South, by the end (following the death of most of her family and an extended and graphically described bout of torture at a Guantanamo-esque detention facility in the Florida archipelago) she realizes that such ideals are moot in the postapocalyptic world. The meaning of "the South," she eventually realizes, is not rebellion but simple ruination, a quality than can have no ethical response. This is alluded to through her conversations with Gaines, during which she asks why the southern guerillas are nicknamed "the Reds," which she assumed stemmed from the first Civil War: "Gaines said [the name] was older than all that, older than the country itself. He said it was about the dirt: in the South there's a mineral in the ground that turns the dirt red. He said when you've leached all the good from the earth, all the nutrients that a seedling needs to grow, the last thing left is the stuff that turns the dirt red. She wondered now if maybe that was the only honest thing he'd ever told her" (307). This rather remarkable passage holds clear implications for the dissolution of Sarat's earlier conception of the South as a mythical land of plenty (as the final sentence overtly points out), marking the region as environmentally impoverished and depleted. Moreover, it subverts the narratives circulated throughout the text (in the form of, among other things, faux-historical documents, public speeches, and newspaper clippings politicizing the conflict) of the second Civil War as a political, economic, or moral concern. Rather, the war finds its genesis in destitution, a desperate struggle for survival in the wake of environmental devastation. The seeming simplicity of its central conflict (North vs. South; environmentalism vs. waste) in its early pages belies the ideologically fragmented, chaotic state in which the characters find themselves later in the novel—though the South appears unitary at first, a political cause and a distinct region, its eventual presence is wholly spectral, a collection of remnants that the reader must parse rather than a viable home for the text's subjects.

Benjamin, writing from the shores of (comparatively climate-immune) Anchorage, Alaska, sees in Sarat's story nothing but these fragments, waste, and "ruin," a metaphor that he repeatedly invokes. And, for the characters of American War, this does seem to be the case; the novel's decentralized conception of evil and its protagonist's susceptibility to narratives of violent vengeance would seem to preclude even the moral sanctimony of the ruin-narrative. Put simply: nobody in American War seems to learn a lesson from the phenomenally bloody and painful events of the novel, with the possible exception of Benjamin, who learns only that the wisest course of action, when surrounded by chaos and violence, is to flee to Alaska. From the reader's contemporary position in the midst of the events that give rise to the theorized future of the novel, however, American War's suspicion toward nationalist and authoritarian environmental messaging and its ambivalence toward the moral implications of taking such stands (as Sarat learns, painfully, over the course of the text) holds relevance. Such applicability is likely not sufficient, in itself, to avert the ruination of the world, but it may offer a notion of how to survive it.

———

The common theme of these three novels seems to be the incapacity of humans to fully comprehend the widespread effects of climate change—in fact, what distinguishes postclimate fiction from the broader category of postapocalyptic fiction is likely its *lack* of the sort of definitive answers that we expect from the latter. Rather than a definite revelation or a call to action, *Orleans* and *American War* would seem to offer only an affirmation that the menacing implications of *Flight Behavior* do, indeed, have world-altering potential. Johns-Putra has noted a tendency in climate fiction toward techniques that "undermine the omniscience of third-person narrators and the reliability of focalizers in a move that simultaneously interrogates realist, imperialist, and anthropocentric constructions of the world" ("The Rest Is Silence" 33). Recent climate fiction's suspicion of definitive, hierarchically arranged knowledge systems (such as those embodied by the scientist-heroes of earlier climate fiction) and tendency toward narrators who lack complete knowledge of science, history, or politics lead naturally to those texts lacking effective syntheses of the fragmented environments that their characters traverse. Instead, those same characters are forced to attempt to comprehend environmental catastrophes without the context that would enable them to craft a complete narrative of their unfolding. Thus, protagonists in both pre- and postclimate fiction typically present fragmentary stories with many missing pieces, uncovering stray bits of previous cultures and histories without recognizing them. If we *expect* the sort of answers from these texts that postapocalyptic fiction is *supposed* to provide, we do not get them. The climate apocalypse, it would seem, is both catastrophic and deeply confusing.

Yet I would argue that the intent of such an aesthetic move is not to suggest that climate change constitutes an immutable and ineffable ruin-narrative; Lawrence Buell notes that such an attitude "undergirds much environmental passivity and quiet desperation today" and in fact "already is being used to help escort us further and further into catastrophe" (Skrimshire 30–31). Rather, these fictions all place the onus of countering such a narrative upon the reader rather than the characters themselves by fragmenting the known world, forcing a reconstitution of what the contemporary reader knows to be true. Resilience, in the present, consists of acknowledging the climate-ruin detailed in the text (and, perhaps, already too familiar to the reader) yet also gathering the remnants of local history, culture, and custom that persist into a recognizable whole. Such a process establishes a dialogue between ruin and resilience, informing the reader of what is necessitated by one fiction of the future or another: what remains of the old world, what meanings persist and which are discarded, and what may be required of those meanings in the world to come.

SIX

No Straight Lines in Nature

The Fantasy of Return in
Postapocalyptic Southern Literature

He will not go behind his father's saying,
And he likes having thought of it so well
He says again, 'Good fences make good neighbors.'
— ROBERT FROST,
"Mending Wall"

IN ROBERT FROST'S FAMILIAR POEM "Mending Wall," the speaker's can-
tankerous neighbor, resistant to the notion of dismantling the outdated and
crumbling titular structure, gives the curt aphorism "good fences make good
neighbors" as the only hint to his predilections. The speaker, a self-described
maker of mischief, attempts to bait the taciturn man, playfully assuring him
that the wall is unnecessary. It does not keep livestock out or in; it draws
meaningless distinctions between divisions (the speaker's apple trees and his
neighbor's pines) that already exist in nature; maintaining it is a tedious and
repetitive task insofar as it is perpetually being disassembled by hunters or,
perhaps, the speaker suggests in a fit of frivolity, "elves." His interlocutor is
unswayed, and, in a rather stunning reversal of tone, the formerly lighthearted
poem casts him as a menacing force of nature: "Bringing a stone grasped
firmly by the top / In each hand, like an old-stone savage armed. / He moves
in darkness as it seems to me, / Not of woods only and the shade of trees."
As is frequently the case with Frost's poetry, whimsical portraits of rural life
conceal deep and terrifying existential reckonings—the wall, in this instance,
serving as a nearly empty signifier that nonetheless acts as the boundary be-

tween the modern, liberated self and the primal Hobbesian survivor. On the other side of the symbolic wall is an unknowable chaos, the "darkness" that is "not of woods only."

Though Frost's poetry stands upon a bedrock of hard-bitten, laconic New England mannerisms, the South, too, has always been a place of walls. There are, of course, the literal walls that any society aspiring to empire constructs: the Civil War forts and redoubts, the massive seacoast citadels. Distinct from these, though serving a similar function, are the whitewashed walls of the Big House and its contemporary counterpart, the massive red-brick designer homes spreading concentrically around Atlanta, Birmingham, Charlotte— walls that insist upon and reinforce the region's unwritten social laws of discrimination, using distance and perfect vertical planes to effect hierarchies of race, class, religion, and place of origin. Walls that exist on maps—the Ohio River, the Mississippi, the Fall Line, the Gulf Coast, the Appalachians—and walls that don't: the color line, the poverty line, lines of descent, lines of migration. And, of course, the ideological wall (always shifting, never, in the postmodern period, stable) by which the region defines itself, the wall between "northern" and "southern," or, frequently, "the South" and "everywhere else."

One means of conceptualizing southern environmentalism from the dawn of modernity to the Anthropocene is the large-scale collapse or decay of such walls. The seemingly impervious "wall" of the Big Woods in Faulkner's short stories yields to the timber industry; levees are overwhelmed in *Their Eyes Were Watching God;* roads penetrate the insular and isolated spaces of Welty's and O'Connor's fiction. These collapsing walls signify, on the one hand, the whelming of old structures by a new uncertainty, the dissolution of an (often fantasized) idea of order, even an injurious and outdated order, into the unparseable flotsam of the remnant South. The southern ruin-narrative believes in the irreparability of such structures; restoring the Big Woods, or permanently securing Belle Glade with a new, impermeable barrier, is as impossible as traveling back in time. The breach of the wall is an act of finality, and the only available course of action following its collapse is that of acceptance and surrender—the path followed by the Missing Person in Russell's "The Gondoliers." The narrative of southern environmental resilience, by contrast, regards the collapse of boundaries as change rather than tragedy, vowing to move on and adapt to the new world. This approach embraces complexity, acknowledges the necessity of change, and leaves anything that is too heavy to carry behind.

However, in southern literature (and, indeed, in much of the region's environmental and social policy) there is a contrary notion that defies both the finality of the ruin-narrative and flexibility of resilience: the notion that the collapse of walls is an opportunity to reestablish the same boundaries, to reinforce the barrier rather than abandon it. This is the fantasy of return that the tall convict totemizes in "Old Man," the notion that, after the wall's collapse, the clock can essentially be reset, with the convict resuming his predisaster life uninterrupted. Yet, while the tall convict's quest is treated quixotically, even (as I have argued elsewhere) satirically, the concept of return, of responding to rapid environmental change by remaining in familiar landscapes and fortifying—or quarantining—them against the trajectory of the world at large, has been proposed repeatedly in southern fiction. Do good fences make good neighbors in the era of rapid change and radical uncertainty heralded by the Anthropocene? Is the fantasy of return simply a fantasy, or can it be a valid alternative to the despair of the ruin-narrative and the uncertainty of resilience?

In this chapter, I will begin by presenting several instances from recent southern literature that respond to sudden and dramatic environmental change by placing walls between themselves and the forces of change, destruction, and anxiety: William Forstchen's *One Second After* (2009), Pat Frank's *Alas, Babylon* (1959), Holly Goddard-Jones's *The Salt Line* (2017), and Michael Farris Smith's *Rivers* (2014). All of these texts might be called speculative fiction, which Finola Prendergast claims is "better equipped than realism to depict climate change," and, indeed, the latter two novels vividly portray the rising waters and rapidly changing ecosystems of a postclimate South (341). However, the former two novels seem altogether more concerned with threats to the United States as a political entity than with threats to the country or region's environment, and Forstchen's novel is overtly suspicious of environmentalist causes. Yet Frank and Forstchen's novels also depict the only walls that remain nominally intact in spite of what their authors avowedly perceive to be a clear and present threat to the integrity of the country: the deployment of technologically advanced weaponry by hostile states. As such, they fulfill what Jimmie Killingsworth and Jacqueline Palmer designate as the archetypal function of postapocalyptic narrative, which "reflects and builds a growing public awareness" and "aims to transform the consciousness that a problem exists into acceptance of action toward a solution" (22). By contrast, *The Salt Line* and *Rivers* are hesitant to proscribe any solutions at all, whether pre- or postapocalypse. However, despite their widely varying ideologies and proposed scenarios, all of these texts fantasize a return to an earlier means of habitation in the South, an opportunity to start over.

———

In its simplest form, the fantasy of return in southern literature is little more than a somewhat more cynical flavor of white American pastoralism, presenting idyllic small towns replete with local color yet menaced by the encroaching specter of modernity. In a text such as *One Second After*, for example, the setting of Black Mountain, North Carolina, is repeatedly compared to a Norman Rockwell painting in the text in an attempt to conjure a romanticized vision of the South, a "sleepy southern mountain hamlet" transformed by the construction of Interstate 40 into a tourist destination: "with the road had come development, traffic, and the floods of tourists on weekends that the chamber of commerce loved and everyone else tried to tolerate" (7). As we have seen in the work of O'Connor and Welty, southern transportation infrastructure can serve as a means of interrogating rapid changes in the character of human relationships with the environment. If *One Second After* is aware of the intricacies of southern history, however, it deals with those notions only in caricature. Women in Black Mountain, we learn, "were addressed as 'ma'am' and doors were held open for them, no matter what their age. If a man spoke inappropriately to a woman in public and another man was nearby, there would be a fight brewing" (39). The catastrophe *du jour* in *One Second After* is the presumptive detonation of an EMP (electromagnetic pulse) weapon above the continental United States, rendering the majority of electronic devices in the country useless. "Boom, and everything electronic in your house is fried, especially delicate stuff with microcircuitry in it," John Matherson, the protagonist, explains.[1] However, the townsfolk quickly discover that certain machines are still functional, all of them predating microchips. John theorizes that the older technologies are immune because "there were no solid-state electronics back in the 1940s, everything was still vacuum tubes" (71). The novel, in nearly enough senses to warrant the use of "literally," thus turns back the world's clock fifty years to a society in which values today perceived as "old-fashioned" become the uniting principles of civilization.

In a novel as nationalist and politically reactionary as this one (the novel's conclusion features a group of patriotic survivors gazing appreciatively at the American flag flying from a military vehicle sent to rescue them), such posturing serves to imagine a community (in Benedict Anderson's terms) defined by social norms and inscribed by gender and, implicitly, race. John Matherson is initiated into this community when he takes a few potshots with a rifle at a band of rednecks sent to haze him; later, when he encounters one of his interlocutors at a bar, the local shakes his hand and proclaims "this Yankee boy's OK." John reflects: "Damn, even then he did love the South" (50). The region appears in the text as a shorthand for a set of homosocial white male values that have been eroded by modernity and which the sudden apocalypse enables to proliferate once more. In short, *One Second After* seems to reincarnate, nearly a hundred years after its inception, many of the most reviled stereotypes of southern pastoralism: the region as a naturally bountiful and socially harmonious zone that embodies the best aspects of an older, distinctly racially homogenous, chivalric age. John and his narrow social group move to fortify the Black Mountain community against raiders by erecting barriers crafted from now-useless automobiles; their conflicts with neighboring towns are compared to skirmishes between "Yankees" and "Rebels," and the final battle is described as "like something from the Civil War" (426). The wall in this novel is thus couched in terms of a barrier between the values of the South and those of the North, or at least the old and new Souths, in language that would not have been unfamiliar to the Agrarians and neo-Agrarians of the past century.

The wall in *One Second After* thus provides a method for distilling simplicity out of chaos, of drawing a distinct and impermeable boundary between a pastoralized southern space and a surrounding world of chaos and confusion. However, despite its general hostility toward environmentalism (Forstchen inserts a scene in which John cruises through Asheville and makes disparaging remarks about "the hippies"), the novel's enclosure of a fantasized pastoral space enables some degree of new eco-awareness. In addition to John's distaste toward the interstate, he understands the toxic effects of the meat industry upon communities and animals, the fragility of supply lines, and the alienation of products from production. He reflects:

> There were hog farms just two hundred miles east of here. They were contemptible, usually rammed into poorer communities, five to ten thousand hogs raised at a clip in sheds where they could barely move from birth until slaughter, the stench and pollution killing property value for miles around. . . . The farms were dependent on hundreds of tons of feed being shipped in each week. If those farms had not already

been looted, the waste going on was most likely beyond imagining. The animals would be starving to death, and people who were used to thinking meat was grown inside a pink foam package would now be trying to chase a hog down, kill it, and dress it. (330)

Despite the red herring concerning property values (an economic index largely made irrelevant by the apocalypse), John's observations here are in line with the well-known and devastating environmental effects of the meat industry in central North Carolina.[2] He notes that such toxic facilities are frequently located in politically disenfranchised lower-class regions (a la Bob Bullard's *Dumping in Dixie*) and rely upon unsustainable networks of supply and demand. And, by the conclusion of the text, he is admiring a group of liberal college students—"the granola crew," whom he notes "were mildly disdained before 'The Day,'" for their foraging skills: "knowing which roots to dig, which plants could be brewed into teas, which had some medicinal value" (387). In a rare pastoral postapocalyptic scene, John watches two such students gathering edible foliage, remarking that "the boy and girl looked like some Rousseau ideal, a fantasy of the way the world was supposed to be if civilization went awry" (388). John's ideal rebirth, for all its thinly disguised heteronormativity, nonetheless suggests that times of great necessity provide a newfound attention to the natural world. However, this is "environmentalism" only in the sense that a book of poetry is valuable as kindling; John seems to have a sense of practicality, but no essential environmental ethic. What the construction of the wall permits, then, is an easy collapse of not only social, but also environmental complexity. The fantasy of return enacted by *One Second Later* permits only "useful" conceptions of nature, just as it allows only one particularly narrow vision of humanity.

What happens when the fantasy of return is enacted in a setting where nonhuman nature plays a larger role? Pat Frank's *Alas, Babylon* (1959) situates a human response to a worldwide nuclear strike in the fictional town of Fort Repose, Florida, based loosely on the town of Mt. Dora north of Orlando and so named because of the "balmy weather and idyllic life" observed by one of the region's pioneers (11). The environment in *Alas, Babylon* is more of an active force than in *One Second After*, distinguishing itself from the less torrid climates to the north; one local resident predicts that some new arrivals to the town from Cleveland will prove inadequate to the demands of the place: "Mrs. McGovern she can't 'bide bugs or little green lizards and she won't go out of the house after dark for fear of snakes. I don't think the McGoverns going to be with us long . . . because what's Florida except bugs and lizards and snakes? I think they leave around May, when bug season starts good" (10). When the nuclear strike wipes out the surrounding larger cities, leaving Fort Repose without electricity or supplies from the outside world, one character gazes into the surrounding vegetation and predicts that "in a few more months the jungle will take over" (211). The characters of *Alas, Babylon* have to contend with and utilize their environment in a way that the protagonists of *One Second After* never seem to conceive of—as providing the raw material for a new society in which civilization had "retreated a hundred years" (144). The family of Randy Bragg, around whom the majority of the plot rotates, harvests citrus from their property and, with the aid of a neighboring poor white family, constructs a system of irrigation. Randy bends his efforts toward uniting the townsfolk and establishing organized systems of hunting and gathering from the wilderness.

The walls in Frank's novel are not, as in other postapocalyptic media, formed out of the physical wreckage of the vanished world, but are rather construed from Fort Repose's isolation; when the bombs fall, all of the nearby Floridian cities are leveled, leaving the residents of the town to fend for themselves. Despite the lack of tangible barriers, the residents of Fort Repose rapidly develop a prejudice toward "outsiders," most of whom seem to be desperate, murderous bandits, and Randy soon declares martial law and arms the populace. Though a similar masculinist impulse seems to drive the protagonists of *Alas, Babylon* and *One Second After,* the former does not so much cling to race and class homogeneity as minimize such distinctions in the postnuclear landscape. In a manner similar to the dissolution of class boundaries between the Braggs and their redneck neighbors, the political history of the region becomes largely obviated. At the beginning of the novel, Randy is a distinct gradualist, believing that "integration should start in Florida, but it must begin in the nursery schools and kindergartens and would take a generation" (8). In the days following the attack, however, such concerns become immaterial. "The economics of disaster placed a penalty upon prejudice," the narrator notes as Randy watches a Black resident of Fort Repose, "a brace of chickens dangling from his belt, drink water, presumably boiled, from a Negro's jug. There were two drinking fountains in Marines Park, one marked 'White Only,' the other 'Colored Only.' Since neither worked, the signs were meaningless" (191).

Similarly, Fort Repose's prejudices and ignorance toward the environment itself—the residents' inability to hunt, fish, and grow food—are steadily overcome in order to ensure the community's survival; features of the environment that once were obstacles become instruments of survival. Florida's perennial problems with invasive species, for example, are metonymized by the proliferation of armadillos in the text and across the state; after escaping from a roadside zoo, the creatures immediately begin "undermining golf greens and dumping over citrus trees from St. Augustine to Palm Beach" (259). The apocalypse hastens the spread of the species owing to the fact that they have "no natural enemies in the state except automobiles," which are in short supply following the nuclear bombardment; Randy predicts that "soon there [will] be more armadillos than people in Florida" (259). The creatures, however, soon become a vital food source for the survivors, in a rare instance of practical and environmental needs aligning. Florida, arguably one of the most threatened and least environmentally inclined of all of the states in the days prior to the apocalypse, becomes (more due, in the text, to its temperate climate and explosive plant and animal life than any human factors, it is worth noting) a place in which humans can create new manners and methods of survival out of the mistakes of the past.[3] At the close of the novel, some remnants of the US military arrive in Fort Repose and offer to transport the survivors to safety, but the community refuses, preferring to remain within the boundaries of the society they have built. It is implied that the small, organic society that Fort Repose has become is, though humble, preferable to the governance of the failed US state.

The walls in both *One Second After* and *Alas, Babylon* prove ultimately to be effective; as in many socially conservative fantasies of return, the community is saved by the ingenuity, resourcefulness, and wise management of heroic white men of action—specifically, the type of "action" oftentimes marginalized by contemporary liberal life: chivalric attitudes toward women, racial and cultural homogeneity, a distrust toward technology, an emphasis on nuclear familial units, possession of significant quantities of firearms, etc. The implication in these novels is that the fantasy of return is a fantasy of liberation from the present, an opportunity to resurrect those "virtues" of violence, survivalism, heterosexuality, and a primitive communion with nature that have been quashed by the technologically mediated and socially progressive modern age. Though the process of doing so is never simple or comfortable— on the contrary, both of these novels contain frequent descriptions of extreme suffering and cruelty—there is nonetheless the implication here that naturally regenerative southern landscapes, enhanced and protected by vanished codes of southern custom wielded by heroic white masculine protagonists, can bring about a return to a more productive relationship between humans and nature than "civilized" society enjoys today. This process only transpires in isolated and fortified pockets, however, behind walls patrolled by those same protagonists; the presence of the wall permits the fantasy of return to be phrased as a necessity, as resilience. Petty human concerns vanish in the face of the impulse to survive: political distinctions become unimportant, racial, cultural, and class difference is a non-issue, nature becomes purely instrumental. The fantasy of return is not simply the fantasy of a return to nature; it is a full-fledged retreat into an imagined vision of the past, made possible by impermeable and vigilantly guarded walls.

———

If the wall in southern postapocalyptic fiction represents a regressive return to a pastoralized southern landscape, then, what goes on beyond the wall? Holly Goddard-Jones's *The Salt Line*, set in what was once North Carolina (but which is referred to throughout, along with its neighboring states, as the "Atlantic Zone") at an indeterminate date in the future, attempts to answer this question. Civilization in the Zones (in addition to the Atlantic, the Midwest and Gulf Zones play a role, with zones in New England and the Pacific coast mentioned as well), we learn, has walled itself off from much of the interior United States on account of the latter becoming infested with ticks carrying the deadly Shreve's Disease. Beyond the barrier (the titular Salt Line), freed from human influence, biotic communities have undergone a rapid revitalization, giving rise to a pocket industry in nature tours beyond the Line. The novel opens, in fact, with Andy, a representative of Outer Limits Excursions, one such tour agency, enticing a group of customers about to embark on a voyage into what once was Great Smoky Mountains National Park with promises of sublime natural beauty:

> You can go see the things your great-great grandparents took for
> granted, that are available to you now only in photographs or simulations. Sunrise from a rock precipice. A hawk circling over your head.
> Trout bellies in a mountain stream. You can listen to cold water dripping
> from the ceiling of a cave, and you can see deer flipping up their white

tails at you before dashing between trees and out of sight . . . you can hike across hillsides covered in reds, golds, and oranges, the scale of which—I promise you—is like nothing you've ever seen before (8).

Andy employs many of the common rhetorical flourishes of nature writing: the concatenation of several striking images that never appear in conjunction with each other (deer are seldom found in caves, for instance), the triangulation of several sensory registers (the sight of a hawk, the feeling of trouts' bellies, the sound of dripping water), and an invocation—twice—of the singularity of the experience, inaccessible in the present and irreproducible by any similar set of stimuli. And, indeed, the sight of the woods beyond the Salt Line is enough to captivate the pilgrims. Edie, one of the narrators, remarks rapturously on "the trees! The ones at home were mostly young, thirty or forty years on the top end, and though there were, in the parks, some of the larger species, the oaks and the cedars, the inner-zone trend was toward small, slim, and ornamental: Japanese maples, crepe myrtle, dogwoods, redbuds. . . . But these outer-zone trees climbed stories" (81). Nature, it seems, has wasted no time in transforming what were once heavily populated areas into sublime vistas. Edie sees rotted telephone poles "leaning under the freight of snarled green vines that dripped down, touched the ground, and rolled off in waves across the surrounding hillsides. Kudzu . . . the scale of it—how much the green sea of vines had consumed—was beautiful and terrifying."[4]

Moreover, *The Salt Line* seems to suggest that the rejuvenation of the southern wilderness has essentially effaced all remnants of "manufactured" or commercial southern culture while leaving its more treasured and "traditional" elements intact. This is made evident when the group of pilgrims pauses at a former rest stop along their tour, now, as Andy states, nothing more than a "museum." The travelers peer in confusion at the roadside stop: "Wes Feingold, shoulders hunched as he leaned in for a better look, raised a hand and said, 'What's a cracker barrel?' 'Beats me,' said Andy. 'But this place was a restaurant with a little store attached, part of a big chain of them'" (83). True to form, the roadside emporium contains a startling array of mass-produced trinkets of dubious provenance and use: "a set of plates glazed with the old American flag pattern," boxes of porcelain dolls marked "Elegant Christmas Angel," and decorative china printed with "a portrait of a long-ago British royal family and their handsome children" (85). Faced with this kaleidoscope of late-capitalist flotsam, Edie finds it difficult to conceive of "the person—the people—who would patronize a place like this, an Old Country Store, but also cared enough about the British monarchy to purchase a commemorative plate in their honor. It made her suddenly and inexplicably sad" (85). Whatever the contents of the Cracker Barrel might have signified to its earlier customers has been thoroughly extinguished by the time Edie and the other travelers from the Atlantic Zone visit the site, and it remains in the novel simply as a defunct reminder of the consumer economy that once saturated the region, a remnant of the South.

If the defunct Cracker Barrel represents the obsolescence and excision of the South's commercialism, however, the tour's eventual destination (after an unexpected course correction caused by a band of agrarian guerrillas), a secret compound of survivors named Ruby City, mysteriously immune to the diseases rampant beyond the Salt Line, resembles nothing so much as a pastoral ecological commune informed by selected "valuable" aspects of southern culture. The residents of Ruby City reside in "trim, simply made cabins comprised, almost charmingly, of scavenged materials as well as new lumber," on a site "cleared to make room for a scattering of structures, each unique, several beautiful enough to imagine they were somewhere back home, perhaps in one of the posh little eco-communities around the university."[5] The emphasis on posterity, community, and future sustainability that Ruby City embodies completes its recreation of a sterilized, welcoming stereotype of Appalachian life, as Edie feels herself "being lulled: by the festive mood among the Ruby City residents, by the beauty of the evening. By the plate of food she held: shreds of juicy smoked pork, some kind of salad with pickled beets and a bitter green, grilled slices of squash, fry bread. The bluegrass trio—men on standing bass and fiddle, a woman on banjo—played with spirit, and Edie had to make a conscious effort to stop her foot from tapping along with the beat" (181). The Salt Line relies upon a perceived affinity between ecological harmony and other aspects of southern culture such as food and music that are here deployed as a means of celebrating the region independently of its troublesome social and political history.[6] Though the bulk of The Salt Line describes a future dystopia in which nonhuman nature has been largely marginalized in favor of a pervasive technocratic corporate future, it also offers a highly selective, spontaneously reinvented southern ecotopia as a counterpoint.

In The Salt Line, the folksy, racially homogenous, southern ecofriendly lifestyle enjoyed by the residents of Ruby City is nearly impossible for the new arrivals to comprehend; "nature" has, by and large, come to signify alienation and danger for them. Marta confesses at the beginning of the expedition that she "had never craved the great outdoors, never registered the nostalgia others felt for bygone days of national parks and waterfalls and hiking trails," and that even viewing film footage of the countryside beyond the Zones had inspired "not wonder or longing but oppression and vertigo. So many trees, so much variation in the landscape, whole chunks of sky blotted out by jagged precipices—she didn't know how people had ever been able to stand it. Even those startling, high-up views, with the landscape rolling away kilometers into the distance: it was too much" (40–41).[7] *The Salt Line* both theorizes an ecotopian future for the southern region that arises spontaneously, almost miraculously, and insists that, for the thoroughly acclimated visitors from that future world, such a paradise is unrecognizable as such. At first, it seems that only the residents of Ruby City, enjoying a blissful preindustrial village existence, are able to appreciate their situation.

Moreover, *The Salt Line* seems to suggest that the fantasy of return, by virtue of its emergence out of scenarios of apocalyptic waste, represents a false dawn for the South—even if the natural world were suddenly and improbably to recover, the opportunity for cooperation between humans and the revived wilderness has already been lost. This is made clear in the text by several references to a children's book titled *The Shaman and the Salt Line*, which at first appears to be a thinly veiled variation on the tragedy of the commons: a community of hunter-gatherers finds that, upon attempting to move beyond a subsistence lifestyle, their impact on the surrounding environment becomes unsustainable: "The forest, which had been so plentiful and yielding of its resources to the tribespeople, grew stingy and unaccommodating. The clear stream water turned bitter and sat uneasily on the stomach. The blueberries shriveled on the bush. The trees refused to yield to the ax, and the rabbits, when shot and skinned, offered up only the thinnest slivers of meat, which the starving children fought over brutally" (71). The titular shaman advises the doomed humans to "withdraw back to their village, salt the earth in a perimeter around it, and vow only to venture into the woods when the greatest necessity required it" (72). In keeping with the narrative of ruin in the South, *The Salt Line* suggests that there can be no effective recovery of a state of equity with nature once the initial ruination (in this case, overconsumption) has occurred; though "in the forest, the water ran sweet, and the blueberries and rabbits came back in abundance" after the humans forcibly isolated themselves, none of the villagers actually witnessed this, ensconced as they were beyond their protective wall (73). Even the ostensibly idyllic sanctuary of Ruby City is revealed, through a convoluted web of connections, to be a front for the production of highly addictive narcotics for the Zones, and its leader, June, comments dolefully on the fleeting nature of her pastoral community's bond with nature in her observation of the still-changing climate: "By 10:00 a.m. it was hot. Summer hot. . . . Each year June allowed herself to be lulled by the occasional runs of seasonally appropriate days into thinking: well, it's not so bad, maybe. There's hope yet. And then she'd see steam wafting off the kudzu, or she'd forget to wear her bonnet and come home with her neck sunburned again, and the despair would settle on her once more" (242).[8] June realizes that, despite the semblance of harmony that Ruby City represents, the walls that insulate it from planetary environmental issues are ultimately illusory; it remains inextricably connected to the larger world, both in terms of its economic livelihood and much broader ills such as climate change. Sure enough, the Ruby City enclave soon proves more vulnerable than it at first appeared, and is summarily destroyed by the technocrats beyond the Salt Line.

Janet Fiskio calls "utopia and apocalypse" two "mutually constituting" forms (13). Fiskio separates such apocalyptic narratives into "lifeboat" and "collective" methodologies, the first in which "competition for scarce resources requires ruthless decisions" and the latter featuring a more "courageous and generous" cooperative vision of humanity (14). While *The Salt Line* advances the possibility of a "collective" society existing in isolation beyond the titular barrier, Ruby City is ultimately little more than an outgrowth of the "lifeboat" future that lurks beyond the line. Essentially, Goddard-Jones's novel suggests that even a fantasized return of the South to a point where humans once again struggle for survival in the wilderness will not create a single isolated pastoral zone, but simply repress the human impulses and failures that necessitated the walls to begin with.

——— .

The fact that walls, be they physical barriers or more abstract dividing lines, proliferate in apocalyptic and postapocalyptic narratives is not difficult to explain: the ruined world is invariably portrayed as more dangerous than our own, replete with hazards that must be contained. Like Frost's frangible interface between the forces of modern order and primal chaos, postapocalyptic walls seek to create and fortify what remains of civilization against encroaching forces of disorder. Such is certainly the case in Michael Farris Smith's *Rivers* (2014), which images a postclimate future for the South in which the southernmost ninety miles of the Gulf Coast is cut off and quarantined by "the Line," described in the novel as "a geographical boundary that said, We give up. The storms can have it. No more rebuilding and no more reconstruction" (10). North of the Line, it is assumed, the northern United States wage their own battle against ever-more severe storms and floods emerging from the Gulf, but the quarantined area is essentially abandoned to its fate. "The Line had been drawn," thinks Cohen, the novel's gruff, reluctant protagonist, "and everything below was considered primitive until the hurricanes stopped and no one knew if that day was ever coming" (10). The "primitive" nature of life below the Line, of course, plays on longstanding stereotypes of the uncivilized or "backward" South, with the implication that anyone foolish enough to voluntarily occupy such a region has essentially abandoned their claim to normative modern existence. The drawing of the Line denotates, for the states to the north, the end of the region, its consignment to ruin, but small communities of survivors remain on the coast, struggling to continue living in the flooded remnants of civilization.

The presence of the Line, and those who remain along the coast in spite of it, thus symbolizes the coexistence of narratives of ruin and resilience in the postclimate South. However, in *Rivers*, neither the ruinous abandonment of the South to hurricanes nor the resilience of the survivors proves sufficient. The survivors who manage to adapt and succeed to the greatest extent in the region are also the most morally bankrupt and physically violent—to wit, the villains: Charlie, an itinerant peddler driven mad by rumors of a buried casino fortune, and Aggie, a polygamous cult leader who inhabits an abandoned plantation with a murderous band of strongmen and sex slaves. In a somewhat unusual narrative choice, Aggie is given a significant number of interior monologues in *Rivers*; he reflects that he "had never been anything but grateful for the calamity of the storms and the subsequent drawing of the Line, this perfect godforsaken land where a man like him could create his own world, with his own people, with his own rules. The rage of God Almighty. The fractured and forgotten order. In his most selfish moments, he believed that this had all somehow come about explicitly for him" (42). As we have seen in Ruby City, Fort Repose, and Black Mountain, catastrophic environmental change offers Aggie an opportunity to remake civilization with a select group of "people," under a new set of "rules." Aggie's rulership, however, is fundamentally corrupt, amounting to little more than a prison camp supported by the banditry that he visits upon other survivors, including Cohen. Early in the novel, Evan and Mariposa, two of Aggie's "people," ambush and nearly kill Cohen, setting a series of events into motion that culminates with Cohen killing Aggie and liberating the plantation. Cohen himself, however, is not necessarily motivated by charitable or humanitarian aims; his first priority is consistently the recovery and protection of his Jeep, in which he has stashed a small fortune stolen from the elusive casino hoard. In the end, *Rivers* suggests that the establishment of the Line and the fantasy of return that it enables is less an opportunity to remake society in productive ways than an embrace of the worst aspects of humanity. Cohen notes that, below the barrier, there was "no law. No service. No offering. No protection," and, absent these securities, the land below the Line becomes a haven for buried horrors of southern history to emerge, as evidenced by Aggie's reinstitution of slavery on the abandoned Crawford Plantation (10).

In *Rivers*, the Line is never breached—but it is revealed toward the end of the novel that its function and entire existence was always purely symbolic. After days of battling their way northward away from the storm-ravaged and bandit-ridden Gulf Coast, Cohen and a small band of survivors of the plantation finally reach the Line. Where they had expected a physical fortification or protected border, however, they find only a miserable assortment of windswept and waterlogged checkpoints. The guards on the Line make no effort to stop the survivors. "The Line ain't nothing more than a line in the sand these days," one guard sagely remarks (247). Cohen and the other survivors cross the Line to find a world startlingly similar to the region they have left behind: the economy has collapsed, law enforcement is a nonpresence, storms swamp the towns and roadways, and theft and violence run rampant. Cohen makes inquiries in a small town about the miserable state of existence above the Line and is told that the Line itself is "bullshit . . . everywhere I know about is like this. Probably as far up as Tennessee, I guess. On the east side. West side is washed out" (260). Seeking further information in an old newspaper, Cohen discovers that the paper now has a "boundaries" section in which the edges of the flooded part of the country are adjusted on a daily basis. Such a landscape mocks the notion of static boundaries and barriers; the Line can neither contain the storms and water surging up from the Gulf nor the breakdown of civilization itself that accompanies catastrophic climate change. The Line may be valuable as a conceptual barrier, but for most intents and purposes life is just as nasty, brutish, and short on either side.

The implication in *Rivers*, as in other instances of postapocalyptic southern literature, is that, even when walls are effective at keeping threats at bay, their protective potential is inevitably squandered by human error. In short: if preapocalyptic southern walls such as the levees surrounding the Mississippi and Lake Okeechobee presented a narrative of human restriction of nonhuman nature being punished by a destructive resurgence of natural forces, as it is figured in *Their Eyes Were Watching God* and "Old Man," postapocalyptic walls similarly attempt to confine and restrict *human* nature. The result, however, is the same: a ruinous outpouring of repressed impulses through the breach in the wall. This is, fundamentally, a highly cynical understanding of human nature itself; the utopian projects of Ruby City and Crawford Plantation are portrayed as doomed by the moral turpitude of their foundations, while the more successful walled encampments of Fort Repose and Black Mountain only prosper through adherence to a fascistic heteronormative social code. The fantasy of return, as articulated in these novels, is in fact a return to the persistent ruin-narrative in southern literature that assigns the blame for the loss, or irrevocable widespread change, inflicted upon southern landscapes to human moral failures. The walls collapse or are rendered irrelevant and the contained societies crumble or spiral into authoritarianism not because they are poorly constructed, but because they were built on the rotten bedrock of human conscience.

––––––

The driving force behind most postapocalyptic narrative is plausibility: the reader must believe that the catastrophes contained within such narratives could be visited upon the earth—could even, in fact, cause harm to themselves. Yet I am less interested in the feasibility of the fantasy of return as portrayed in these novels than in the wellsprings of the fantasy—what crucial assumptions does it make about the southern environment and its potential transformation in the future? In other words, it is less important to understand whether the walls remain standing than why they were built in the first place. To that end, I would advance several observations about the fantasy of return as it appears in these texts:

— The fantasy of return reinforces the narrative of southern environmental ruin—there would be no need to "start over" if the initial attempt at reconciling southerners and their environment had not failed to a catastrophic extent.

— The fantasy of return also implies that any putative improvement of the relationship between southerners and their environment necessitates a conscious limitation, a barrier or wall, between zones of recovery and zones of loss.

— The fantasy assumes that a closer union of humans and their environment in the South is inherently a desirable state of affairs.

It is worth remarking that these assumptions are spread unevenly across these four texts; Forstchen and Frank's doomsday scenarios do not necessarily engage with the reparation of southern environmentalism, though they do distinctly believe in the necessity of walls. To a greater or lesser extent, then, it is possible to critique these four novels as a group, and, as such, these texts are all deeply critical of the fantasy of return. Even under the drastically altered environmental conditions that pervade the various scenarios that they present, efforts in the South to return to older patterns of interaction with nature fail drastically. In *The Salt Line*, a theoretically utopian organic community is torn apart by corruption and greed, while *Rivers* graphically details the nightmarish conditions suffered by those who attempt to build a community in a "primitive" zone—the boundaries of which were always meaningless to begin with. Even the novels in which the project of constructing a well-contained and functional society seems to succeed—*One Second After* and *Alas, Babylon*—only achieve that success via a heavy toll on the basic human rights of their characters. It would seem that, even in imagined settings, the fantasy of return does not seem to be an attractive alternative to the familiar narratives of ruin and resilience that animate southern environmental fiction.

Moreover, as I have hinted already, the postapocalyptic future that these narratives envision is a quite particular, exclusionary model of the times to come; Audra Mitchell and Aadita Chaudhury may be correct in their assertion that the new societies posited by works such as those I have cited in this chapter, "despite their claims to universality... are more specifically concerned [with] protecting the future of whiteness," with "whiteness" here symbolizing a certain familiar unequal racial/hierarchical configuration of humanity (310). *One Second After* and *Alas, Babylon* are fairly overt in their reincarnation of a socially and racially homogenous future, though *The Salt Line* effects a seemingly more inclusive, progressive, and organic reproduction of the same—Goddard-Jones's novel invokes latter-day reifications of "authentic" Southern culture in bleached terms. Mitchell and Chaudhury contend that, in contemporary postapocalyptic narratives, white protagonists "are framed as saviors able to protect and/or regenerate and even improve Western forms of governance and social order by leveraging resilience, scientific prowess, and technological genius," a trope that is evident in several of the texts I have addressed in this chapter (313). The "reborn" postapocalyptic society, in other words, looks very similar to the "lost" previous society, with all of its inequalities, colonialist impulses, and fantasies of white male dominance intact.

Does the idea of return have a utility, then, beyond a certain variety of weak self-critique—the notion that contemporary society is "wrong" in a superficial manner that can be resolved via a return to a falsely imagined past? Can more productive or tangible ecocritical lessons emerge from narratives of reinstating more basic relationships between southerners and their environment? A new potential direction for this line of inquiry comes from Jeff VanderMeer's *Southern Reach* trilogy (2014), whose three volumes— *Annihilation, Authority,* and *Acceptance*—constitute a highly unusual rethinking of the fantasy of return. Set in a fictionalized version of what is commonly interpreted (but never explicitly identified) as the St. Mark's Wildlife Refuge near Tallahassee on the Florida Panhandle, *Annihilation* chronicles the sudden appearance of "Area X," a wild profusion of kaleidoscopic flora and fauna surrounding a mysteriously abandoned lighthouse. The protagonist, unnamed throughout and referred to primarily (as are all the members of her group) in terms of her profession, is "the biologist," determined to unravel the mystery of her husband's doomed expedition in Area X some years before. And there is much to discover: the region acts in bizarre manners on the group's psyche; one of the group members has distinctly ulterior motives and controls the others by uttering mnemonic phrases; past expeditions into Area X have failed catastrophically, and alien life-forms are everywhere, menacing the expedition and progressively warping their psyches in bizarre ways. Overwhelmingly present among all of the assorted mutations and permutations of nature in Area X, however, is the concept of "transitional" environments—in biological terms, the space between adjacent biomes, but reinterpreted in *Annihilation* to mean hybridizations of humans, animals, and plants. Hulking elephantine abominations speak with human voices; a passing dolphin peers out from the waves with a human eye; a ghastly glowing hybrid of human, plant, and fungal matter scrawls words written in spores across the walls of a living tower.

Annihilation has frequently been interpreted as a parable for the process of "global weirding" that accompanies planetwide environmental collapse, detailing the spiderweb of unexpected and even incomprehensible natural changes resulting from the steadily advancing tide of destruction. Area X can be read as an analogue for both the pace and the drastic uncertainty surrounding world-altering environmental change, with one of the novel's characters ominously hinting: "The border is advancing. For now, slowly, a little bit more every year. In ways you wouldn't expect. But maybe soon it'll eat a mile or two at a time" (87). Yet Joshua Rothman, in a 2015 article, asserts that "there's not much that's post-apocalyptic about VanderMeer's novels. They're not interested in how life ends, but in how it changes, and they are fascinated by the question of persistence through change" ("The Weird Thoreau"). The distinction between "destruction" and "change" is vital to our understanding of Anthropocene fiction, as I have contended in a previous chapter, and VanderMeer's emphasis on the latter over the former suggests a revision of the fantasy of return—drawing a boundary around a region not as an act of forsaking it (as *Rivers* and *The Salt Line* do, and as *One Second After* and *Alas, Babylon* attempt for the world beyond their own walls) but as an effort to interrogate the possibility of endless adaptation and transformation. From this perspective, the process of "returning to nature" as it appears in the fantasy of return, becomes an uncanny colonization of and by nature, oftentimes grotesque and deeply morally ambiguous. Gry Ulstein identifies the question of "whether it is really 'such a bad thing' to be colonized, assimilated, altered, and forcefully evolved by Area X's monstrous system" as central to the trilogy (92). In the face of the alternative—violent resistance to Area X's native inhabitants, which is always met with sudden and gruesome death—it seems altogether more wise and prudent to adapt to change than accept destruction.

VanderMeer thus consciously attempts to counteract the narrative of ruin in his consistent emphasis on transformation over destruction—even the human lives that are lost in Area X (no expedition sent into the zone ever returns intact) are replicated and repurposed by the mysterious natural forces at work there. VanderMeer himself has placed the genesis of *Annihilation* and its sequels in his own resistance to narratives of environmental destruction, specifically the "anger and grief over the BP Gulf Oil Spill," which carved a "dark, horrible spiral through [his] mind" at the time of its writing ("Annihilation to Acceptance"). The landscape of *Southern Reach* is tainted—or, rather, rapidly transitioned from a blighted state to unexpected and effusive verdancy. In fact, a later narrator in *Authority* notes that the term "environmental boon" has frequently been applied to Area X by the scientists who study it, signifying the purging of all anthropogenic toxins from the area, its conversion to "pristine wilderness" (169).[9] And, indeed, when the biologist wanders through the wilderness of Area X in a contemplative state, the reader's thoughts are naturally drawn to Wordsworthian accounts of the sublime emotions that accompany a raw experience of nature. She states:

> It was as if I traveled through the landscape with the sound of an expressive and intense aria playing in my ears. Everything was imbued with emotion, awash in it, and I was no longer a biologist but somehow the crest of a wave building and building but never crashing to shore. I saw with such new eyes the subtleties of the transition to the marsh, the salt flats. . . . The strange quality of the light upon this habitat, the stillness of it all, the sense of *waiting*, brought me halfway to a kind of ecstasy. (59)

It is worth mentioning that, at this point in the novel, the biologist has been infected by a peculiar organism that infuses her with "brightness," that is, a superhuman clarity of perception, but it is not simply the "new eyes" that she possesses that saturate the landscape in such vivid colors. The omnipresence of "emotion" that the biologist feels seems to emerge as spontaneously as the flora of Area X itself out of the intersection of humanity and untrammeled wilderness, a pattern familiar to Romantic environmental aesthetics. However, *Southern Reach* revises this pattern by way of presenting and contemplating ravaged, depleted, and forcibly altered landscapes—environments that are, in a word, southern.[10] On several instances over the course of *Annihilation*, the biologist's narrative of exploring Area X is broken up by reminiscences from her past set in "'dead' spaces . . . transitional environments that no one saw, that had been rendered invisible because they were not 'of use.'" (104). The biologist describes her encounters with an overgrown swimming pool and an abandoned city lot in the same manner and with the same detail that she addresses the fairyland foliage of Area X, suggesting that "transitional" environments are not denied the sublimity generally attributed to more remote and dramatic landscapes—precisely the opposite. What the biologist finds compelling is the constancy of change, the proliferation of life even in difficult or drastic circumstances.

The *Southern Reach* trilogy is not as preoccupied with plausibility as the other postapocalyptic novels in this chapter; rather, it proposes a radical uncertainty for the future that necessitates an unprecedented degree of adaptability on the part of humans who live through the Anthropocene. Area X appears sinister, even terrifying at times, in the *Southern Reach* trilogy, but much more often it is simply uncanny, disturbing, and, as many critics have asserted, invoking Poe, Lovecraft, and others, "weird."[11] Gözde Ersoy, in fact, contends that the strangeness of the environment and the biologist's uncertainty toward her own role in discovering the secrets of the zone are one and the same: "The fantastic rural space that VanderMeer creates distances the protagonist from her daily routine, which helps her to discover the unknown aspects of her identity" (262). Indeed, *Annihilation* reveals very little about the nature, history, biology, or source of Area X; at the end of the novel, the mysteries introduced early in the text, by and large, keep their secrets. Finola Prendergast, in fact, contends that these unanswered questions are essential to the novel's cultivation of an environmentalist ethos: "Area X's uncanniness saves *Annihilation* from the rhetorical mistake of aggressive optimism. . . . *Annihilation* evokes the disorientation and fear that might attend humanity's acceptance of nonhuman life's value and, in consequence, the admission that human life is not uniquely valuable. . . . With this intermingling of horror, confusion, and human-nonhuman affinity, *Annihilation* makes a weird, persuasive case for biodiversity's value" (347). Prendergast's comments on the value of nonhuman life in *Annihilation* are well taken; the text repeatedly emphasizes the strong (and oftentimes blurry) link between human and nonhuman nature. However, I would contend that the most important revelations in the trilogy are not centered on the strangeness of the nonhuman environment, which largely appears as an enigma throughout, but on the human characters who encounter it. In other words, it is more important that we learn about those humans' history, opinions, and relationships with each other over the course of *Southern Reach* than reach an understanding of what is *really* going on in Area X. Though VanderMeer critiques the fantasy of return by making the union of humans and nature deeply uncanny, he also suggests that it is ultimately the responsibility of humans to be the arbiters of their own encounters with nature.

Though, on the surface of things, *Southern Reach* seems to evince a desire to wipe the slate of southern environmental history clean, to turn the clock back on generations of ecological devastation and purely celebrate the landscape, such an ambition, VanderMeer reveals, is dependent on an acute consciousness of lack, an awareness of previous failures in land stewardship. The biologist in *Annihilation* reflects frequently and rhapsodically upon the natural beauty of Area X: "This water was so dark we could see our faces in it, and it never stirred, set like glass, reflecting the beards of gray moss that smothered the cypress trees. If you looked out through these areas, toward the ocean, all you saw was the black water, the gray of the cypress trunks, and the constant, motionless rain of moss flowing down . . . the effect of this cannot be understood without being there. The beauty of it cannot be understood, either, and when you see beauty in desolation it changes something inside you. Desolation tries to colonize you" (4). VanderMeer construes the scene using the language of lack ("it never stirred," "all you saw," "cannot be understood") in order to effectively conclude with the concept of "desolation." The biologist reflects that the landscape surrounding her is unparseable without the perspective granted by emptiness; the environment is consumed by the opacity of the smothering, obscuring Spanish moss, and the water itself merely reflects what is above. Though *Annihilation* has the notion of unrestrained biological plenitude at its core, effectively making sense of its presence is only possible because of the simultaneous existence of "desolation." In this novel, narratives of ruin (the environmentally marginalized southern landscape surrounding Area X) are intertwined with narratives of resilience (the rampant growth and constant change within the boundaries of the zone), and each grants legibility to the other. The fantasy of return, in *Annihilation*, is the fantasy that the two can be extricated, that a "return to nature" can be enacted within a limited zone independent from the human attitudes toward the environment that proliferate beyond its boundaries. For VanderMeer, the wall does not permit, but impedes a more holistic understanding of the relationship between southerners and their environment.

———

At the beginning of this chapter, I argued that literary chronicles of southern environmentalism can be conceived of as a history of the *failure* of walls, and the postapocalyptic (or pseudoapocalyptic) texts I have assembled here predict the collapse, or irrelevance, of such walls in the future. In almost all cases, the crumbling of the wall is a disaster, symbolizing the implosion of ordered societies and the destruction of utopian dreams. As such, these texts subscribe to the philosophy of southern environmental ruin—the walls fail because walls have always failed in the past, because nature (whether the environment itself or human nature) abhors such boundaries, and erecting them can only result in disaster. However, alloying the ruin of the wall's collapse with resilience, which regards such decay as morally neutral change rather than destruction, permits a way forward. To return to Frost's reconstruction of his own largely symbolic wall with the help of his gruff companion, in the Anthropocene South good walls would seem to make rather *bad* neighbors indeed, but they are a good pretense for reaching across to one's *actual* neighbors.

Against Resilience

Rain and river, frost and thaw, wind and wave, however much they
may differ among themselves, agree in this—that they are, upon the
whole, slow and certain agents of destruction.
— THOMAS HENRY HUXLEY,
quoted in *The Skies and the Earth*

Shall our blood fail? Or shall it come to be
The blood of paradise? And shall the earth
Seem all of paradise that we shall know?
The sky will be much friendlier then than now,
A part of labor and a part of pain,
And next in glory to enduring love,
Not this dividing and indifferent blue.
— WALLACE STEVENS,
"Sunday Morning"

WRITING ABOUT THE ENVIRONMENT in the Anthropocene has to constitute a resistance to the concept of ruin. Even if we recount devastating
losses, we are still *here*, still alive, still able to change the course of the world to
whatever small extent. This book began as such a gesture of resistance toward
the ruin-narrative in southern literature, with the assumption that, as difficult
and unattractive the concept of resilience in the face of ruin might be, it was
surely preferable to the alternative. In the end, however, I have begun to call
this premise into question.

What are the consequences of accepting a narrative of environmental
ruin? In its most extreme form, it suffocates activism; if the world is irre-

vocably consigned to decline and inevitable destruction, or if the important environmental battles of the region have already been fought (and lost), efforts to slow or stop that process are quixotic at best. Moreover, this syllogism has, in the past, been used to justify exploitive environmental practices. In 1981, James Watt, Secretary of the Interior under Reagan, a devout Christian and a staunch promoter of extractive industry at the cost of undeveloped areas, was asked whether it was ethical to preserve the earth for future generations. "I do not know how many future generations we can count on before the Lord returns," was Watt's reply. He later added, after his remarks stirred controversy among environmentalists, "it's been 2,000 years since the last coming of Christ and it might be another 2,000 before the second coming."[1] Needless to say, Watt's millenarian, anthropocentric, and quite ecologically hostile philosophy risks producing (and did produce, during the Reagan years) disastrous environmental policies, and certainly his beliefs are not widespread. But in the South, where religious belief is strongest and environmental policy weakest, we cannot discount their sway, or the temptation to simply abdicate the responsibility for redeeming landscapes that would seem, for all intents and purposes, to be beyond repair.

Internalizing narratives of ruin also de-emphasizes individual agency in the face of global environmental change, producing deleterious psychic results. Renée Lertzman has written of what she calls "environmental melancholia," a psychic process in which a sense of loss, "when unattended to and unresolved," creates "a condition in which even those who care deeply about the well-being of ecosystems and future generations are paralyzed to translate such concern into action" (4). Implicit in Lertzman's definition is the notion that this process might be interrupted by giving voice and expression to a festering sense of deprivation; melancholia, whether environmental or otherwise, only results from a lengthy period of unaddressed depression. Lauren Dockett, in a 2019 article discussing the "combined sense of primal loss and paralyzing powerlessness" resulting from the ongoing process of climate change, concurs with this assessment (11). As climate change steadily worsens, Dockett suggests, we should anticipate further cases of "eco-anxiety" in addition to "increased levels of helplessness, fatalism, suicide, and aggression as natural disasters increase," but she recommends that the process can be alleviated by allowing patients to vocalize their feelings of dread and "find[ing] empowerment through action" (12). Such measures, however, are unlikely to appreciably impact the environmental causes of eco-anxiety, which tend to be rooted in forces beyond the control of individuals. The preexisting sense of fatality and loss of individual agency stemming from the pervasive narrative of ruin combines toxically with the seeming impossibility of producing any discernible change in large worldwide environmental threats through simple behavioral alterations.

I have repeatedly seen these same patterns in my own students, who, though almost universally enthusiastic about preserving and recuperating nonhuman nature, are overwhelmingly skeptical about their own capacity to effect environmental change. Paradoxically, such pessimism has an inverse relationship to these students' levels of education; the more they know about major threats to their biosphere, the less confident they are in a positive outcome. There is evidence, however, that such fatalism is far more deeply rooted than developments among college-age students would suggest. A 1999 study of Australian teenagers found that "feelings of 'powerlessness' to affect positive environmental change are prominent" (Liu & Lin 82). More worryingly, a second (2002) survey found that, among children aged five to twelve years, "the older the children, the less positive they felt about the future environment," and that "few students were able to express optimism about making a difference in caring for their future environment, or provide ways of acting that went beyond picking up litter, not shooting animals and not chopping down trees" (Liu & Lin 82).[2] Such largely symbolic actions serve more as coping mechanisms than as genuine movements toward large-scale behavioral changes.

Finally, accepting and normalizing a narrative of ruin, especially in the South, worsens the conditions of marginalized and vulnerable populations. Mark Haller and Markus Hadler have concluded, in a 2008 article, that there are heavily entrenched racial, political and economic factors facilitating environmental disenfranchisement. Though they note that "the economically well-off have more possibilities to evade bad environmental conditions," this does not necessarily translate into a converse concern with environmental issues among the lower class, for whom "other problems tend to be more pressing . . . than background environmental concerns" (284). Haller and Hadler thus note a prevalence of "pessimistic-resigned environmental orientation," in other words, the belief that environmental issues are overemphasized today and there is little, in any case, that can be done about them, in poorer countries and regions (294–95). Their findings seem to indicate that environmentalism itself may be a "postmaterialist" value system that manifests itself only when a certain level of material wealth, education, and comfort is achieved (295). Ironically, this means that social groups that most *need* environmental causes (the poor, the marginalized) are those least interested in them. In fact, the study concluded that "better education and higher income," coupled with "a good environmental knowledge and a high risk assessment improve readiness and lower fatalism," seemingly drawing a direct relationship between economic and social success and environmental engagement (301). Such, at least, is the dominant narrative; Mitchell and Chaudhury, writing of Afro-Futurist conceptions of the world's ultimate fate, contend that "BIPOC are often represented in [apocalyptic] narratives as embodiments of ecological collapse and threat, embedding the assumption that 'black people don't care about the environment,' and that the global 'poor' will always prioritize short-term economic needs above ecological concerns" (315). Mitchell and Chaudhury's comments are well-taken; economic and racial factors define, but do not necessarily reinforce, the narratives that they identify, and the assumption of their truth-value shows a distinct myopia on the part of ecocritics. The stereotype of the uninvolved poor and the fetishized but degraded BIPOC subject further entrenches obstacles to any attempt at environmental resuscitation in the South. Such common rhetorical modes bend the fate of the region toward tragedy and ruin, and there would seem to be little hope for a revision of this situation. If environmental activism and policy changes are strongly tied to political beliefs—as both history and more recent studies such as Haller and Hadler's suggest—there is scant room for optimism. Recent years have shown political policies across the South moving further toward polarization rather than cooperation, and the lack of effective federal action on the environment emerging over that same span of time would seem to suggest a lack of solutions in the near future and an ever-increasing sense of inevitable decline.[3] And the narrative of ruin, as we have seen, robs already disenfranchised subjects of agency and leads to inaction and anxiety rather than resolve.

———

Faced with the ever-present narrative of ruin, environmentalist authors in the South and elsewhere have turned to narratives of resilience as the only tenable alternative. It is not necessarily a desirable one. On the contrary, most of us living today would prefer *not* to have to be resilient—we would prefer not to have our lives violently upended, our health gravely threatened, and our homes imperiled. Rather, we are forced into resilience out of necessity. Or so we are told.

In the South, we can see evidence of environmental resilience emerging, though often only under the most exigent circumstances imaginable. In "Cancer Alley," a massive cluster of refineries and factories extending along the Mississippi River between New Orleans and Baton Rouge, conditions have become almost unlivable for large sectors of its disproportionately Black residents, with the likelihood of developing cancer from airborne contaminants at seven hundred times the national average. Astonishingly, the violence inflicted by these factories against adjacent residential neighborhoods is not always the slow violence of pollution and disease, but fast, fiery violence as well. In 1973, gas leakage from a plant near Norco, Louisiana, was ignited by a spark from a lawnmower operated by sixteen-year-old Leroy Jones, incinerating both the boy and Helen Washington, who was sitting on her porch nearby. For nearly thirty years after the 1973 explosion, the residents of Norco were embroiled in a legal, scientific, and media battle against the Shell plant, which directly adjoins a residential neighborhood. Ronnie Greene's *Night Fire* (2008) focuses on the efforts of one woman, Margie Richard, to seek justice from Shell for its longstanding environmental crimes. Richard correctly realizes that the actions of the corporation are part of a longstanding pattern of oppression and violence inflicted upon predominantly Black residents of Diamond, the neighborhood of Norco closest to the plant: "As the familiar plants in Margie's backyard flared anew, a truth took hold of her. It wasn't that her Diamond neighbors had been dealt a poor hand, she realized. Rather, they had never been given a hand at all. . . . Politicians and Shell officials spoke often of the economic jewels industry provided, but all the people of Diamond knew was their four-street neighborhood sandwiched between a chemical plant and a refinery" (47). Environmental racism in the South is, of course, all-pervasive and notoriously difficult to dislodge, based as it is upon long-existent patterns of oppression. Frequently this difficulty contributes to a narrative of ruin for the region, phrased thusly: vulnerable and disadvantaged populations such as the Black residents of Diamond have always disproportionately suffered from pollution due to environmental racism and will continue to do so until the power configuration between toxic corporations and the public is disrupted (that is to say, never, or within some distant utopian future). The counter to that narrative is resilience: to take an active role in responding to environmental change and fight for survival. In the case of the people of Diamond, that fight took thirty years, but was, in the end, successful; Shell's 2002 Good Neighbor Initiative guaranteed the purchase of vulnerable homes in Diamond at a fair price to allow its residents to move to less toxic environments. Notably, this is only a positive outcome to the story in the sense that it prevents further ongoing harm to the residents of Diamond, halting at the horizon of the sickness already embedded in their bodies and in the land itself.

Nonetheless, we are meant to take the story of Margie Richard, like that of Erin Brockovich or Robert Bilott (the corporate defense lawyer who pursued large-scale legal action against the DuPont corporation after finding toxins in the drinking water of Parkersburg, West Virginia) as, in a word, inspirational.[4] This and similar stories imply that, even in the face of widespread and monolithic environmental destruction, people (especially the Black, indigenous, and other people of color who overwhelmingly suffer those effects) can improve their lot through great feats of determination, activism, and patience. They posit ingenuity and resilience as effective counters to ruination. In doing so, however, they fetishize the lives of populations existing under hazardous environmental conditions without necessarily interrogating the structural forces that brought about those conditions to begin with. In *Night Fire*, Greene writes: "In dollars and cents, many, though not all, of the families in Diamond were poor. But the roots were rich, and on Mother's Day or Thanksgiving or Christmas, the grills and stoves burned late and the mingling stretched on past midnight and into a new day, the chatter rising to the chorus of a family get-together" (13). Greene is clearly attempting to cultivate sympathy for the residents of Diamond, appealing to their "rich roots" and their many acts of domestic kindness; such an approach constitutes essential empathy-building in a book such as *Night Fire*. Yet we are not called upon by the text to contemplate why these families are compelled to live in this place, the injustices that have already been perpetrated, the toxins that already run through their bloodstreams. We do not necessarily ask what the place was used for before the corporations arrived.[5] Resilience does not orient itself toward history, does not necessarily ask or know how the environment came to be in its current state. It acknowledges—and encourages us to accept—the value, beauty, and power of human agency, the power to defy ruin, but in doing so it turns away from that ruin and its origins, its injustices. It pushes the survivors, in their reduced state, to keep moving, keep adapting, and not ask questions.

When we speak of such "survivors," however, we frequently are invoking, either implicitly or directly, a certain homogenous experience of white privilege, with "resilience" itself becoming a watchword of the contemporary Afro-Pessimist movement, which, as Sebastian Weier writes, in 2014, "proposes a critique of (post-) modernity's theorization of the subject whose claims within civil society are based on a supposed possession of the self and right thereto that are constitutionally opposed to the literal possession of the slave or prison-inmate as commodity and chattel" (421). In short, to discuss "survivors" in this context assumes a solid state of said survivors' being—in reality, the subjectivity and conditions of said survivors' survival are always in question. Moreover, the fantasy of return, as invoked in the sixth chapter of this volume, is exceedingly complicated in regards to people of color in the South; as Weier notes, "the black person living within white civil society cannot claim redress in the form of a return of the land and a rewriting of history" (423). Clearly the notion of resilience in the form of naked futurity is insufficient; it is not enough to simply insist upon a movement *away from* a past of injustice—rather, the motion must be *toward* something positive and productive, which the ruin-narrative has no consciousness of. Jasmine Syedullah calls Afro-Pessimism, which regards the afterlives of slavery as a "project of loss mitigation, a viable alternative to dispositions of dispossession that animate unrest, in the academy, in cities and communities, and in the U.S. as a whole," a "first step on the road to seeking reparation for the conditions so many black people are subject to living within, that intimate union of national belonging and domestic violence that is the reward for legal legibility" (Gordon 129). In this sense, the flexible structures and paths to activism that animate contemporary protest (including, among many others, the Black Lives Matter movement) fall broadly within the category of resilience insofar as they insist upon a viable path forward for the nation that does not involve the illegal and unconscionable deaths of BIPOC citizens. Resilience, we are encouraged to believe, is the path forward, the viable and acceptable attitude toward the vicissitudes of the world.

Yet resilience is not a valid alternative to ruin; it is a narrative, a story that masquerades under the moniker of hope or inspiration, but in fact can easily deepen environmental injustice and further environmental damage. There are three broad rhetorical problems with the narrative of resilience that make it far more insidious than it may at first appear.

First, the burden of resilience is unequal. People of color, the poor, and other marginalized groups are forced to be more resilient than others, and this power imbalance becomes an expectation on the part of majority groups. Images of poor people of color struggling for survival in the wake of natural disasters, environmental destruction, or toxic events emerge from the South with astounding frequency. The (white, middle-class, distant) viewer is invited, by both popular media and art, to empathize with these victims, to admire their resilience. And, further: to acknowledge the beauty, the dignity, of their lives, which are implied to be simpler and less fraught than the viewer's own. These valedictions cloak the patterns of slow violence that necessitate the possession of resilience itself. Resilience thus becomes a rhetorical tool to further entrench injurious race and class hierarchies.

Second, resilience sees only its surroundings. Resilience does not challenge the larger power structures inflicting environmental harm. It does not dabble in politics or argue for corporate reform; it is instead oriented toward the survival of the individual, the household, the community. Regional or global environmental concerns are beyond its purview, and contemplating their relationship to these smaller social units inspires ennui, despair, and paralysis. Resilience can react to a fallen tree, a flooded basement, the hunger and wounds and disease of a single person or familial unit, but not to the presence of larger and stronger hurricanes brought on by warmer ocean waters or drinking water befouled by generations of agricultural runoff. In so doing, resilience permits structural violence and slowly unfolding global environmental catastrophes to continue unabated.

Finally, *resilience works in the currency of responsibility.* Resilience places the onus on the individual rather than the state, the corporation, or the legal system. It is incumbent upon said individuals to react to the environmental damage wreaked by such entities rather than relying upon them for refuge and remuneration. The individual must attend to their own health without necessarily asking why they are sick and repair their home without knowing why it was damaged. Resilience phrases these demands as the "responsibility" of singular people, implying that the possession of resilience is an intrinsic element of constituting a modern state; this is "good citizenship." In doing so, it fails to hold the state, the corporation, the congress, and the court accountable for their actions.

Willie Jamaal Wright claims, in a 2021 article, that "the outrage around the poisoning of impoverished Black residents" too frequently ignores the fact that "a regulatory entity has, first, contaminated the air, water, and/or land upon which [such] residents subsist" (794). Thus, the narrative of resilience, which generally places the onus upon the individual rather than the "entity" that Jamaal cites, is largely insufficient. Likewise, Jamaal compellingly asks:

"How can impacted communities escape the malediction of environmental degradation when the prominent tactic employed by activists, scholars, and politicians is redress through environmental policies and the state and federal agencies charged with enforcing them?" (800–801). The banality and abortiveness of resorting to ineffective structural agencies reinforce the individual's responsibility to take matters into their own hands, insisting upon the necessity of resilience against ruin's pervasive progress. In the face of overwhelming and persistent violence coupled with the lack of effective responses and solutions from those in power, the only effective course of action frequently manifests itself as reluctant resilience, a sense of vague and pacifying futurity that insists that the most vital necessity is continuation—survival at all costs.

Yet, I repeat, resilience is not a valid alternative to ruin; it is an anodyne, a panacea that can, in fact, inspire hope and endurance, but can also be used to maintain a slowly decaying status quo. It makes the preservation of life paramount without the perspective necessary to determine whether that life is entirely worth living, whether it is the best life that the world, in its current state, can provide. What the narrative of resilience lacks is a consciousness of history, the capacity to contemplate and learn from past environmental failures, and to insist upon accountability for those mistakes. This perspective is provided, of course, by the ruin-narrative, which preoccupies itself with such historical losses. As I have argued over the course of this volume, resilience and ruin are intimately connected, but in truth they are mutually constitutive, interdependent, and essential. Resilience is necessary to continue in the face of ruin, but resilience also presupposes ruin. Margie Richard and the people of Diamond would not need to engage in a thirty-year struggle against the Shell Corporation if their lives had not been irrevocably altered (and, in many cases, ended) by either the direct or indirect actions of that entity. In the Anthropocene, the strength that animates resilience needs to be born out of the trauma of ruin. There is no choice to be made between ruin or resilience; there is only ruin *and* resilience.

———

Ike McCaslin goes, one last time, to the gum tree. He has walked this path many times, both in his own childhood and within the pages of countless syllabi for environmental literature classes. Old Ben and his canine adversary are dead. Sam Fathers is dead. The forest itself is dying, hewed and planked and packed away. The air of tragedy hangs heavy in the air; all that remains for Ike to do is speak his last lines before curtain. Yet his final vision of his departed mentor as he leaves Sam Fathers's grave is not of loss, but of decomposition and reintegration into natural systems:

> There was no death, not Lion and not Sam: not held fast in earth but free in earth and not in earth but of earth, myriad yet undiffused of every myriad part, leaf and twig and particle, air and sun and rain and dew and night, acorn oak and leaf and acorn again, dark and dawn and dark and dawn again in their immutable progression and, being myriad, one: and Old Ben too, Old Ben too; they would give him his paw back even, certainly they would give him his paw back: then the long challenge and the long chase, no heart to be driven and outraged, no flesh to be mauled and bled (313).

In the end, Ike denies the ruin-narrative of linear loss and retribution that has consumed so much of "The Bear," suggesting instead a cyclicality that ultimately leads to a more reciprocal relationship with nature—whereas the hunt was phrased as a recreational challenge and ritual of manhood at the story's outset ("those fine fierce instants of heart and brain and courage and wiliness and speed") and Old Ben himself as a challenge to be overcome, these epic trappings and the narrative they shape are revealed by the story's ending to simply guide humans toward environmental devastation (190). In the story's concluding scene, Ike realizes that the androcentric ruin-narrative is inextricably bound up in nonhuman nature's inherent resilience.

Can environmental trauma become a source of enduring strength? Can trauma itself become the basis of a new environmental ethic? Or does the co-existence of narratives of ruin and resilience place us into a paralyzing binary, a dialectic between the two? Are these narratives directed only toward the actions of humans toward their environment, or (as the ending of "The Bear" implies) also means of identifying patterns that carry meaning in nature itself? Southern literature is uniquely positioned to address itself to these questions as the region, increasingly freighted with vulnerabilities, makes its slow and winding way through the twenty-first century.

NOTES

INTRODUCTION: Against Ruin

1. Blister and her three sisters, in fact, show *genetic* as well as *cultural* adaptation to the flooded streets of New Florida; through a largely obscure mix of heredity and exposure to toxins, the gondoliers have developed a form of batlike echolocation that they use to communicate with each other over great distances. The Missing Person regards this adaptation as hideous, more evidence of his generation's failure, and refers to Blister by a number of derogatory pet names such as "little bat," as the gondola moves along.

2. Cronon's central formulation, in "The Trouble with Wilderness," is that humanity needs to realize that wilderness is not a "pristine sanctuary where the last remnant of an untouched, endangered, but still transcendent nature can at least for a little while longer be encountered" (69). Cronon instead advances the idea that "wilderness" is in fact a "product of . . . civilization" in the same manner as the South fashions itself (69).

3. "How the Laws of Political Servitude Relate to the Climate," and "Of Laws in the Relation They Bear to the Nature of the Soil," http://www.constitution.org/cm/sol.txt, accessed April 1, 2020. Montesquieu is perhaps the most well-known, yet hardly the first, writer to posit a correlation between climate and politics; Eduardo Cadava, in *Emerson and The Climates of History* (1997), for one, has traced the idea back to Herodotus, Plato, and Aristotle. However, despite these early instances and the examples offered by multiple sixteenth- and seventeenth-century writers, he states that these theories "blossom most fully in eighteenth-century writers" and "perhaps most importantly" in Montesquieu's work (20).

4. Perhaps even more worryingly, Morris portrays this persistent theme as continuing in the twenty-first century as well: "Echoes of Elliott and Jones can be heard today in, for example, the language of Duke University photographer and folklorist Tom Rankin, who has explained, 'Our weather—cultural, political, social, and climatic—has marked us and our land, demonstrated so recently and dramatically by Katrina/Rita and our failed response to it'" (585).

5. This gap helps, in part, to explain the paradox that Bullard and others have noted—why are poor people of color, the most frequent victims of environmental racism, only "marginally involved in the nation's environmental movement?" (1). Bullard implies that said movement, in its current incarnation, does not effectively address the concerns of these populations. Eddy Harris contemplates something of the same question in *Mississippi Solo* (1988): "I went to a wonderful bluegrass music festival in Park City, Utah, high up in the Uinta Mountains. Sunshine, spectacular scenery, fabulous musicians. I was the only black

face there. Why? Because blacks don't want to listen to certain kinds of music? Because blacks don't like the mountains and crisp clear air? Or because blacks feel there are certain places where they don't belong, certain things they can and cannot do? Is the exclusion self-imposed or by hints both subtle and overt?" (14).

ONE. The Region in Ruins: William Faulkner and Natasha Trethewey

1. Historically, Christopher Morris contends in a 2009 article, scholars have fallen in line with Muir, finding little room for attention to the southern environment amidst the multitude of other topics available for study: "With few exceptions southern historians could not stop thinking about war, slavery, race, and gender long enough to think about the environment" (581). Like the southern landscape itself, academic environmentalism in the South was always present, but tended to be overshadowed by more present social concerns.

2. Byrd 21. Anthony Wilson has also written that southern swamps in general prove exceedingly problematic for environmentalists informed primarily by Romantic concepts of nature, calling it "the antithesis of the pastoral ideal" (xvii).

3. In some sense, the ruin-narrative in southern environmental rhetoric springs from much more widespread narratives of human failure broadly conceived, which Andrew Murphy, in a 2003 article, traces as far back as classical antiquity, historically representing a perpetual present as "the culmination of a long period of decline set into motion by a specific set of mistaken and/or harmful ideas" (95).

4. This holds true to an extent sufficient for Lewis Simpson, in 1980, to claim that "the permutations of the image of America as an explicit recovery of Arcadia are well known" (*The Brazen Face of History* 117).

5. Christine Cloud writes that "[Columbus's] Biblically-inspired accounts of a paradisical environment awaiting European inhabitation and domination . . . established the mythopeic framework that America, 400 years later, is still struggling to transcend" (Hamilton and Jones 63).

6. Even Byrd's idealistic portraits presage both the human suffering and environmental depletion already at work in the South. He notes that the inhabitants of the regions he traverses "seem to be all mine-mad, and neglect making of corn for their present necessities, in hopes of growing very rich hereafter." The extractive economy takes an immediate and visible toll upon the residents, as Byrd describes encountering "a tall, meager figure, which I took at first for an apparition. . . . I concluded that the unwholesome vapours arising from the copper mine had made this operator such a skeleton, but upon inquiry understood it was sheer famine had brought him so low. He told us his stomach had not been blessed with one morsel of meat for more than three weeks, and that too he had been obliged to short allowance of bread, by reason corn was scarce."

7. Jacqueline Megow sees something of the same notion of an "improved" paradise in Crevecoeur's writings, which suggest that, "free from the shackles of European monarchy and state-sponsored religion, all of America is a potential Eden . . . an earthly paradise

where self-determination allows its citizens to create an ideal society based on agriculture and local industry" (Hamilton and Jones 77).

8. MacKethan 3. Jack Kirby, among many others, has remarked on the irony of plantation owners claiming this harmony: "At its very heart . . . the plantation tradition seems to present consistently, over at least five sad centuries, not only a purgatory (if not hell) for workers but a disaster for landscapes. Logically (although ironically, too) in the American South it was planters themselves who persistently proclaimed the intimate relationship between plantations, forced labor, and the breaking of the land" (79).

9. Annette Kolodny also notes, in *The Land before Her* (1984), that "until the outbreak of the Civil War in 1861, nineteenth-century Americans were repeatedly admonished to believe that 'we are still in Eden,'" according to an 1841 lecture by Thomas Cole (5). Nonetheless, historical accounts as recent as Gail Fishman's *Journeys through Paradise: Pioneering Naturalists in the Southeast* (2000) do not hesitate to effervesce about the region using distinctly prelapsarian rhetoric: "though [these naturalists] made no great speeches, fought no military battles, and seemingly left no spectacular history, they led extraordinary lives. We are, indeed, fortunate that they possessed an astounding desire to study and to describe this paradise" (xv).

10. Of all of the environmental catastrophes visited upon the region, deforestation tends to provoke the most heated denunciations. Thomas D. Clark's *The Greening of the South* (1984) deploys nigh-apocalyptic rhetoric to describe the early destruction of southern forests: "These were soulless trails of torture that ground men and teams down without mercy or surcease. Then in the end there was a desolate void. . . . Behind the departing millmen were the smouldering slab and sawdust piles, the blackened sweep of wanton forest fires left free to consume the last iota of green promise" (xii, Preface).

11. Davis is, however, fully aware that his perspective is informed by a modern sense of ethics and conservation. For the first settlers, he acknowledges, "the southern mountains were a wilderness to be tamed, a landscape to be transformed into an earthly paradise. . . . Civilization, as the Europeans understood it, demanded large expanses of open, unobstructed land. For the early pioneer, dark primeval forests and dense imposing canebrakes were uninhabitable landscapes hardly compatible with pastoral ways of life" (97).

12. These efforts were not necessary founded, but certainly catalyzed, by the publication and subsequent popularity of Janisse Ray's *Ecology of a Cracker Childhood* in 1999, which encouraged its readers to reimagine the value of "ugly" or "useless" regions of the South in environmental terms.

13. Wilson 40. Several recent writers have attempted to revisit regions where environmentalism has historically been weak in the interest of showing resilience rather than crafting tales of ruin. Donald Davis, for instance, recalls an interview with Hazel King, an activist from a postcoal town in eastern Kentucky in which environmental ethics are inflected with religious belief: "Although Hazel has witnessed firsthand the perennial exploitation and debasement of her mountainside community, she knows little about the growing 'Green Party' movement in North America. . . . No, she has not heard of Edward Abbey, Arne Naess, Murray Bookchin, Dave Foreman, Kirkpatrick Sale, and George Sessions.

She has, however, heard of Al Fritsch, the director of Appalachia—Science in the Public Interest. . . . Hazel says she reads Fritsch's books because they speak to her needs as both a Kentuckian and a Christian. The words are both familiar and comforting and ring not of philosophy but of spiritual faith, commitment, and mystery" (*Homeplace Geography* 19).

14. Anecdotally, these are descriptors that I hear regularly from students enrolled in my Southern Literature and the Environment class—predominantly young, liberal students pursuing environmentally focused majors and careers.

15. According to Don Doyle, these landscapes stem from personal experience; Faulkner "grew up in a land torn apart by gullies that ran down the hillsides, with creeks and rivers clogged by quicksand sludge, a landscape also of denuded fields pocked with stumps left by the lumbermen who had cut their way through the woods like locusts" (*Clear-Cutting Eden* 137).

16. Lawrence Buell similarly marks class- and race-based divisions as essential to comprehending ecological catastrophe in *The Future of Environmental Criticism* (2005): "At such a historical moment, one might argue that it is a virtue for critics from the dominant subculture to take pains to stress the difference between their positions and those for whom ecocultural struggle or immiseration has been compounded by having been racially or ethnically marked as social others" (119).

17. Timothy Clark links Abadie's "epiphenomenon" to Murray Bookchin's idea that "the very idea of dominating . . . nature has its origins in the domination of human by human," suggesting that, in the text as elsewhere, "ecological problems are seen to result from structures of hierarchy and élitism in human society, geared to exploit both other people and the natural world as a source of profit" (2).

18. Ike's repeated use of Sam and Sam's forefathers as imaginative mirrors for his own interpretation of the wilderness carries troublesome implications for Faulkner's narrative as a whole, which, while it treats native inhabitants of Yoknapatawpha sympathetically, also verges upon the common pitfall of reducing said inhabitants to symbols for the exercise of Western ideas of natural purity and the tragic loss of indigenous systems of knowing. When Ike enters the Big Woods, he encounters "the same solitude, the same loneliness through which frail and timorous man had merely passed without altering it, leaving no mark nor scar, which looked exactly as it must have looked when the first ancestor of Sam Fathers' Chickasaw predecessors crept into it and looked about him, club or stone axe or bone arrow drawn and ready" (192). Of course, Ike has no means of knowing this, and the soft-focus dreamy recollection of now-vanished native hunters renders the scene almost ludicrous.

19. As an anecdotal demonstration of the narrative flexibility of this passage in particular, I have been teaching "The Bear" for over a decade, and I have never seen students identify Sam's "foreknowledge" as an objectively true element of this passage. Much more frequently, students believe that Sam identifies the paw print as belonging to Old Ben, or that Sam predicts Old Ben's death. Sam's prophecy in this passage is extremely difficult to parse for anyone who has not read the story at least once already (Lion has not even been introduced as a character at this point), and Ike's presentation of Sam's thought process is fairly unintuitive.

20. *Go Down, Moses* 347. It may be possible that Ike's symbolic, even apocalyptic, environmentalism leads to a set of moral or ethical principles that are themselves *not* sym-

bolic but behavioral; Zackary Vernon, for instance, has written that, while Ike's first kill as a hunter "may seem to be a violation of strict deep ecological principles," his "insistence on a thoughtful killing . . . suggests a mature ecological philosophy that recognizes the interconnectedness of the biosphere" (76).

21. In "Miscegenation," the poem that follows "Pastoral" in *Native Guard*, Trethewey compares herself to Joe Christmas, noting that her first name derives from the word "nativity," commonly used to describe Christmas, with an additional pun on the title of the volume.

22. Trethewey 1. Not by coincidence, Ship Island contains Fort Massachusetts, a prison for Confederate soldiers during the Civil War. The Louisiana Native Guards, for whom the volume of poetry is named, were tasked with guarding the fort.

23. See Narayan et al., 2019.

24. Trethewey 8. Hughes's poem also mimics the structure and meter of blues lyrics, though "The Weary Blues" switches between 8- and 12-bar blues rhythms.

25. Undoubtedly the most famous use of the villanelle in this context is Elizabeth Bishop's "One Art," the last line of which features the poet berating herself for being reluctant to deliver the rhyming word ("disaster") that she knows must complete the poem.

26. "Elegy" also takes a passage from Allen Tate's "Ode to the Confederate Dead" as its epigraph, suggesting a slightly different outcome for the Native Guards than Tate's tragic narrative.

TWO. Resilient Routes: Infrastructure and Loss in Eudora Welty and Flannery O'Connor

An earlier version of this chapter appeared as "Welty on the Interstate: Mobility and Mass Culture on I-55 and the Natchez Trace," *Eudora Welty Review* 9 (2017), 55–74.

1. One of the comments on Alison Willmore's review of *General Orders No. 9* for *The Onion A.V. Club* refers to the movie as a "southern-fried *Koyaanisqatsi*" (Willmore).

2. Significantly, many elements of the narration—and even some of its content—borrow from Faulkner's *The Town*, and specifically the imagistic description of Jefferson and its environs contained in chapter 20, narrated by Gavin Stevens: "First is Jefferson, the center, radiating weakly its puny glow into space; beyond it, enclosing it, spreads the County, tied by the diverging roads to that center as is the rim to the hub by its spokes." Faulkner was recorded reading this section of *The Town* at the University of Virginia in 1957, so it is somewhat better known than the rest of the novel.

3. It is worth noting that, though *General Orders No. 9* is clearly interested in southern history (one of the earliest shots in the film is a map, likely from the early mid-eighteenth century, of the southeast, and a portion of the first segment is devoted explicitly to discussing the Civil War), the film, like the Agrarian and neo-Agrarian work that precedes it, tends to elide the conditions of slavery that made the South's pre-industrial system of agriculture possible.

4. Transcriptions from the film are my own; the script is not publicly available.

5. In fact, various elements of southern industrial development appear in the valedictory first section of the film; the procession of pastoral natural images is peppered with

shots of high-tension power lines, tire tracks, radio towers, and grain elevators. Even rail trestles and freight trains appear—the film's critique, though it appears more general at first, is in fact quite specific: industry itself is not to blame, nor mass transit, but large-scale car culture and the infrastructure that supports it.

6. In reality, the "spokes on a wheel" system of roadbuilding that underlies many small towns across the South was designed to enable the transportation of produce and livestock simultaneously from the farms in outlying areas. These products were then delivered to other towns by rail. Such a system does, indeed, connect farms to towns, but makes large-scale travel between distant towns difficult and, in the South, led to railroad monopolies that brought immense economic hardship to producers.

7. The Trace itself terminates just outside of Nashville, only a few miles south of where I-40 traverses the state. The contrast between the two roads is stark; while the interstate pushes relentlessly west toward the Mississippi flood plain across a landscape littered with billboards, rest stops, and service stations, the Trace meanders southwest through rural areas of Tennessee, Alabama, and Mississippi largely untouched by tourism or the exigencies of mass transit.

8. See "The Aeneid of the Natchez Trace: Epic Structure in Eudora Welty's 'The Wide Net,'" *Southern Review* 19.3. Cluck observes that, structurally, "The Wide Net" strongly resembles both traditional and folk epic plots.

9. Welty's "A Fairy Tale of the Natchez Trace," first delivered as a talk to the Mississippi Historical Association in 1975 and later independently printed in small quantities, also makes clear the author's application of traditional folktale (in this particular case, the Brothers Grimm story "The Fisherman's Wife") to the environments of the Trace.

10. Faulkner takes this argument a step further in *Requiem for a Nun* (1951), in which the transportation of the jail's lock from Nashville to Jefferson (implicitly, along the Trace) becomes "a gesture of salutation . . . of civilization to civilization across not just the three hundred miles of wilderness to Nashville, but the fifteen hundred to Washington: of respect without servility, allegiance without abasement to the government which they had helped to found and had accepted with pride" (11).

11. Today, only vestiges of this road scattered across the South remain; in many instances stretches of the Dixie Highway were converted to US routes, and in others it still retains its original route and name. In late 2015, the city of Riviera Beach, Florida, renamed a nearby stretch of the Dixie Highway the President Barack Obama Highway.

12. *One Writer's Beginnings*, 44. We can find Welty expressing a similar sentiment in a 1983 letter to William Maxwell: "In those days," she writes, referencing the early days of travel on the Natchez Trace, "a trip was really a trip, and if you asked somebody to 'tell me your trip,' here was what you got" (388).

13. It is worth noting, however, that the narrator of "The Wanderers" immediately steps in to correct Virgie's lament: "Though that was like a sad song, it was not true: the road still went the same, from Morgana to MacLain, from Morgana to Vicksburg and Jackson, of course. Only now the wrong people went by on it. They were all riding trucks, very fast or heavily loaded, and carrying blades and chains, to chop and haul the big trees to mill. They were not eaters of muscadines, and did not stop to pass words on the season and

what grew" (435). The narrator implies that the issue may not be with the road *per se*, but a much broader cultural and economic shift.

14. Quoted in Brigham, pp. 58. Cohen may be phrasing the issue in somewhat deceptive terms; Mississippi state highway commissioner John D. Smith, in a 1960 interview, asserted that "the automobile has become a part of the American way of life, and the public road is as necessary to economic health as food is to the human body," suggesting that participation in car culture is less a marker of the embrace of capitalist ideals and more a matter of necessity (Hills 8).

15. Throughout the mid-1950s, *Clarion-Ledger* articles tend to express some suspicion toward federal road-building enterprises, though many of these critiques seem to be rooted in a general suspicion toward large government projects rather than toward any intrinsic qualities of the roads themselves. A 1956 column entitled "Them's Our Sentiments," for example, looks askance at Eisenhower's nascent interstate bill, direly predicting that "the Federal government will tell Mississippi what kind of highways it can build with money that came out of Mississippi pockets." There are similar critiques of the proposed gasoline tax slated to help cover the enormous costs of building the highway systems, anxiety toward displacement of homes and businesses, and concerns about potential increases in accident fatalities.

16. To be fair, public opinion toward the new interstates in Mississippi was by no means unilateral, and the *Jackson Clarion-Ledger* certainly did its fair share to promote the highways as well, noting that they would bring more jobs, open up more of the land surrounding the city, and connect Mississippians more easily to other cities. A February 28, 1958, editorial titled "It Is Good Here and It Will Get Better" presents the results of a survey by the Jackson Chamber of Commerce: "Every available reliable indicator points toward a continued healthy economic situation in . . . the 'Crossroads of the South'" (20). The article lists ongoing interstate construction as one of the factors leading to this economic success.

17. Travel in Welty's work is frequently linked to death or the threat of death—most prominently in "The Hitch-Hikers," "The Wide Net," and *The Optimist's Daughter*, but also more obliquely, as suggested by the quilt covering the ailing Solomon in "Livvie"—"a big feather-stitched piece-quilt in the pattern 'Trip Around the World,' which had twenty-one different colors, four hundred and forty pieces, and a thousand yards of thread" (*Collected Stories* 228–29). The "disruption" to which Brigham alludes likely should not be taken as a gentle process of beneficial change, but must also be expanded to include the possibility of fear, trauma, and death.

18. It is worth noting that the woods, and specifically the tree line (a repeated symbol in O'Connor's work), are used to indicate Fortune's general ignorance of not only ecological but also spiritual matters. Eventually, the woods that strike him as mundane are transformed by the red light of the setting sun into "an uncomfortable mystery that he had not apprehended before. He saw it, in his hallucination, as if someone were wounded behind the woods and the trees were bathed in blood" (*Everything That Rises* 71).

19. This theme of placelessness persists throughout *Wise Blood*, from Hazel's oft-cited (and delivered from the hood of his car, no less) proclamation that "where you come from is gone, where you thought you were going to never was there, and where you are is no

good unless you can get away from it. Where is there a place for you to be? No place" to the laconic mechanic who rescues his car from one of its frequent breakdowns's lugubrious assertion that "some things'llget some folks somewheres" (165, 125). Given that these moments of unrootedness are so frequently linked to the highway and the cars that travel it, O'Connor may well have been thinking of how rapid interstate transit impacted the sense of place in the South.

20. Vande Brake also notes that, in her letters, O'Connor herself was insistent on Fortune, in "A View of the Woods," being "damned" to an extent that surprised even the editor of her correspondence (21). Brian Abel Regan, in fact, links O'Connor's concern with highways and cars with "a denial of Original Sin," insofar as her "manipulation of the image of the automobile in several novels and stories . . . develops a critique of the myth of the American hero free from the constraints imposed by women, society, and God" (56).

21. In the case of the Dixie Highway, the road that was expected to foster national unity and amicability between regions eventually drove those regions toward greater sectionalism and feuding. Ingram writes: "While organizers of the Dixie Highway had predicted that it would unify North and South, during the winter and spring of 1914–15, the routing competition only magnified existing regional divisions. The contest revealed vast differences in the local resources of the hundreds of communities along rival routes between Chicago and Miami" (74).

22. Nall 395. In addition to redrawing economic and political lines, interstate construction frequently served as an opportunity for local politicians to sequester, marginalize, and in some cases obliterate minority communities, coded as "blight" in planning documents. This is another instance of a means of travel and contact (the public road) being reified as a tool of isolation and segregation. See Eric Avila, *The Folklore of the Freeway: Race and Revolt in the Modernist City* (University of Minnesota Press, 2014).

23. The rape scene itself is described in surprisingly muted language; rather than using the language of violence and resistance, Welty writes: "a rude laugh covered her cry, and somehow both the harsh human sounds could easily have been heard as rejoicing, going out over the river in the dark night" (*Collected Stories* 258). "Rejoicing" is the operative term here, throwing into question the ethical character of what is happening to Jenny and leaving the reader in a state of deep and abiding doubt at the conclusion of the story.

24. Westing extends her view of Welty's fetishization of wilderness by fetishizing Welty herself: "Is it possible for Welty to celebrate the land and the fecundity and independence of the world of nature so comfortably because she feels the same way about herself as woman [sic] and understands the ancient identification of the land as feminine? I think the answer must be yes" (7).

THREE. Of Yams and Canned Pasta: Southern Foodways as Discourse in Toni Morrison and Fannie Flagg

An earlier version of this chapter appeared as "Southern Foodways and Visceral Environmentalism" in *Ecocriticism and the Future of Southern Studies*, Zackary Vernon, ed. (Louisiana State University Press, 2019).

1. Similarly, Casey Clabough invokes the "visceral" in the writing of another influential southern author, James Dickey, claiming that his novels follow intellectual Romanticism by "assum[ing] the existence of a natural form" but eschew "the traditional romantic formula" in favor of "a more visceral and elemental sensibility" (7).

2. Southern cookbooks are a contributing factor to the discourse surrounding the linkage between southern food, people, and landscapes. Joseph Dabney's *Smokehouse Ham, Spoon Bread, & Scuppernong Wine* (1998), for instance, pairs one selection of recipes with bits of folk wisdom: "everyone in the hill country knows that you should never attempt to kill a hog on a dark moon, otherwise some of your meat will just vanish. It's always best to slaughter your swine when the moon is shrinking" (60).

3. There is also a tendency to regard southern food and its significance as overriding the frequently complex or painful circumstances underlying its development. Tara Powell, in "Foodways in Contemporary Southern Poetry" (2014), regards southern foodways as "a safe location in which to perform Southernness. It is possible to find community at the table across divisions of race, class, and gender" (*Writing in the Kitchen* 217).

4. Though this concept has gained new currency in the postsouthern age, historical accounts of the pastoral, fruit-bearing South come to similar conclusions. Michael Bennett writes that, for Frederick Douglass, the "real travails" of the world are "obfuscated and kept in place by a mythic understanding of the relationship between humans and their environment" (199). "The world Douglass lived in," Bennett contends, "is one in which the myth that 'the fruitful earth unforced bare . . . fruit abundantly and without stint' can only be maintained by the erasure of the slave labor that brought the fruits of Southern agriculture and husbandry to the tables of the white ruling classes" (199).

5. Miller claims that white southerners, desirous of restoring their elite status following the Civil War, "often observed these conspicuous communal and public celebrations from afar and got grist for their mill of endless stereotyping" (31).

6. In some ways, Frank Money's poor diet in the years following the war mirrors the behavior of Plum in Morrison's *Sula*, who, upon his return from the Second World War, consumes only heavily sweetened junk foods. Parker writes of a scene set in Plum's room that contains what appears to be a strawberry soda: "The strawberry crush is as ironic as the *Liberty* magazine, since it transpires that it is actually blood-tainted water. The blood that taints the water evokes the blood that Plum has lost as a result of injuries sustained fighting for the freedom of others and recalls the blood black men have given to a flawed democracy" (627). It might be said that *Home* is both an account of Frank and Cee's homecoming and one of Morrison's return to *Sula*, one of her first novels.

7. "Problematic History" 344–45. Of Wendell Berry in particular, Vernon writes, "it remains vexing that Berry has rededicated his allegiance to the Southern Agrarians in recent years. While it is possible to locate within the pages of *I'll Take My Stand* some semblance of contemporary theories of localism and agriculture, one has to read carefully and interpret generously; moreover, to find elements of the manifesto that are relevant to contemporary environmental politics, one must sift through vast amounts of racism and elitism as well as countless examples of reactionary, revisionist histories of the American South" (348).

8. Moreover, Ninny's apprehension of racially coded foodways is fairly inconsistent; while she praises the barbecuing skills of "colored people" in this scene, elsewhere she describes ostensible instances of pica among African American women: "I know for a fact some of those colored women ate clay right out of the ground" (125).

9. The Franco-American brand is now owned by Campbell's, so twenty-first-century readers may not recognize the brand as referring to popular varieties of canned noodles and soups, including Spaghetti-Os. Ninny misconstrues the brand name to refer to actual French cuisine.

10. Such, at least, is the schism currently active in southern food studies, which in recent years has fractured along the lines of what might be roughly called "celebration," championed by university-affiliated southern culture centers, most prominently the Southern Foodways Alliance, and "critique," largely deployed by scholars of the humanities and southern studies at research universities. The divide is encapsulated by Catarina Passidomo in a 2018 article criticizing the planned publication of a volume, edited by two prominent southern studies scholars, titled *Against Cornbread Nationalism: How Foodways Partisans Misrepresent the South*, the title itself being a clear shot across the bow of the Southern Foodways Alliance's popular *Cornbread Nation* series. Passidomo counters that the SFA's original mission to "celebrate" southern foodways (though, as she notes, this language has been changed in subsequent years) is in no way inconsistent with "a robust body of scholarship that uses the foodways of the South as an entry point for investigations into or documentations of the various and changing people, values, identities, and biases that co-exist within the region" (16).

11. It is worth noting that the term "yam" in North America is usually applied to the sweet potato (*Ipomoea batatas*) rather than the true yams of west Africa, which occupy an entirely different genus (*Dioscorea*), and what the Invisible Man is consuming in Harlem is almost certainly the former.

12. Thus, a paean to the virtues of elemental living on the order of Barbara Kingsolver's *Animal, Vegetable, Miracle* (2007), an account of the author and her family moving from Tucson to a farm in Virginia and raising their own food and livestock over the course of a year, may well be as much a critique of modernity as it is a visceral appeal to agricultural simplicity. According to Kingsolver, the family leaves the urban hellscape of Arizona "like rats leaping off the burning ship" in search of a place "where rain falls, crops grow, and drinking water bubbles right up out of the ground" (2−3).

FOUR. Leaving the Ruins: Mobility and Southern Disaster-Narratives in Zora Neale Hurston, William Faulkner, and *Beasts of the Southern Wild*

An earlier version of this chapter appeared as "Slow Violence and the (Post)Southern Disaster Narrative in Hurston, Faulkner, and *Beasts of the Southern Wild*" in *Mississippi Quarterly*, Spring 2015, 145−66. Copyright © 2015 Mississippi State University. Published with permission by Johns Hopkins University Press.

1. Richard 162. Chester Hartman and Gregory Squires, in their introduction to *There Is No Such Thing as a Natural Disaster* (Routledge, 2006), also call Katrina "a shorthand for a set of economic, social, and political conditions that characterize most of metropolitan America," implying that the disaster itself is symptomatic of much larger structural factors (3). And Anthony Dyer Hoefer, in a 2010 article, writes that disasters arising from "the attempts to control the river through a system of levees cannot be considered distinct or separate from the institutions of Jim Crow segregation, sharecropping, the Delta plantocracy, or the New Orleans elite; all are implicated in the effort to harness the economic dynamo of the River and the rich topsoil in its floodplain" (552).

2. See Bone, *The Postsouthern Sense of Place in Contemporary Fiction* (Louisiana State University Press, 2005), Romine, *The Real South* (Louisiana State University Press, 2008), Duck, *The Nation's Region* (University of Georgia Press, 2006), Peacock, *Grounded Globalism* (University of Georgia Press, 2007). See also John Smith and Deborah Cohn, eds., *Look Away!* (Duke University Press, 2004), Suzanne Jones, ed., *South to a New Place: Region, Literature, Culture* (Louisiana State University Press, 2002), and Fred Hobson, ed., *South to the Future* (University of Georgia Press, 2002).

3. The editors of *Look Away!* (2004), in fact, offer their choice of title as a straightforward rebuke to this early criticism: "by taking, with deep irony, [their] title from 'Dixie'" they "wish to refute for good the fetishization of community, hierarchy, place, and so on of another 'Dixie'-titled anthology: the paradigm of white southern nativism, *I'll Take My Stand*" (Smith & Cohn 13).

4. Michael O'Brien's *Rethinking the South* (Johns Hopkins University Press, 1988) claims that, if the old South had a unique "mind" (*pace* Cash), it was adumbrated by the cultivation of an idealized, pastoral relationship between southerners and the land. Much early criticism surrounding modern southern literature similarly capitalized on its connection to place.

5. Similarly, Michel Laguerre argues, in *Minoritized Space* (1999), that the creation of the titular spaces is coincident with the formation of the social rights of ethnic minorities. Spatial divisions, according to Laguerre, permit the majority to naturalize hierarchical relations between groups.

6. It is worth noting that the novel frequently juxtaposes productive and destructive representations of nature, as with the combination of fecundity and devastation in the quoted passage. Christopher Rieger observes, in *Clear-Cutting Eden* (University of Alabama Press, 2009), that these juxtapositions are particularly frequent in reference to female physiognomy, claiming that Hurston "retains the association of the female body with landscape, but empowers both with an active, threatening aspect that counteracts more circumscribed versions of femininity" (99).

7. Hurston's emphasis on the process of interment evokes the controversial casualty rates from the Okeechobee Hurricane: body counts are difficult to obtain, since the majority were washed out to the Everglades and lost. The remaining bodies were frequently dumped in mass graves—one such burial site is commemorated in West Palm Beach.

8. Admittedly (and unfortunately), this is of particular relevance to Floridian land-scapes, which historically and to this day have been represented as temporary, subject to sudden and frequently violent elision—whether brought on by nature, human action, or simply the dictates of convenience and desire.

9. See also Amy L. Ai et al., "Character Strengths and Deep Connections Following Hurricanes Katrina and Rita: Spiritual and Secular Pathways to Resistance among Volunteers," *Journal for the Scientific Study of Religion* 52.3 (2013), 537–56.

10. Hartman and Squires, too, state that "those with means left when they knew the storm was coming: they had access to personal transportation or plane and train fare, money for temporary housing, in some cases second homes" (4). Michael Eric Dyson's *Come Hell or High Water* (2005) also asserts that "blacks of means escaped the tragedy; blacks without them suffered and died. In reality, it is how race and class interact that made the situation for the poor so horrible on the Gulf Coast" (144).

11. The screenplay is less ambiguous about the fact that the Bathtubbers are leaving than the film itself; the screenplay reads "the Bathtub gang marches across the marsh road. Hands touch the town sign, saying goodbye," while in the film itself, the only clear indication of the direction the crowd is taking is the placement of the "Isle de Charles Doucet" sign on the western side of the causeway—the same sign affectionately caressed by the residents at the beginning of the film.

12. See Klein and Zellmer, 5.

13. These violations included displacement of black laborers from their homes, promising them a wage of one dollar a day, then reneging on the payment when the waters receded. See Spencer, "Contested Terrain," 171–74.

14. For more on the linkages between the flood of 1927 and later hurricanes, see Anthony Dyer Hoefer, "'They're Trying to Wash Us Away': Revisiting Faulkner's *If I Forget Thee, Jerusalem [The Wild Palms]* and Wright's 'Down by the Riverside' after the Flood.'" *Mississippi Quarterly*, 22 June 2010, 537–54.

15. Though citing the author's recorded statements is thin beer at best, owing largely to his discomfort at making such statements and their characteristic flippancy, Faulkner did mention, in response to a student question during his time at the University of Virginia, that he made the tall convict's shipmate a (pregnant) woman because he thought it would be "funnier" (Gwynn & Blotner 176).

16. Faulkner's description of the flood does not seem to be inaccurate; one witness described the waters as "a torrent ten feet deep, the size of Rhode Island; it was 36 hours coming and 4 months going; it was deep enough to drown a man, swift enough to upset a boat and long enough to cancel a crop year" (Spencer 170).

FIVE. Glimpses of the Whole: Climate Fiction and Resilience in the Remnant South

1. Easily misperceived as unalloyed ruination, the environment in *The Road* can, with effort, be recognized by the reader as familiar, albeit deprived of the context that gives it meaning, and there has been significant scholarly attention paid to the actual locations

detailed therein. For example, in "The Routes and Roots of *The Road*" (2007), Wes Morgan painstakingly tracks each step of the main characters' journey, even giving illustrative photographs of prominent locations. An accompanying map (https://www.arcgis.com/home/item.html?id=fdd2d58cf68c4f3a96c6248b63d44c10) gives the path of the travelers.

2. To return, briefly, to *The Road*, Johns-Putra acknowledges that the novel "is not easily identifiable" as climate fiction, but also contends that "at the heart of climate-change discourse resides an anxiety about whether we have cared enough, not just about and for each other and the planet but about and for the future" and that this "collective disquiet" is "the context for the popular reception of *The Road*" ("My Job Is to Take Care of You," 520). Johns-Putra, however, suggests that *The Road* eschews an environmentalist (or "eco-apocalyptic") message in favor of a focus on "the necessity of care—particularly care for the people of the future" that "offers a relatively manageable sphere" in which to contemplate issues such as climate change.

3. Chakrabarty attempts, though ultimately abandons, the endeavor of linking climate change to existing political practices, concluding that its legibility instead rests upon speciated conceptions of humanity: "The current crisis has brought into view certain other conditions . . . that have no intrinsic connection to the logics of capitalist, nationalist, or socialist identities. They are connected rather to the history of life on this planet, the way different life-forms connect to one another, and the way the mass extinction of one species could spell danger for another. Without such a history of life, the crisis of climate change has no human 'meaning'" (217).

4. Baucom explicitly notes that "the epoch of the Anthropocene poses two key challenges to thought: that of reconceiving the 'planet' (as a now-living hybrid of 'human' and 'natural' history) and—as Dipesh Chakrabarty and many other scholars have indicated— that of rethinking the 'human'" (139).

5. Baucom 140. Christian Parenti also suggests that radical alterations of social and legal structures are potentially as daunting as any tangible changes in sea level and global temperature: "The physical impacts of climate change—rising sea levels, desertification, freak storms, and flooding—are certainly frightening, but so are the emerging social and political aspects of adaptation, which too often take destructive and repressive forms" (12).

6. Mayer 22. Southern studies have also, at least since their second, globalizing wave, endeavored to establish links between large worldwide phenomena and much more particularized southern subjects and communities. This issue is particularly visible in the realm of local southern responses to global environmental issues. In south Louisiana, for example, Gregory Button writes, the environmental degradation and public health disasters devastating small communities are the product of a toxic cocktail of "powerful multinationals such as Standard Oil and the state government, the political economy of the state, and a lack of government transparency" (94).

7. As is frequently the case in Kingsolver's novels, nonhuman environmental conditions in *Flight Behavior* tend to mimic the psychological makeup of primary characters. This is made overt in the text when the entomologist Ovid Byron asks Dellarobia what she would do if one of her children had a four-degree fever. "At a hundred and three I'd head for the emergency room. That's four and a half degrees. More than that, don't make me think

about" (279). Byron's aim, of course, is to link ideas of human illness, with which Dellarobia is familiar, to the imperiled state of the planetary ecosystem, with which she is not.

8. Kingsolver 14. Elsewhere, the butterflies are described as possessing "unearthly beauty"; they are "a vision of glory" that looks like "the inside of joy" (15). The passages describing the butterflies are, as a rule, stylistically breathless and effusive, deliberately contrasting with the mundanities of Dellarobia's domestic life elsewhere in the text.

9. The reader may, in fact, have heard of the precipitous decline in monarch populations in the American West, or the disruption of their migration patterns, both phenomena that have been attributed to climate change. For a brief summary, see Jaclyn Diaz, "What Happened to the Butterflies?," https://www.npr.org/2021/02/26/971650046/climate -change-deforestation-threaten-monarch-butterfly-migration.

10. Kermode 46. Stefan Skrimshire also notes the common knowledge that "etymologically the Greek *apokalyptein* has its roots in *apo-* 'from,' and *kalyptein*, 'to cover or conceal.' Apocalypse is therefore an uncovering, a *revelation*" (ix).

11. Ovid Byron occupies something of this role in *Flight Behavior;* the vitriol he directs at the local news station late in the text has all the hallmarks of the courageous, articulate scientist torpedoing the nefarious peddlers of misinformation.

12. Elsewhere, Daniel contemplates how Orleans continues living contrary to all logic and circumstance: "Yes, the Delta was dangerous, but it was still very much alive. . . . The Outer States had almost everything that Orleans didn't. But the Delta still lived on" (246).

13. Michael Clark has linked subjects such as those in *American War*'s drowned South to William Ophuls's condition of "energy slavery," causing characters to "inhabit an infrastructure and economy in which their choices are not only very constrained but in which most of them, unwittingly or not, have a cumulative and negative environmental impact" (Clark et al. 16). El Akkad arguably treats southerners more sympathetically than other US factions, as a populace made helpless by the changing climate.

14. In fact, in its early pages, *American War* does a passable job of *mimicking* the language of typical postapocalyptic fiction, as Benjamin delivers exposition by way of leafing through a box of old postcards from "the last decades before the planet turned on the country and the country turned on itself. [The postcards] featured pictures of the great ocean beaches before rising waters took them; images of the southwest before it turned to embers; photographs of the Midwestern plains, endless and empty under bluest sky, before the Inland Exodus filled them with the coastal displaced. A visual reminder of America as it existed in the first half of the twenty-first century: soaring, roaring, oblivious" (3). The final descriptor, "oblivious," would seem to indicate a conveyance (either here or later in the novel) of crucial lessons not learned by the earlier world in the manner of much postapocalyptic fiction, but Sarat's story tends toward a different trajectory.

SIX. No Straight Lines in Nature: The Fantasy of Return in
    Postapocalyptic Southern Literature

1. Forstchen 71. John's attitudes are transparently reactionary; he "wonder[s] for a second if maybe all the pocket-size computer toys were gone . . . if so, no regrets there at least"

(74). He regards environmentalism as largely secondary to military preparedness, and he is frustrated by the fact that threats to the planet's ecosystem have received less wide-scale attention than theoretical new weapons of war. "Global warming, sure, spend hundreds of billions on what might have been a threat, though a lot say it wasn't," he remarks. "This, though, it didn't have the hype, no big stars or politicians running around shouting about it" (76).

2. For a partial investigation of some of the environmental impacts of the pork industry in North Carolina, see https://www.theguardian.com/us-news/2017/sep/20/north-carolina -hog-industry-pig-farms.

3. In another reversal of environmental fortune, it is revealed at the end of the novel that, with the country's oil fields aflame and coal country contaminated with radioactive fallout, the nation has resorted to redeploying its nuclear weapons in power plants. "Our big hope is atomic power," an army colonel sent to seek survivors claims. "Thank goodness we still have a big stockpile of nuclear fuel" (313).

4. Goddard-Jones 134. There is a visual reference here to Andrei Tarkovsky's *Stalker* (1982), one of the central influences on countless pieces of postapocalyptic media. Tarkovsky's famous full-color reveal of the verdant "Zone" after a wash of urban sepia scenes features telephone poles buried beneath vegetation in precisely the same manner that Goddard-Jones represents the technocratic society east of the Line giving way to the "snarled green vines" covering the defunct poles.

5. Goddard-Jones 147. The comparison that the narrator draws between this ecotopian community and third-wave environmentalist reappropriation and revival of previous orthodoxies permeates the whole of Ruby City; the camp leader, June, points out a pair of heavy wooden doors on the meeting hall salvaged from an Episcopal church in Asheville, and the hall itself is situated atop an old Cherokee mound. June helpfully notes: "It would have had a roundhouse structure on it similar to this one, so we decided to base our design on that. . . . The Cherokee interest me very much. I feel a kinship with them" (156).

6. Later in the novel, it is revealed that June has an extensive cache of digital audio files, though she prefers "country singers from a long-gone age: Loretta Lynn, Hank Williams, Johnny Cash, Conway Twitty, Tammy Wynette" (239).

7. Even Andy, who evokes the transcendental beauty of nature in his speech to the travelers early in the text, admits: "I do what I've got to do to make a living. To feed my kids. Maybe once I was sold on that nature bullshit, but that goes away" (17).

8. There are also strong hints that the Ruby City society is held in line, as utopias frequently are, by restricting personal liberties and threatening the use of force. As Werner Christie Mathisen writes of several other fictional ecotopias, "ecological consciousness is strongly internalised . . . and deviation from ecopolitical correctness is sanctioned by a high degree of informal social control" (67).

9. Elsewhere in *Authority*, it is revealed that "analysis by Southern Reach scientists of the most recent scientists of the most recent samples . . . showed no trace of human-created toxicity remained in Area X. Not a single trace. No heavy metals. No industrial runoff or agricultural runoff. No plastics. Which was impossible" (213).

10. Though there are few references to overtly southern tropes in *Southern Reach*, some aspects of the text do invoke rural north Florida. For example, Control, the narrator of *Au-*

thority, lives in Hedley, a small town in which "some of the bars just off the waterfront had long been notorious for sudden, senseless violence—places you didn't go unless you could pass for white, or maybe not even then. A town that seemed trapped in time" (174–75).

11. Though Area X *literally* fuses together human and inhuman nature on many occasions, with many of its characters transformed into sentient plants, giant talking pigs, waves composed of eyeballs, and (somewhat less spectacularly) owls, Neal Baker has suggested that the language of texts that depict drastic environmental change are frequently chimeric as well: "The authors must model a complex environmental aberration—earthquakes—via literary devices, so as to appeal to lay readers not necessarily cognizant of scientific terminology. Earthquakes are consequently depicted through analogy . . . 'tears in the skin of the earth widen . . . into mouths that gulp . . . the boulders, people, trees, buildings, and boats near its lips'" (251).

CONCLUSION: Against Resilience

1. See "The Watt Controversy," https://www.washingtonpost.com/archive/politics /1981/06/30/the-watt-controversy/d591699b-3bc2–46d2–9059-fb5d2513c3da/.

2. The only students who tended to have a *positive* outlook on their environmental futures, Liu and Lin found, were those who believed in a miraculous wave of futuristic technology that would suddenly and drastically improve the situation: "students who are more optimistic about the realisation of their preferred future visions tend to believe that techno-science will have positive influence on the future" (91).

3. Brockovich's story was adapted for film in *Erin Brockovich* (2000) and Bilott's in *Dark Waters* (2019); Richard's has yet to receive such treatment.

4. It is worth noting, however, that the intervening time between the writing of this book and its publication saw the passage of the 2022 Inflation Reduction Act, the most aggressive piece of environmentally-centered legislation of the last fifty years. It remains to be seen whether the Act's stipulations will effect a change of climate, both in terms of temperature and public discourse / attention.

5. The land that is now Diamond was once the Diamond sugar plantation, which the New Orleans Refining Company purchased in 1916. The Black sharecroppers at Diamond found themselves settled upon land that would eventually become one of the largest refineries in the United States.

WORKS CITED

Agee, James, and Walker Evans. *Let Us Now Praise Famous Men.* Mariner: 2001.

Ai, Amy L., et al. "Character Strengths and Deep Connections Following Hurricanes Katrina and Rita: Spiritual and Secular Pathways to Resistance among Volunteers." *Journal for the Scientific Study of Religion* 52.3 (2013), 537–56.

Atkins-Sayre, Wendy, and Ashli Quesinberry Stokes. "Crafting the Cornbread Nation: The Southern Foodways Alliance and Southern Identity." *Southern Communication Journal* 79.2 (April–June 2014), 77–93.

Baker, Neal. "Imaginative Forecasting, Models, and Environmental Chaos." *Extrapolation* 39.3 (Fall 1998), 249–57.

Barry, John M. "After the Deluge." *Smithsonian* (November 2005), 114–20.

Baucom, Ian. "'Moving Centers': Climate Change, Critical Method, and the Historical Novel." *Modern Language Quarterly* 76.2 (June 2015), 137–57.

Bell, Karen. *Diversity and Inclusion in Environmentalism.* Routledge, 2021.

Benjamin, Walter. "Theses on the Philosophy of History." In *Illuminations: Essays and Reflections.* Shocken, 2007.

Bennett, Michael. "Anti-Pastoralism, Frederick Douglass, and the Nature of Slavery." In Karla M. Armbruster and Kathleen R. Wallace, eds., *Beyond Nature Writing: Expanding the Boundaries of Ecocriticism.* University Press of Virginia, 2001, 195–210.

Berry, Wendell. *Farming: A Hand Book.* Counterpoint, 2011.

Black, Jane. "The Next Big Thing in American Regional Cooking: Humble Appalachia." *Washington Post,* June 29, 2016. Accessed April 25, 2017.

Bonneuil, Christophe, and Jean-Baptiste Fressoz. *The Shock of the Anthropocene: The Earth, History, and Us.* Verso, 2016.

Branch, Michael P., ed. *Reading the Earth: New Directions in the Study of Literature and Environment.* University of Idaho Press, 1998.

Brigham, Ann. *American Road Narratives: Reimagining Mobility in Literature and Film.* University of Virginia Press, 2015.

Brune, Michael. "Pulling Down Our Monuments." July 22, 2020. https://www.sierraclub.org/michael-brune/2020/07/john-muir-early-history-sierra-club. Accessed June 15, 2021.

Buell, Lawrence, "Faulkner and the Claims of the Natural World." In Donald Kartiganer and Ann Abadie, *Faulkner and the Natural World.* University Press of Mississippi, 1996, 1–18.

——. *The Future of Environmental Criticism: Environmental Crisis and Literary Imagination.* Blackwell Publishing, 2005.

Bullard, Robert. *Dumping in Dixie: Race, Class, and Environmental Quality.* Westview Press, 1990.

Button, Gregory. *Disaster Culture: Knowledge and Uncertainty in the Wake of Human and Environmental Catastrophe.* Left Coast Press, 2010.

Byrd, William F. *A Journey to the Land of Eden.* Jazzybee Verlag, 2018.

Canavan, Gerry, and Kim Stanley Robinson, eds. *Green Planets: Ecology and Science Fiction.* Wesleyan University Press, 2014.

Carruth, Allison. "'The Chocolate Eater': Food Traffic and Environmental Justice in Toni Morrison's *Tar Baby.*" *Modern Fiction Studies* 55.3 (Fall 2009), 596–619.

Chakrabarty, Dipesh. "The Climate of History: Four Theses." *Critical Inquiry* 35.2 (Winter 2009), 197–222.

Chesnutt, Charles. *Conjure Tales and Stories of the Color Line.* Penguin Classics, 2000.

Clabough, Casey. *Elements: the Novels of James Dickey.* Mercer University Press, 2002.

Clark, Thomas D. *The Greening of the South: The Recovery of Land and Forest.* University Press of Kentucky, 1984.

Clark, Timothy. *The Cambridge Introduction to Literature and the Environment.* Cambridge University Press, 2011.

Clarke, Michael Tavel, Faye Halpern, and Timothy Clark. "Climate Change, Scale, and Literary Criticism: A Conversation." *Ariel: A Review of International English Literature* 46.3, 1–22.

Cluck, Nancy Anne. "'The Aeneid' of the Natchez Trace: Epic Structure in Eudora Welty's 'The Wide Net.'" *Southern Review* 19.3 (1 July 1983), 510.

Cohen, Lizabeth. *A Consumer's Republic: The Politics of Mass Consumption in Postwar America.* Vintage, 2003.

Coetzee, J. M. *Elizabeth Costello.* Penguin, 2003.

Cowdrey, Albert E. *This Land, This South: An Environmental History.* University Press of Kentucky, 1996.

Cronon, William. "The Trouble with Wilderness." In William Cronon, ed., *Uncommon Ground: Rethinking the Human Place in Nature.* W. W. Norton, 1995.

Dabney, Joseph E. *Smokehouse Ham, Spoon Bread, & Scuppernong Wine: The Folklore and Art of Southern Appalachian Cooking.* Cumberland House, 1998.

Dafoe, Allan. "On Technological Determinism: A Typology, Scope Conditions, and a Mechanism." *Science, Technology, & Human Values* 40.6 (November 2015), 1047–1076.

Dallmeyer, Dorinda G. *Elemental South: An Anthology of Southern Nature Writing.* University of Georgia Press, 2004.

Davis, David A., and Tara Powell, eds. *Writing in the Kitchen: Essays on Southern Literature and Foodways.* University Press of Mississippi, 2014.

Davis, Donald E., *Homeplace Geography: Essays for Appalachia.* Mercer University Press, 2006.

———. ed. *Southern United States: An Environmental History.* ABC-CLIO, 2006.

———. *Where There Are Mountains: An Environmental History of the Southern Appalachians.* University of Georgia Press, 2005.

Davis, Jack E., and Raymond Arsenault. *Paradise Lost? The Environmental History of Florida.* University Press of Florida, 2005.

Davis, William C. *A Path through the Wilderness: The Natchez Trace and the Civilization of the Southern Frontier.* HarperCollins, 1995.

Diaz, Jaclyn. "What Happened to the Butterflies? Climate, Deforestation Threaten Monarch Migration." NPR. https://www.npr.org/2021/02/26/971650046/climate-change-deforestation-threaten-monarch-butterfly-migration. Accessed August 15, 2020.

Dobraszczyk, Paul. "Sunken Cities: Climate Change, Urban Futures and the Imagination of Submergence." *International Journal of Urban and Regional Research* 41.1 (2017), 868–87.

Dockett, Lauren. "The Rise of Eco-Anxiety." *Psychotherapy Networker,* January/February 2019, 11–14.

Dyson, Michael Eric. *Come Hell or High Water: Hurricane Katrina and the Color of Disaster.* Basic Civitas, 2005.

Edmondson III, Henry T. "Modernity versus Mystery in Flannery O'Connor's Short Story 'A View of the Woods.'" *Interpretation* 29.2 (Winter 2001), 187–204.

Egerton, John. *Southern Food: At Home, on the Road, in History.* University of North Carolina Press, 1993.

Eisenhower, Dwight D. "Special Message to the Congress Regarding a National Highway Program," address to 84th Congress, 1st Session, 22 February 1955. Transcript at *https://www.presidency.ucsb.edu/documents/special-message-the-congress-regarding-national-highway-program.* Accessed July 20, 2022.

Ellison, Ralph. *Invisible Man.* Vintage, 1995.

Engelhardt, Elizabeth S. D. "Appalachian Chicken and Waffles: Countering Southern Food Fetishism." *Southern Cultures* 21.1 (Spring 2015), 73–83.

Ersoy, Gözde. "Crossing the Boundaries of the Unknown with Jeff VanderMeer: The Monstrous, Fantastic, and 'Abcanny' in *Annihilation.*" *Orbis Litter* 74 (2019), 251–63.

Farris, Teresa Parker. "Picturing the Road's End: Art and Environment in the New Deal and New Millennial South." *Southern Cultures* 25.1 (Spring 2019), 72–87.

Faulkner, William. *Absalom, Absalom!*. Vintage, 1990.

———. *Essays, Speeches, and Public Letters.* James B. Meriwether, ed. Random House, 1965.

———. *Faulkner in the University: Class Conferences at the University of Virginia, 1957–1958.* Frederick L. Gwynn and Joseph L. Blotner, eds. University of Virginia Press, 1959.

———. *Go Down, Moses.* Vintage, 1990.

———. *Requiem for a Nun.* Vintage, 1975.

———. *The Town* (excerpt). http://www.people.virginia.edu/~sfr/FAULKNER /finish.html. Accessed June 18, 2020.

———. *The Wild Palms [If I Forget Thee, Jerusalem].* Vintage, 1995.

Ferris, Marcie Cohen. *The Edible South: The Power of Food and the Making of an American Region.* University of North Carolina Press, 2014.

Fishman, Gail. *Journeys through Paradise: Pioneering Naturalists in the Southeast.* University Press of Florida, 2000.

Fiskio, Janet. "Apocalypse and Ecotopia: Narratives in Global Climate Change Discourse." *Race, Gender, and Class* 19.1-2 (2012), 12–36.

Flagg, Fannie. *Fried Green Tomatoes at the Whistle-Stop Cafe.* Ballantine, 1997.

Flanagan, Christine. "Social Distortion: Displaced Landscapes and Machines of Progress in Flannery O'Connor's 'The Displaced Person' and 'A View of the Woods.'" *Flannery O'Connor Review* 15 (2017), 18–34.

Forstchen, William R. *One Second After.* Tor, 2009.

Frank, Pat. *Alas, Babylon.* HarperCollins, 2005.

Gaard, Greta. "From 'Cli-Fi' to Critical Ecofeminism: Narratives of Climate Change and Climate Justice." In Mary Phillips and Nick Rumens, eds., *Contemporary Perspectives on Ecofeminism.* Routledge, 2016.

Garrard, Greg. *Ecocriticism.* Routledge, 2004.

General Orders No. 9. Directed by Robert Persons. New Rose Window Inc., 2011.

Glotfelty, Cheryll, and Harold Fromm, eds. *The Ecocriticism Reader: Landmarks in Literary Ecology.* University of Georgia Press, 1996.

Goddard-Jones, Holly. *The Salt Line.* Penguin: 2017.

Gordon, Lewis R., et al. "Afro Pessimism." *Contemporary Political Theory* 17.1 (2017), 105–37.

Gould, Kenneth A., and Tammy L. Lewis. "Viewing the Wreckage: Eco-Disaster Tourism in the Wake of Katrina." *Societies without Borders* 2 (2007), 175–97.

Graybill, Mark S. "O'Connor's Deep Ecological Vision." *Flannery O'Connor Review* 9 (2011), 1–18.

Greene, Ronnie. *Night Fire: Big Oil, Poison Air, and Margie Richard's Fight to Save Her Town.* Amistad, 2008.

Haller, Mark, and Markus Hadler. "Dispositions to Act in Favor of the Environment: Fatalism and Readiness to Make Sacrifices in a Cross-National Perspective." *Sociological Forum* 23.2 (June 2008), 281–311.

Hamilton, Geoff, and Brian Jones, eds. *Encyclopedia of the Environment in American Literature.* MacFarland & Company, 2013.

Harris, Eddy. *Mississippi Solo: A River Quest. Holt Paperbacks, 1998.*

Hartman, Chester, and Gregory D. Squires. *There Is No Such Thing as a Natural Disaster: Race, Class, and Hurricane Katrina.* Routledge, 2006.

Henderson, Laretta. "*Ebonyjr!* and 'Soul Food': The Construction of Middle-Class African American Identity through the Use of Traditional Southern Foodways." *MELUS* 32.4 (Winter 2007), 81–97.

Herman, Bernard L. "Drum Head Stew: The Power and Poetry of Terroir." *Southern Cultures* 15.4 (Winter 2009), 36–49.

Hills, Charles M. "Good Highways and Progress Go Together." *Jackson Clarion-Ledger,* June 24, 1960. Newspapers.com electronic archives, pp. 39.

Hoefer, Anthony Dyer, "'They're Trying to Wash Us Away': Revisiting Faulkner's *If I Forget Thee, Jerusalem [The Wild Palms]* and Wright's 'Down by the Riverside' after the Flood.'" *Mississippi Quarterly* June 22, 2010, 537–54.

Howell, Elmo. "Southern Fiction and the Pattern of Failure: The Example of Faulkner." *Georgia Review* 36.4 (Winter 1982), 755–70.

Hulme, Mike. "Four Meanings of Climate Change" in Stefan Skrimshire, ed., *Future Ethics: Climate Change and Apocalyptic Imagination.* Continuum: 2010.

Hurston, Zora Neale. *Their Eyes Were Watching God.* Harper Perennial, 2006.

Ingram, Tammy. *Dixie Highway: Road-Building and the Making of the Modern South, 1900–1930.* University of North Carolina Press, 2014.

Isles, George. *The Skies and the Earth.* Doubleday, 1902.

"It Is Good Here and It Will Get Better." Editorial. *Jackson Clarion-Ledger,* February 28, 1958. Newspapers.com electronic archives, pp. 20.

Jenkins, David, Joanne Bauer, Scott Bruton, Diane Austin, and Thomas McGuire. "Two Faces of American Environmentalism: The Quest for Justice in Southern Louisiana and Sustainability in the Sonoran Desert." In Joanne Bauer, ed., *Forging Environmentalism: Justice, Livelihood, and Contested Environments.* East Gate, 2006.

Johns-Putra, Adeline. "Care, Gender, and the Climate-Changed Future: Maggie Gee's The Ice People." In Gerry Canavan and Kim Stanley Robinson, eds., *Green Planets: Ecology and Science Fiction.* Wesleyan University Press, 2014, 127–42.

———. "'My Job Is to Take Care of You': Climate Change, Humanity, and Cormac McCarthy's *The Road.*" *MFS Modern Fiction Studies* 62:3 (Fall 2016), 519–40.

———. "The Rest Is Silence: Postmodern and Postcolonial Possibilities in Climate Change Fiction." *Studies in the Novel* 50.1 (Spring 2018), 26–42.

Jones, Suzanne W., and Sharon Monteith, eds. *South to a New Place: Region, Literature, Culture.* Louisiana State University Press, 2002.

Kelting, Lily. "The Entanglement of Nostalgia and Utopia in Contemporary Southern Food Cookbooks." *Food, Culture & Society* 19.2 (2016), 361–87.

Kermode, Frank. *The Sense of an Ending: Studies in the Theory of Fiction.* Oxford University Press, 1967.

Killingsworth, Jimmie, and Jacqueline Palmer. "Millennial Ecology: The Apocalyptic Narrative from *Silent Spring* to Global Warming." In Carl G. Herndl and Stuart C. Brown, eds., *Green Culture: Environmental Rhetoric in Contemporary America.* University of Wisconsin Press, 1996.

Kingsolver, Barbara. *Animal, Vegetable, Miracle: A Year of Food Life.* Harper Perennial, 2008.

———. *Flight Behavior: A Novel.* HarperCollins, 2012.

Kirby, Jack Temple. *Mockingbird Song: Ecological Landscapes of the South.* University of North Carolina Press, 2008.

Klein, Christine A., and Sandra B. Zellmer. "Mississippi River Stories: Lessons from a Century of Unnatural Disasters." *SMU Law Review,* Fall 2007, 1437–1537.

Klein, Naomi. *The Shock Doctrine: The Rise of Disaster Capitalism.* Metropolitan Books, 2007.

Kolodny, Annette. *The Land before Her: Fantasy and Experience of the American Frontiers, 1630–1860.* University of North Carolina Press, 1984.

Kreyling, Michael. "Faulkner in the Twenty-First Century: Boundaries of Meaning, Boundaries of Mississippi." In Robert W. Hamblin and Ann J. Abadie, eds., *Faulkner in the Twenty-First Century.* University Press of Mississippi, 2003, 14–30.

———. *Inventing Southern Literature.* University Press of Mississippi, 1998.

Laguerre, Michel S. *Minoritized Space: An Inquiry into the Spatial Order of Things.* University of California Institute of Governmental Studies, 1999.

Latham, Rob. "Biotic Invasions: Ecological Imperialism in New Wave Science Fiction." In Gerry Canavan and Kim Stanley Robinson, eds., *Green Planets: Ecology and Science Fiction.* Wesleyan University Press, 2014.

Leach, Sara Amy. "The Daughters of the American Revolution, Roane F. Byrnes, and the Birth of the Natchez Trace Parkway." In Claudette Stager and Martha Carver, eds., *Looking Beyond the Highway: Dixie Roads and Culture.* University of Tennessee Press, 2006, 99–114.

Lefler, Lisa J. *Southern Foodways and Culture: Local Considerations and Beyond.* Newfound Press, 2013.

Lertzman, Renée. *Environmental Melancholia : Psychoanalytic Dimensions of Engagement.* Taylor & Francis Group, 2015.

Liu, Shu-Chiu, and Huann-shyang Lin. "Envisioning Preferred Environmental Futures: Exploring Relationships between Future-related Views and Environmental Attitudes." *Environmental Education Research* 24:1 (2018), 80–96.

Longfellow, Rickie. "Back in Time: The Evolution of Mississippi Highways." Federal Highway Administration, https://www.fhwa.dot.gov/infrastructure /back0503.cfm.

MacKethan, Lucinda Hardwick. *The Dream of Arcady: Place and Time in Southern Literature.* Louisiana State University Press, 1980.

Marrs, Suzanne, and Tom Nolan, eds. *Meanwhile There Are Letters: The Correspondence of Eudora Welty and Ross MacDonald.* Arcade Publishing, 2015.

Marx, Leo. *The Machine in the Garden: Technology and the Pastoral Ideal in America.* Oxford University Press, 1964.

Masserand, Ann M. "Eudora Welty's Travellers: The Journey Theme in Her Short Stories." *Southern Literary Journal* 3.2 (Spring 1971).

Mathisen, Werner Christie. "The Underestimation of Politics in Green Utopias: The Description of Politics in Huxley's Island, Le Guin's The Dispossessed, and Callenbach's Ecotopia." *Utopian Studies* 12.1 (2001), 56–78.

Mauldin, Erin Stewart. *Unredeemed Land: An Environmental History of Civil War and Emancipation in the Cotton South.* Oxford University Press, 2018.

Mayer, Sylvia, "Exploration of the Controversially Real: Risk, the Climate Change Novel, and the Narrative of Anticipation." In Sylvia Mayer and Alexa Weik von Mossner, eds., *The Anticipation of Catastrophe: Environmental Risk in North American Literature and Culture.* Universitätsverlag Winter GmbH, 2014.

Mayer, Sylvia, and Alexa Weik von Mossner, eds. *The Anticipation of Catastrophe: Environmental Risk in North American Literature and Culture.* Universitätsverlag Winter GmbH, 2014.

McCarthy, Cormac. *The Road.* Knopf, 2017.

McGuire, Olivia. "'Incarnational Art': Thing Theory and Flannery O'Connor's *Wise Blood.*" *Religion and the Arts* 17 (2013), 507–22.

McWhirter, David. "Eudora Welty Goes to the Movies: Modernism, Regionalism, Global Media." *MFS: Modern Fiction Studies* 55.1 (Spring 2009), 68–91.

Meeker, Joseph. *The Comedy of Survival: Literary Ecology and a Play Ethic.* University of Arizona Press, 1997.

Meriwether, James B., compiler. *Lion in the Garden; Interviews with William Faulkner, 1926–1962.* Random House, 1968.

Miller, Adrian. *Soul Food: The Surprising History of an American Cuisine, One Plate at a Time.* University of North Carolina Press, 2013.

Miller, Monica. "'No man with a good car needs to be justified': Preaching Rock and Roll Salvation from O'Connor's *Wise Blood* to Ministry's 'Jesus Built My Hotrod.'" *Flannery O'Connor Review* 12 (2014), 82–98.

Mitchell, Audra, and Aadita Chaudhury. "Worlding beyond 'the' 'end' of 'the world': White Apocalyptic Visions and BIPOC Futurisms." *International Relations* 34.3 (2020), 309–32.

Morgan, Wes. "The Routes and Roots of *The Road*." 2007. http://web.utk.edu/~w morgan/TR/route.htm. Accessed December 2, 2019.

Morris, Christopher. "A More Southern Environmental History." *Journal of Southern History* 75.3 (August 2009), 581–98.

Morrison, Toni. *Home*. Vintage, 2012.

Moss, Robert F. *The Fried Green Tomato Swindle and Other Southern Culinary Adventures*. https://books.google.com/books/about/The_Fried_Green_Tomato _Swindle_and_Other.html?id=iR9LED-AsxgC. Accessed September 19, 2019.

Muir, John. *A Thousand-Mile Walk to the Gulf*. Mariner, 1998.

Murphy, Andrew. "Environmentalism, Antimodernism and the Recurrent Rhetoric of Decline." *Environmental Ethics* 25 (2003), 79–98.

Nall, Clayton. "The Political Consequences of Spatial Politics: How Interstate Highways Facilitated Geographic Polarization." *Journal of Politics* 77.2 (April 2015), 394–406.

Narayan, Siddharth, et al. "Valuing the Flood Reduction Benefits of Florida's Mangroves." Nature Conservancy Gulf of Mexico Program, 2019. http://www .conservationgateway.org/SiteAssets/Pages/floridamangroves/Mangrove _Report_digital_FINAL.pdf. Accessed June 22, 2021.

Nixon, Rob. *Slow Violence and the Environmentalism of the Poor*. Harvard University Press, 2011.

O'Brien, Michael. *Rethinking the South: Essays in Intellectual History*. University of Georgia Press, 1988.

O'Connor, Flannery. "The Agriculturalist." Flannery O'Connor Papers, Series 2, Stuart A. Rose Manuscript, Archives, and Rare Book Library, Emory University, Atlanta, GA.

———. "The Crop [draft]." Flannery O'Connor Papers, Series 2, Stuart A. Rose Manuscript, Archives, and Rare Book Library, Emory University, Atlanta, GA.

———. *Everything That Rises Must Converge*. FSG Classics, 1965.

———. *A Good Man Is Hard to Find and Other Stories*. Harcourt Brace, 1977.

———. *Unpublished Letter, Edward F. O'Connor to Flannery O'Connor*. February 13, 1939. Flannery O'Connor Papers, Series 1, Stuart A. Rose Manuscript, Archives, and Rare Book Library, Emory University, Atlanta, GA.

———. *Unpublished Letter, Flannery O'Connor to John J. Sullivan*. April 30, 1945. Flannery O'Connor Papers, Series 1, Stuart A. Rose Manuscript, Archives, and Rare Book Library, Emory University, Atlanta, GA.

———. *Unpublished Letter, Flannery O'Connor to Robert D. Franklin*. July 8, 1952. Flannery O'Connor Papers, Series 1, Stuart A. Rose Manuscript, Archives, and Rare Book Library, Emory University, Atlanta, GA.

———. *Wise Blood: A Novel*. FSG Classics, 2007.

Omar El Akkad. *American War*. Borzoi, 2017.

Opie, Frederick Douglass. *Hog and Hominy: Soul Food from Africa to America*. Columbia University Press, 2008.

Parenti, Christian. *Tropic of Chaos: Climate Change and the New Geography of Violence*. Nation Books, 2011.

Parker, Emma. "'Apple Pie' Ideology and the Appetite in the Novels of Toni Morrison." *Contemporary Literature* 39.4 (Winter 1998), 614–43.

Parrish, Susan Scott. "Faulkner and the Outer Weather of 1927." *American Literary History* 24.1 (Spring 2012), 34–58.

Passidomo, Catarina. "Southern Foodways in the Classroom and Beyond." *Southern Quarterly* 56.1 (Fall 2018), 12–28.

Phillips, Dana. *The Truth of Ecology: Nature, Culture, and Literature in America*. Oxford University Press, 2003.

Porter II, William W. "William Bartram's "Road to Xanadu" on Modern Florida Maps." *Proceedings of the American Philosophical Society* 118.6 (December 27, 1974), 514–18.

Prendergast, Finola Anne. "Revising Nonhuman Ethics in Jeff VanderMeer's *Annihilation*." *Contemporary Literature* 58.3 (Fall 2017), 333–60.

Ray, Janisse. *Ecology of a Cracker Childhood*. Milkweed, 1999.

Regan, Brian Abel. *A Wreck on the Road to Damascus: Innocence, Guilt, and Conversion in Flannery O'Connor*. Loyola University Press, 1989.

Richard, Brad. "A Poetics of Disaster: Katrina in Poetry, Poetry after Katrina." *New Orleans Review*, December 2010, 162–81.

Rieger, Christopher. *Clear-Cutting Eden: Ecology and the Pastoral in Southern Literature*. University of Alabama Press, 2009.

Romine, Scott. *The Real South: Southern Narrative in the Age of Cultural Reproduction*. Baton Rouge: Louisiana State University Press, 2008.

Roos, John. "The Political in Flannery O'Connor: A Reading of 'A View of the Woods.'" *Studies in Short Fiction* 29.2 (Spring 1992), 161–80.

Rothman, Joshua. "The Weird Thoreau." *New Yorker*, January 14, 2015. https://www.newyorker.com/culture/cultural-comment/weird-thoreau-jeff-vandermeer-southern-reach. Accessed February 3, 2020.

Rousell, David, Amy Cutter-Mackenzie, and Jasmyne Foster. "Children of an Earth to Come: Speculative Fiction, Geophilosophy and Climate Change Education Research." *Educational Studies* 53:6 (2007), 654–69.

Rubin Jr., Louis D. *Southern Renascence: The Literature of the Modern South.* Johns Hopkins University Press, 1953.

Russell, Karen. "The Gondoliers." In *Orange World and Other Stories.* Vintage, 2020.

Saikku, Mikko. *This Delta, This Land: An Environmental History of the Yazoo-Mississippi Floodplain.* University of Georgia Press, 2005.

Selbert, Pamela. "Mississippi's Scenic Highway." *Trailer Life,* June 2015, 31–36.

Shields, David. *Southern Provisions: The Creation & Revival of a Cuisine.* University of Chicago Press, 2015.

Simpson, Lewis P. *The Brazen Face of History: Studies in the Literary Consciousness in America.* University of Georgia Press, 1997.

———. *The Dispossessed Garden: Pastoral and History in Southern Literature.* University of Georgia Press, 1975.

Smith, Jon. "Hot Bodies and 'Barbaric Tropics': The U.S. South and New World Natures." *Southern Literary Journal* 36.1 (2003), 104–20.

Smith, Jon, and Deborah Cohn, eds. *Look Away!: The U.S. South in New World Studies.* Duke University Press, 2004.

Smith, Michael Farris. *Rivers: A Novel.* Simon & Schuster, 2013.

Smith, Sherri L. *Orleans.* Penguin, 2013.

Spencer, Robyn. "Contested Terrain: The Mississippi Flood of 1927 and the Struggle to Control Black Labor." *Journal of Negro History* 79.2 (Spring 1994), 170–81.

Stokes, Ashli Quesinberry, and Wendy Atkins-Sayre. *Consuming Identity: The Role of Food in Redefining the South.* University Press of Mississippi, 2016.

Sutter, Paul, and Christopher J. Manganiello. *Environmental History and the American South: A Reader.* University of Georgia Press, 2009.

Theide, Brian C., and David L. Brown. "Hurricane Katrina: Who Stayed and Why?" *Population Research and Policy Review* 32 (2013), 803–24.

"Them's Our Sentiments." Editorial. *Jackson Clarion-Ledger,* May 27, 1956. Newspapers.com electronic archives, pp. 38.

Thomas, Lynnell L. "'Roots Run Deep Here': The Construction of Black New Orleans in Post-Katrina Tourism Narratives." *American Quarterly* 61.3 (September 2009), 749–68.

Thompson, Victor H. "The Natchez Trace in Eudora Welty's 'A Still Moment.'" *Southern Literary* Journal 6.1 (Fall 1973), 59.

Toomey, Diane. "How Green Groups Became So White and What to Do about It." June 21, 2018. https://e360.yale.edu/features/how-green-groups-became-so-white-and-what-to-do-about-it. Accessed June 14, 2021.

Trefzer, Annette. "Tracing the Natchez Trace: Native Americans and National Anxieties in Eudora Welty's 'First Love.'" *Mississippi Quarterly* 55.3 (Summer 2002), 419.

Trethewey, Natasha. *Beyond Katrina: A Meditation on the Mississippi Gulf Coast.* University of Georgia Press, 2010.

———. *Native Guard.* Mariner, 2006.

Turner, Alan. "Dick Hall: Mississippi's Economic Future Is Tied to Its Highway System." *Mississippi Business Journal* May 1, 2015, 32.

Ulstein, Gry. "Brave New Weird: Anthropocene Monsters in Jeff VanderMeer's *The Southern Reach.*" *Concentric: Literary and Cultural Studies,* March 2017, 71–96.

Urgo, Joseph R., and Ann J. Abadie, eds. *Faulkner and the Ecology of the South.* University Press of Mississippi, 2007.

Vande Brake, Timothy R. "Thinking Like a Tree: The Land Ethic in O'Connor's 'A View of the Woods.'" *Flannery O'Connor Review* 9 (2011), 19–35.

VanderMeer, Jeff. "From Annihilation to Acceptance: A Writer's Surreal Journey." *Atlantic,* January 28, 2015. https://www.theatlantic.com/culture/archive/2015/01/from-annihilation-to-acceptance-a-writers-surreal-journey/384884/. Accessed February 3, 2020.

———. Area X: *The Southern Reach* Trilogy: *Annihilation; Authority; Acceptance.* Farrar, Straus & Giroux, 2014.

Veldman, Robin Globus. "Narrating the Environmental Apocalypse: How Imagining the End Facilitates Moral Reasoning among Environmental Activists." *Ethics & the Environment* 17.1 (2012), 1–23.

Vernon, Zackary. "'Being Myriad, One': Melville and the Ecological Sublime in Faulkner's Go Down, Moses." *Studies in the Novel* 46.1 (Spring 2014), 63–82.

———. "The Problematic History and Recent Cultural Reappropriation of Southern Agrarianism." *Interdisciplinary Studies in Literature and Environment* 21.2 (Spring 2014), 357–72.

———. ed. *Ecocriticism and the Future of Southern Studies.* Louisiana State University Press, 2019.

Watson, Jay. "The Other Matter of the South." *PMLA* 131.1 (January 2016), 157–61.

Weber, Lynn, and Lori Peek. *Displaced: Life in the Katrina Diaspora.* University of Texas Press, 2005.

Weier, Sebastian, "Consider Afro-Pessimism." *Amerikastudien / American Studies* 59.3 (2014), 419–33.

Welling, Bart H. "A Meeting with Old Ben: Seeing and Writing Nature in Faulkner's Go Down, Moses." *Mississippi Quarterly* 55.4 (2002), 461–96.

———. "Grounding Southern Ecocriticism" (review). *Southern Literary Journal* 45.1 (Fall 2012), 129–33.

Welty, Eudora. *Collected Stories of Eudora Welty.* Houghton Mifflin, 1982.

———. "No Place for You, My Love." *New Yorker,* September 20, 1952, 37.

———. *One Writer's Beginnings.* Harvard University Press, 1995.

———. *The Optimist's Daughter.* Vintage, 1990.

————. *The Robber Bridegroom*. Harcourt Brace, 1978.

Welty, Eudora, and William Maxwell. *What There Is to Say We Have Said: The Correspondence of Eudora Welty and William Maxwell*. Houghton Mifflin, 2011.

Westing, Louise. *Sacred Groves and Ravaged Gardens: The Fiction of Eudora Welty, Carson McCullers, and Flannery O'Connor*. University of Georgia Press, 1985.

"Wide Open Spaces Vanishing." Editorial. *Jackson Clarion-Ledger*, March 2, 1958. Newspapers.com electronic archives, pp. 39.

Wilkes, J. D. *The Vine That Ate the South*. Two Dollar Radio, 2017.

Willmore, Alison. Review of *General Orders No. 9* for *The Onion* A.V. Club, June 23, 2011. http://www.avclub.com/review/general-orders-no-9-57971. Accessed July 28, 2016.

Wilson, Anthony. *Shadow and Shelter: The Swamp in Southern Culture*. University Press of Mississippi, 2006.

Wright, Beverly. "Race, Place, and the Environment in the Aftermath of Katrina." *Anthropology of Work Review* 32.1 (2011), 4–8.

Wright, Willie Jamaal. "As Above, So Below: Anti-Black Violence as Environmental Racism." *Antipode*, 53.3 (2021), 791–809.

Yaeger, Patricia. "*Beasts of the Southern Wild* and Dirty Ecology." *Southern Spaces*, February 13, 2013. https://southernspaces.org/2013/beasts-southern-wild-and-dirty-ecology/. Accessed June 15, 2020.

Zeitlin, Benh, Lucy Alibar, Dan Janvey, Josh Penn, Michael Gottwald, Chris Carroll, Matt Parker, Quvenzhane Wallis, Dwight Henry, Levy Easterly, and Dan Romer. *Beasts of the Southern Wild*. Toronto: Entertainment One Films Canada, 2012.

INDEX

www.ingramcontent.com/pod-product-compliance
Lightning Source LLC
Chambersburg PA
CBHW030305100426
42812CB00002B/577